Laura Ide
Sato

HOUGHTON
★ MIFFLIN ★
REGIONAL STUDIES
PROGRAM

★ ★ ★

WORLD REGIONAL STUDIES

HOUGHTON MIFFLIN COMPANY / BOSTON

Atlanta / Dallas / Geneva, Illinois / Hopewell, New Jersey / Palo Alto

India

REVISED EDITION

(Including Pakistan and Bangladesh)

Hyman Kublin

Editorial Consultant: Howard R. Anderson

HYMAN KUBLIN

A specialist in non-Western history, Dr. Kublin received his Ph.D. from Harvard University. At present he is Professor of History at Brooklyn College of the City University of New York. He has also taught at the University of Hawaii and Waseda University in Japan. Dr. Kublin has written many articles on the history and cultures of the non-Western world for scholarly and educational publications and is general editor for the World Regional Studies series.

HOWARD R. ANDERSON

Dr. Anderson, consulting editor, has taught social studies in the secondary schools of Michigan, Iowa, and New York. He has also taught at the University of Iowa and at Cornell University, and has served as Provost of the University of Rochester and as President of the National Council for the Social Studies.

Title page: The design illustrates the "eternal wheel" of Hinduism and Buddhism. The twenty-four spokes correspond to the twenty-four cycles of time which make up eternity according to Indian thought.

Printed in the U.S.A.

Library of Congress Catalog Card Number: 72–3351

ISBN: 0–395–13928–7

CONTENTS

Indian nationalism. 3. Nationalists shifted their goal from self-government to independence. 4. World War II changed the political situation in India. 5. India and Pakistan became nations under the most trying of circumstances.

1. Independent India constructed a new system of government. 2. India has made slow economic headway. 3. India's social needs are of gigantic proportions. 4. India seeks its place in the world order. 5. Pakistan has had a stormy existence. 6. Bangladesh is the newest nation in South Asia.

MAPS

CHARTS

WORLD REGIONAL STUDIES

In recent years the teaching of history has reflected two trends: (1) a growing appreciation of the fact that the past of "Western man" constitutes only a small part of the history of the human race, and (2) recognition that discovery and analysis, interpretive thinking, and use of the inductive method provide important roads to learning. The first calls for the use of instructional materials that deal in depth with the lands, peoples, and cultures of the great world regions. The second is facilitated by the introduction of materials that encourage extensive reading and provide the necessary basis for analysis and inductive learning. The World Regional Studies series has been planned with both of these trends in mind.

Basal Texts. The World Regional Studies series includes a number of texts dealing in depth with important regions or leading nations of the world. Each of these regional volumes develops concepts that are derived from many fields of study — not only history but also the other social sciences and the humanities. Political and economic systems, geography, methods of communication, social organization, human values, the fine arts, and religion have all received attention.

Selected Readings. For each of the regional study texts there is a companion volume of selected readings. These books illuminate the evolution of ways of life which have been and continue to be different from our own. They include primary sources, selections from literary and religious works, and excerpts from readable books written by scholars. These readings provide opportunity not only for developing deeper understanding but also for further analysis and inductive learning. They may also be used advantageously to supplement other "area books" as well as any of the standard textbooks in world history.

The goal of the World Regional Studies series is to provide a well-rounded treatment of human experience in important areas around the globe. Without knowledge of traditions and ways of life different from our own, there can be no adequate understanding of the present-day world.

INTRODUCTION

. . . .

Next to China, India is the greatest nation in the world in terms of population and historical tradition. Yet, until the twentieth century, Americans gave it little thought. The impression we had of India was gained by reading stories written by such men as Rudyard Kipling. But during the early 1900's, when Indians began agitating for freedom from British rule, American interest was aroused. Perhaps because their struggles reminded us of our own revolutionary heritage, Americans began to follow closely the efforts of the great Indian nationalists, Gandhi and Nehru. Since 1947, when India achieved independence, that country has come to play an important part in world affairs. For this and other reasons, it has become necessary for Americans to acquire a better understanding of India and its people.

India has an ancient and great culture. As Americans have learned more about India, they have discovered that the vast country has a record of five thousand years of civilized life. Indian creativity has left lasting marks on religion, philosophy, the arts, and science. Since numerous centuries-old Indian writings are now being translated into English, many Americans have become enthusiastic students of Indian civilization. Those with artistic tastes are dazzled by India's heritage of beautiful architecture, sculpture, painting, music, and the dance. Scholars are intrigued with India's religions and philosophies, which collectively comprise one of the richest storehouses of faith and thought in the world. In recent times Indians have continued to make important contributions to civilization. Rabindranath Tagore, winner of the Nobel Prize for literature; C. V. Raman, recipient of the Nobel Prize in physics; and Mahatma Gandhi, the incomparable philosopher, are among the Indians who contributed much to the twentieth century's cultural history.

Americans long had an unrealistic view of Indian life. If Americans at one time were ignorant of India's cultural achievements, they also were misinformed about Indian life. For many years visitors to India brought back tales of wealthy maharajas (princes); of beautiful temples; of palaces filled with treasures of gold, silver, and precious stones; of thrilling tiger hunts, regal pageants, and eye-arresting festivals. To be sure, all of these things were found in India. But were they representative of Indian life?

The legend of India's wealth has dimmed as Americans have learned more about the country. We have come to understand that India actually is one of the poorest lands in the world. Many Indians live on less than five cents a day — and earn in a year less than an American worker does in a week. To several hundred million Indians, hunger, sickness, and utter misery are the normal course of life. Few of the benefits stemming from advances in science, technology, agriculture, and industry have reached the great mass of the Indian people. An American accustomed to plenty can hardly grasp the depths of India's poverty.

India must cope with serious problems. Poverty is but one of India's many serious problems. So dark was the outlook on India's twentieth birthday as an independent nation that no national holiday was proclaimed and no celebrations were planned. Drought had led to woefully inadequate crops two years in a row, and millions of people were on the verge of starvation. India was at odds with both Pakistan and Communist China, two of the countries on its border. Plans for industrial expansion were being scrapped or cut back because there was no money to put them into effect. The Congress Party, which had guided India since independence, was seriously divided. And because of a shortage of trained workers, India was unable to complete even the on-going programs for national improvement.

But, in spite of difficult problems, India has made considerable progress since achieving independence. During its first 20 years as an independent nation, India's industrial production increased 150 per cent and food production 75 per cent. Few nations in the world could match that rate of growth. Nevertheless, India's population has grown so rapidly that the people's needs outrace production increases. As a result, there has been little rise in the Indian standard of living. Unless India can limit population growth, its outlook for the future is dim.

Pakistan has charted its own course since 1947. Until 1947, when the British withdrew from India, the nation now called Pakistan was part of the Indian tradition. It was in Pakistan that the subcontinent's earliest civilized life was found, and it was also this region that gave birth to the Muslim way of life in South Asia. Thus Pakistan can justly take credit for some of the subcontinent's most significant developments. But Muslim leaders were afraid their people would be submerged in the Hindu majority in a united, independent India, so they successfully agitated for a separate Muslim nation. Bitter feelings between Hindus and Muslims, which had been smouldering for several centuries, erupted into near-warfare before and immediately after the two new nations were created. Independence has in no way lessened the tensions between India and Pakistan. India's assistance of the secession of East Pakistan in 1971 greatly added to the hostility between the two countries. Today each considers the other its most dangerous enemy.

American interest in the subcontinent has increased in recent years. For a number of years following World War II the cold war and crises all over the world claimed America's attention. In the East, the problems of India and Pakistan seemed less important than the Communist takeover of China, the military occupation of Japan, and the war in Korea. By the 1970's these were past crises, but the United States still was deeply involved in Asian affairs. Besides playing an active economic and military role in Southeast Asia, the United States government maintained a close interest in the nations of South Asia.

India and Pakistan, as developing nations, had seemed to be likely targets for Communist influence during the early postwar years. The United States, in line with its cold war policy of "containing" communism, stood ready to aid both countries in opposition to Soviet expansion. Pakistan especially benefited from all kinds of American aid and became a member of SEATO, a defensive alliance sponsored by the United States to oppose communism in Asia. Not wishing to become aligned with either of the two power blocs (the United States and its allies vs. the Communist countries), India, at first, would not take military aid but did accept economic and technical assistance. Communism failed to gain a strong foothold in India or Pakistan, but neither did American aid solve the many problems that continued to burden both countries. Nevertheless, American interest in the nations of South Asia remains strong.

THE WORLD OF INDIA

Many civilizations have evolved in Asia during the past 7000 years. Few, if any, have exerted more widespread influence upon man than the Indian. The ways and ideas of the Indian people are derived from the patterns of living of several hundred generations of the inhabitants of the South Asia region. Indian civilization, moreover, has spread into lands to the north and south, to the east and west. Over the centuries India has adopted the customs, thought, and inventions of many other peoples. But she also has freely shared her unusually rich cultural heritage with her many neighbors.

All civilizations have unique qualities and "personalities" of their own. But there is something special about India which requires extra effort to understand. Indian civilization is "Asian" in the sense that it emerged and endured on the Asian continent. Yet the Indian way of life is the least "typical" of the many that have flourished in Asia. It is not only Westerners, with their distinct way of life, who have found Indian society, culture, and life difficult to fathom. Other Asian peoples too have found this to be true.

Indian civilization unfolded in an immense land. The variety of its natural features makes Europe seem geographically dull by comparison. Considering her great diversity of terrain and climate, of animal and plant life, India can best be compared with such continental land masses as Africa or Latin America. Because of its size and geographic complexity scholars traditionally have been reluctant to refer to the Indian part of South Asia as a country. They have preferred to call it a subcontinent.

The many differences in the physical environment of the Indian subcontinent have been rivaled only by the richness of its life. A magnet of civilization, India has attracted, as invaders and migrants, peoples representing all the major races of the Eurasian land mass. It perhaps has fostered the growth of more languages and dialects than may be found in any area of comparable size in the entire world. And as a breeding ground of religious faiths the Indian region of South Asia enjoys a proverbial fame. Yet, with all this diversity of race, language, and religion the peoples of India fashioned a civilization that still serves the needs of one sixth of mankind.

In the following chapters the term "India" is used before 1947 to include the present-day nations of India, Pakistan, and Bangladesh.

1. India's Imposing Boundaries Have Not Prevented Invasion

To look at a topographical map, one would think that the Indian subcontinent was the most secure of lands. The entire northern region is encircled by the most massive peaks in the world. In the north and northwest the Kirthar (kir-*tahr'*), Sulaiman (soo-lay-*mahn'*), and Hindu Kush (*hin'*doo-*koosh'*) mountain ranges mark a natural border between the subcontinent and the long-settled plateau of Afghanistan and Iran. These mountains fuse with the towering Himalaya (him-uh-*lay'*uh) system, which extends in a southeasterly direction for more than 1500 miles. The jagged and forbidding peaks of the Himalayas separate northern India from Tibet, now a part of the People's Republic of China. Farther east the mountainous land of Burma protects the northeastern part of the subcontinent from overland invasion. The rest of the subcontinent is separated from other parts of the settled world by vast expanses of ocean and sea. Yet despite these natural defenses, the subcontinent never has been free from attack. Its history has been changed time and again by invaders in search of empire, riches, or fame.

Invasion of India depended on conditions beyond the mountain frontier. Since the most ancient times, peoples from beyond the mountain wall have forced their way into the Indian subcontinent. Rarely did they come in peace. Most of them burst upon the subcontinent as plunderers or would-be conquerors. In making their way into India they were troubled far more by the Indian peoples who sought to bar their way than by the mountainous terrain. Almost

The Himalaya

The Himalaya system of mountain ranges towers above every other landform on the globe. Composed of three parallel ranges, it arcs northward from the Indian subcontinent for some 1500 miles. The southernmost range, called the Siwalik (si-*waul'*ik) or Outer Himalaya, rises out of the Indo-Gangetic Plain to an elevation of 5000 feet. The second range, the Lesser Himalaya, has peaks of 7000–15,000 feet. The third range, the Great Himalaya, forms the southern boundary of China. The crests average 20,000 feet. The world's highest peak, Mount Everest (29,028 feet), and many of the other famous mountain peaks of the world are found in this range.

The name "Himalaya" is a combination of two words taken from Sanskrit, the ancient language of India. The word "him" means "snow" while "alaya" means "abode." "Himalaya" is an appropriate name for the ranges, for the blanket of snow on the higher peaks never disappears. So high are the mountains that the climate changes sharply from the foothills to the crests. A Himalayan mountain climber would pass from steaming jungles at the base of the Siwaliks to below-freezing temperatures in the second range. Only a handful of men have climbed Mount Everest; the temperatures are so low, and the air has so little oxygen, that the human body can scarcely survive. Some of the peaks in the Great Himalaya never have been climbed.

To the northwest of the Himalaya, and included by some geographers in the Himalaya system, are the Karakoram (kăr-uh-*kore'*um) Mountains. These are said to be the snowiest and iciest mountains between the two polar ice caps. The second highest mountain in the world, Mount Godwin Austen (also called K²), is in the range. It rises to a height of 28,250 feet.

without exception they came from the northwest. There easily traveled passes cut through the mountain wall. The most commonly used entrance was the Khyber (*kye'*ber) Pass, made famous in later years by Rudyard Kipling's stories of adventure and war.

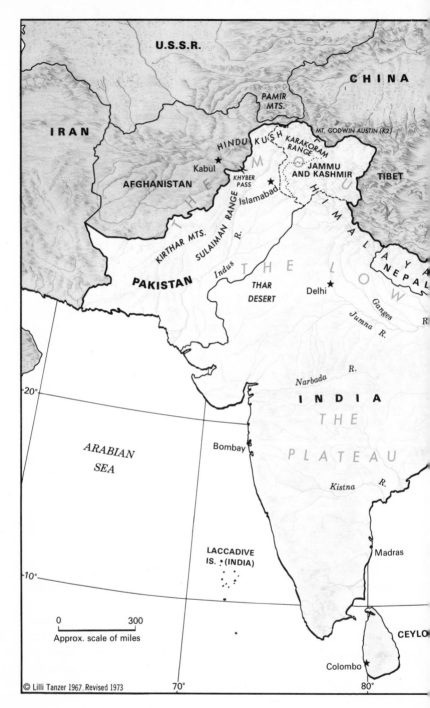

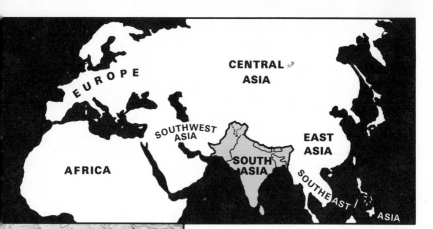

THE REALM OF SOUTH ASIA. Asia, the world's largest continent, is made up of five regions, shown on the above map. South Asia consists largely of the Indian subcontinent. Dominated by India and Pakistan, the subcontinent also contains Bangladesh, Nepal, Bhutan, and Sikkim. (Another South Asian land, Ceylon, is an island.) The subcontinent has three prominent geographic features: the mountain wall; the lowland; and the interior plateau. Cut off from most of Asia by the mountain wall, the people of the subcontinent could expect invasions only from the northwest. They were comparatively free to develop their own way of life. India's great civilizations developed in the vast northern lowland where the Indus and Ganges river systems provided a reliable source of water. The plateau region, called the Deccan, is separated from the lowland by mountain ranges of moderate height. The Deccan depends upon the fickle summer monsoon for water, for its rivers dry up in the winter months. At the outward edges of this plateau are fertile coastal strips.

5

India's northwest came under attack so often because it adjoins one of the oldest inhabited areas in the world. This is the highland region of Afghanistan and Iran. Many civilizations, empires, and kingdoms have risen and fallen in this part of the world during the past 4500 years. Time and again the peoples of the highlands have seen galloping horsemen and armies on the march, for many an aspiring world ruler has attempted to make the region a part of his domain. Often the military rumblings in the highlands were felt in India. Great conquerors such as Cyrus the Great, Alexander the Great, and Genghis Khan (*jeng'gis kahn'*) have overrun the highlands and advanced into the plains of northwestern India.

Until recent times India's north central and northeastern boundaries have been secure. In these regions Tibet and Burma are gateways to India. The Tibetans were so pathetically poor and so few in number that they could not think of annexing Indian soil. Burma was settled much later than India. When aggressive kingdoms finally emerged in Burma, they rarely had enough power to seize and hold territory in the subcontinent. But modern times have seen a change. In World War II Japan easily overran Burma and stopped at India by choice, not because of Indian opposition. During the 1950's the Chinese Communists virtually took over Tibet. In 1962, operating from Tibet, Chinese troops advanced into Indian territory. A cease-fire agreement was reached and the Chinese withdrew, but the border between the two countries continues to be disputed.

India's sea barriers were breached by traders. In the south, the only barrier is the sea. The Indian peninsula occupies the lower half of the subcontinent. The largest peninsula on the globe, it lies athwart the sea routes between the Western World and East and Southeast Asia. Historical records tell of Roman and Chinese traders breaching the sea barrier before the beginning of the Christian era — but for trade, not conquest. Roman traders came to southern and western India. Recent archaeological discoveries indicate that the Romans might have had trading settlements on the west coast of India, but none of these survived. The Chinese merchants brought cargoes to eastern India. However, aside, possibly, from the few Roman trading posts, peninsular India had no foreign "enclaves."

Foreigners began to settle in peninsular India in the early centuries of the Christian era. During this time Arabs and Chinese became middlemen in the Indian trade, transporting goods in both directions around the wedge of the subcontinent. Many of the Arabs stayed in

India, establishing important Muslim trading communities on the east coast. Because they came for purposes of commerce they lived at peace with their Indian neighbors. They had to retain the good will of the Indians if they expected their trade.

During the 1500's and 1600's various European countries established trading centers on both the east and west coasts of India. Eventually the English gained the upper hand. From the late 1700's on Britain controlled most of the seaward approaches, and consequently most of the trade, to the subcontinent. Gradually the English position in the subcontinent changed from privileged visitor to ruler. Using their trading center in Bengal as a base, the English extended their influence and power over the entire subcontinent. By the mid-1800's Britain had made India a part of its great empire. Thus the last and greatest of India's conquerors came not by land but by sea.

The British inherited the problem of making India secure. The last of India's conquerors had to assume the burden of defending the subcontinent against potential invaders. Since Britain controlled the seas, peninsular India was in little danger. To guard the landward approaches from the east, the British took over Burma. To the north, the British made protectorates of the weak Himalayan states of Nepal (neh-*pahl'*), Bhutan (boo-*tan'*), and Sikkim (*sik'*kim). British power and influence was also extended, but with less success, into Tibet.

Britain's chief problem of defense was one that had faced all of the great empire builders of India — to control the passes in the northwest. In the decades before World War I this involved making Afghanistan and Persia (modern-day Iran) buffers against Russian advances that might threaten the passes. During World War II the British erected anti-tank defenses in the passes. The history of British India attests to the success of the British in defending India's mountain wall. Not once during the century of British rule did another power successfully invade the subcontinent.

Independence has magnified the problems of defense. In 1947 the British created two independent states out of their holdings in the subcontinent. The larger portion (some 1,262,000 square miles) became the Republic of India. It occupies the peninsular part of the subcontinent and much of the northern part. Today India is the seventh largest country in the world. The second state created in 1947, the Republic of Pakistan, had two parts. The larger section occupied much of the northwestern region of the subcontinent; the other lay a thousand miles to the east. The two parts of Pakistan embraced an area of over 365,000 square miles.[1] No country in Europe, except European Russia, was as large as Pakistan.

When India and Pakistan became independent, they took on responsibility for their own defense. Again, as in past centuries, the peoples of the subcontinent uneasily watched the lands and peoples beyond the "protecting" mountains. Of special concern to India was its border with China. Pakistan was more wary of Afghanistan, a country that talked about "reclaiming" certain Pakistani lands that have large Afghan populations. But of greatest concern to each of the neighbors on the subcontinent has been defense against the other. Pakistan and India are on anything but friendly terms. In fact, in 1971 India helped the people of East Pakistan break away from West Pakistan and set up a new nation called Bangladesh.

● CHECK-UP

1. What are the "natural defenses" of the Indian subcontinent? Why have most invaders first attacked northwestern India?

2. In this century, why have India's northern and northeastern boundaries become less secure?

3. How did India become a "middleman" in commerce with lands to the east and to the west? How did trade with Western nations lead to occupation?

4. How did Britain's withdrawal from the subcontinent complicate the defense problem?

2. India is a Land of Many Lands

India is both an integral part and a distinct portion of Asia. One noted geographer has summed up this fact as follows:

There is perhaps no part of the world better marked off by nature as a region or a "realm" by itself than the Indian subcontinent. Although there is great diversity within the subcontinent — from scorching deserts to steaming evergreen forests and from seemingly endless plains to the loftiest mountain chains in the world — the features which divide it as a whole from surrounding regions are too clear to be overlooked.[2]

[1] These statistics are approximate because the two countries disputed ownership of the northern province of Kashmir.
[2] L. Dudley Stamp, *Asia: A Regional and Economic Geography*, 11th ed. (London, Methuen & Co., Ltd., 1962), p. 188.

Over the great span of history many divisive factors have been at work in the subcontinent. The issues of religion and language especially have been critical. But these and other issues are to a great extent the result of geographical conditions. Geography has made the subcontinent "a world apart," but it also has helped to splinter it into several distinct regions. The three main divisions are North India, the Deccan, and South India.

North India has long been the heartland of the subcontinent. For many centuries the most heavily populated and most highly developed part of India has been the north. Because it has fertile soil and water for irrigation, North India has always had a large agricultural population. It is here that Indian civilization evolved and where most of India's great empires and kingdoms were founded.

Hindustan — the "land of the Hindus" — is an old and popular name for North India. The region extends from the mountainous frontier in the west to the hills and jungles of Burma in the east. Its northern limits are bounded by the crests of the Himalayas. The southern limit of Hindustan is marked by the Vindhya (*vin'*dyuh) Hills and other, similar ranges. These ramble across most of the neck of the Indian peninsula. The ranges are of moderate height and may be crossed without difficulty. However, they have always slowed the north-south movement of peoples, cultures, and armies.

Hindustan is dominated by the Indo-Gangetic Plain. The rich soil of North India is part of a broad, seemingly endless plain cut by three important river systems: the Indus, the Ganges (*gan'*jeez), and the Brahmaputra (brahm-uh-*poo'*truh). This Indo-Gangetic Plain contains most of Pakistan, part of Bangladesh, and the most heavily populated regions of India. The plain is well described by L. Dudley Stamp:

Inside the mountain wall, and forming a great curve from the Arabian Sea to the Bay of Bengal, is one of the most important plains in the world. It is more than 2000 miles from end to end, and usually from 150 to 300 miles broad. There are several outstanding features of this amazing area. One is the dead flatness of the plain — not a hill, scarcely a mound to break the monotony of the level surface. . . . True, there are foothills, such as the Siwaliks, . . . but they occupy . . . a zone which is inconspicuous in its width. . . .[3]

[3] *Asia: A Regional and Economic Geography*, p. 188.

Although the Indo-Gangetic Plain is a broad, flat ribbon running across Hindustan, all parts of it are not the same. Climatic differences separate it into distinct geographic areas. The two most important regions are the Indus Valley and the Ganges Valley.

The Indus Valley is the center of life in northwestern Hindustan. Since ancient times most of the inhabitants of the northwestern part of the subcontinent have lived in the Indus River Plain, the vast stretch drained by the Indus River and its five tributaries. This area was the home of India's first civilization, the Harappan (huh-*rahp'*-uhn) (pages 34–41). Much of the Plain is now desert, but several thousand years ago it was covered by forest and vegetation. Over the centuries the climate changed from wet and humid to dry. During the same time settlers slowly upset the rhythm of nature by cutting down forests, uprooting the vegetation, and draining the marshes. Nature and man working together gradually turned much of the region into dust bowls and deserts.

The parts of the Indus Valley which are inhabited today support some 50 million people. Most of this large population is concentrated on irrigated lands along the Indus River and its tributaries. These lands, principally in Pakistan, extend into neighboring India.

The practically impassable Thar Desert almost isolates the northwest from other parts of the subcontinent. Most of this desert region is an uninhabited wasteland of shifting sands or scrubby brush. The ancient city of Panipat lies at the extreme western edge of the region in a corridor between the settled part of the northwest and the Ganges Valley. Travel between the two regions usually has flowed through the opening. Because of this, many decisive battles have been fought in the corridor between inhabitants of the Ganges Valley and potential invaders.

The fertile Ganges Valley dominates modern Hindustan. As the Harappan civilization declined, the center of population in the subcontinent shifted from the Indus Valley to the Ganges Valley. For

NORTH INDIA. One can learn how geography has affected the history and culture of North India by studying the map on the facing page. The rugged mountains to the north, east, and west reduced foreign influences on Indian civilization. Desert and mountains helped to protect the Ganges Valley from potential invaders who had entered northwest India through mountain passes. Mountains and hills slowed the spread of civilization from North India into the Deccan.

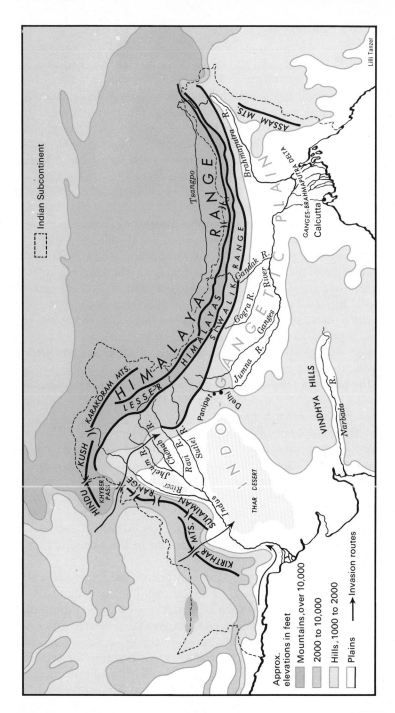

Indian Subcontinent

Indian Subcontinent (legend box)

KARAKORAM MTS.

HIMALAYA RANGE

LESSER HIMALAYAS

SIWALIK RANGE

Tsangpo

Brahmaputra R.

ASSAM MTS.

GANGETIC PLAIN

Gandak R.

Gogra R.

Ganges River

Ganges

GANGES-BRAHMAPUTRA DELTA

Calcutta

Jumna R.

Panipat

Delhi

HINDU KUSH

KHYBER PASS

RANGE

Jhelum River

Chenab R.

Ravi R.

Sutlej R.

Indus River

SULAIMAN MTS.

KIRTHAR RANGE

THAR DESERT

INDO

VINDHYA HILLS

Narbada R.

Lilli Tanzer

Approx.
elevations in feet

Mountains, over 10,000

2000 to 10,000

Hills, 1000 to 2000

Plains

→ Invasion routes

several thousand years this part of the Indo-Gangetic Plain has been the focal point of Indian life. Almost all the great empires of Indian history rose and fell in this region. The Ganges Valley is famous for its many historic cities, several of which were the capitals of empires.

Today the Ganges Valley is one of the most densely populated regions in the world. It supports some 125 million people. But like the rest of India, the region contains few really large cities. Of all the settlements in the Valley only Delhi, India's capital, has more than a million people. Most of the people are peasants who reside in the Valley's countless villages.

The long arc of the Indo-Gangetic Plain ends in the Ganges-Brahmaputra Delta, a region east and southeast of the Ganges Valley. The Delta's rich soil was deposited by the many fingers of the Ganges and Brahmaputra rivers as they reached towards the sea. Many of the fingers no longer exist. Once filled with sediment, they were converted to farming land. Two thirds of the Delta lies in Bangladesh. With a population over a hundred million, the Delta has more people per square mile than even the Ganges Valley. For centuries the city of Calcutta, in the Indian portion of the Delta, has been one of the largest cities in the world.

The northern reaches are characterized by rugged terrain. Completing the area traditionally known as Hindustan are two mountainous regions, one north and northwest of the Indo-Gangetic Plain and the other northeast of the Ganges-Brahmaputra Delta. The northwestern area is known as the Western Frontier. Throughout history it was the first region to feel the attack of invaders, for it guards the main passes of the northwest. The Western Frontier has none of the subcontinent's largest cities and only a few cities of moderate size. Most of the limited number of settlements are villages and small towns. However, for reasons of security, the Pakistani government is building its new capital city of Islamabad in the Western Frontier. Construction is to be completed by 1976.

The northeastern frontier area was one of the last regions of the subcontinent to be settled. It still contains many primitive tribes. The Assam Mountains cover a large part of the area, and much of the rest is blanketed by thick forests and jungle. There is little arable land. A few middle-sized cities exist, but most of the people live in villages and small towns. The region lies largely within the boundaries of India. However, Bangladesh separates it from the main part of the parent nation. Northeastern India is joined to the rest of India

GEOGRAPHY OF INDIA. From the Himalayas in Kashmir (top) to the rice fields of South India (bottom), the subcontinent has an endless variety of landscapes. The topography of the subcontinent's heartland, the Indo-Gangetic Plain (center pictures), is uniform, but climatic differences alter the appearance of the landscape. The photo at left shows the Thar Desert, viewed from a desert city; at right is a field in the Ganges Valley.

only by a narrow strip of land. This corridor also separates Bangladesh from the three small Himalayan kingdoms to the north.[4]

The northeast is not completely devoid of agriculture. The hilly country in the interior is excellent for tea raising, an industry which developed while the region was under British rule. Bringing in tea bushes from China, the British in time established flourishing plantations. Rice is grown in many parts of the northeast. Another important crop is jute, especially in that area that was once East Pakistan and is now Bangladesh. Sacking made from the jute fiber is exported to all parts of the world.

The Deccan lies to the south of Hindustan. Most of the southern two thirds of the Indian peninsula is a large upland plateau. Called the Deccan, this region is almost completely enclosed by hills and mountains. The Vindhya Hills and other heights mark the line of separation from North India. The Western Ghats (gotz), a long range of low but rugged peaks, isolates the interior plateau from the narrow plain along the western coast. A similar range, the Eastern Ghats, separates it from the long eastern coastal plain. In the south the Western and Eastern Ghats join, dividing the southern part of the subcontinent from the Deccan.

For centuries, the mildly rugged terrain of the northern Deccan isolated the region from North India. It was not until the British constructed railway lines in the late 1800's that the Deccan was effectively joined to North India. Because the upland region also had hindered troop movements from the north, kingdoms in the Deccan usually were able to resist invaders from the Ganges region. But isolation had its bad points. Coastal traders seldom visited the Deccan. The navigable rivers in the Deccan flowed to the sea, thus discouraging merchants from fighting their way upstream to the towns. Since the Deccan saw little trade, few large cities developed in the region.

The coastal strips are a vital part of India. Running along the sides of the Deccan, and joining at the tip of India, are narrow, fertile strips of coastal plain. These are heavily settled. Long ago the arable land was converted into farming tracts, with rice becoming the main crop. The many countries which sought trade with India established trading posts on the long coastal strips. Some of the largest cities on the subcontinent owe their growth to a favorable location for ocean trade. The third largest city in India, Calcutta, is the center of trade

[4] Two of the three kingdoms (Bhutan and Sikkim) are protectorates of India. The third (Nepal) is independent.

on the east coast; the largest, Bombay, is the most important trading center on the west coast. The fourth largest city, Madras, overcame poor harbor facilities to become the most important port in South India.

South India is a world of its own. The term "South India" is associated with an undefined region lying south of the Kistna River. This southern region is largely a tropical zone of mountains, hills, and forests. Tillable land in South India is found mainly on that region's share of the coastal strips. Because most South Indians live along the coasts, and because the region is accessible to sea routes, South India has always led the subcontinent in emigration to other countries. Tens of thousands of Indians have crossed the twenty-two mile strait to Ceylon or have left South India for Malaya, Singapore, the South Pacific, and East and South Africa.

In modern times Kerala, a province in South India, has become the most advanced section of the subcontinent. In a nation where three fourths of the people are illiterate, a majority of the Keralese can read and write. Throughout South India irrigation systems are highly developed, and the area has flourishing leather-working and textile industries. Of all parts of the subcontinent, South India might well have the brightest future.

• CHECK-UP

1. What are the chief characteristics of the Indus Valley? of the Ganges Valley? of the northeast? of the Western Frontier? of the Deccan? of South India?

2. How has the Indus Valley changed over the past 4000 years? What caused the changes?

3. What geographic features have been obstacles to Indian unification?

3. India's Sources of Water Have Been Forces of Life and Death

Since ancient times rivers and rainfall have been of vital importance to India. Perhaps no region of the world places as much importance on them as does this subcontinent. Every Indian knows of the three mighty rivers of Hindustan: the Indus, the Ganges, and the Brahmaputra. The Ganges is the sacred river of Hinduism, and many Hindus come to bathe in its holy waters. The summer monsoon, the winds that usher in and end the subcontinent's rainy season, is the subject of Indian art, music, and literature. Wherever a person goes in India he finds that water is the overriding concern.

Each year countless Hindus bathe in the Ganges, seeking purity of soul or healing for the body. Some come to die near the stream so that their ashes may be cast upon the sacred waters.

The Indus River makes the northwest habitable. Life in Pakistan and in the neighboring portions of India depends upon the Indus River. Descending from its source in the high Himalayan plateau through breaks in the mountain wall, the Indus flows onto the Indo-Gangetic Plain and then turns southward to the Arabian Sea. It is fed by five large tributaries: the Jhelum (*jay′*loom), Chenab (chee-*nahb′*), Ravi (*rah′*vee), Sutlej (*sut′*ledg), and Beas (*bee′*ahz). The importance of the tributaries is reflected in the name of the land through which they flow: the Punjab, meaning "five waters." Sind, the lower region of the northwest, has only the Indus River.

Much of the arable land in the Punjab and Sind was settled after the British came to India. Because rainfall was inadequate for crops, irrigation was needed before the fertile land could be transformed into farms. The British built thousands of miles of irrigation canals in the northwest. These have helped to turn the deserts into valuable wheat- and cotton-producing lands.

The Ganges system determines the fate of much of Hindustan. Through the centuries, the difference between food and famine for people in the Ganges Valley has been the Ganges and its four main tributaries: the Jumna (*joom′*nuh), Gogra (*goh′*gruh), Rapti (*rahp′*tee), and Gandak (*gun′*duk). These rivers begin in snow-crowned mountains to the north, flow through central Hindustan, and join the

Ganges before it empties into the Bay of Bengal. The Ganges also is joined by the Brahmaputra, and the two rivers form the delta described on page 12.

The Ganges system irrigates thousands of acres of sugar cane and cotton in central Hindustan. But unlike peasants in the Indus Valley, who depend almost exclusively on irrigation, farmers in the Ganges Valley often use river water as a supplementary supply. Most of the region gets enough moisture from the summer monsoon to produce one crop. Irrigation enables peasants to produce two crops a year. It also makes possible the cultivation of "marginal" land which does not have quite enough rainfall for farming. When the summer monsoon fails, irrigation prevents the total destruction of crops.

The Brahmaputra River bisects the northeast. The Brahmaputra River is the easternmost of the three major rivers of India. Its source of water is literally inexhaustible. Not only does the river begin in the mountains, where it is fed by melting snow, but it flows through one of the rainiest regions on the globe. Unfortunately, much of the water is wasted. A large part of the land across which the Brahmaputra flows is almost uninhabitable. Only after the waters reach West Bengal do they become useful.

The rivers of peninsular India are undependable for irrigation. Peasants in the region of the three great river systems of Hindustan are the only Indians who can depend on river water for irrigation. The rivers of Hindustan are fed by melting snow in the northern mountains, and the flow does not vary a great deal from year to year. In the Deccan and South India, however, rivers are fed only by the summer monsoon. They flood surrounding fields during the monsoon season, but in a particularly wet year the flooding exceeds normal bounds and destroys crops, homes, and lives. On the other hand, in years when the summer monsoon fails, rivers literally dry up. Moreover, in even "normal" years the rivers do not supply a steady source of water for irrigation. In peninsular India the climate is so hot that water evaporates rapidly, and the soil is so porous that a great deal of water seeps out of the river banks. Rivers in the peninsula generally hold water for only a few months a year.

Because Indians in peninsular India cannot depend on the rivers, they count more heavily on monsoon rains than do Indians in Hindustan. And since they can never know how much water the monsoon winds will bring, they must have as a food crop something which grows in either wet or dry seasons. Jowar, a type of sorghum,

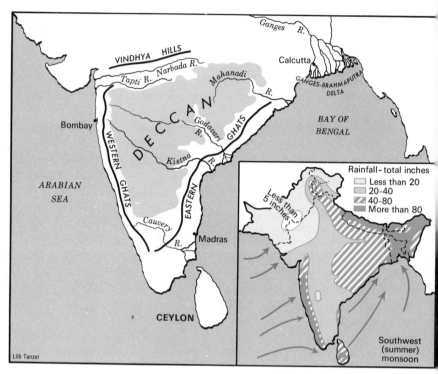

PENINSULAR INDIA. One reason the Deccan developed more slowly than North India is that the former lacked a dependable water supply. The southwest monsoon, which brings rain to much of Asia, may drench the land one year but fail the next. Though the *average* rainfall for peninsular India is adequate, most sections have dry years when crops fail.

meets this requirement, and it has been the principal crop in peninsular India for centuries.

"Tanks" are a common sight in peninsular India. Reliance on the monsoon does not mean that irrigation is unknown in the Deccan and South India. Most villages have reservoirs, or "tanks" as they are called in India. Reservoirs range in size from small, shallow ponds to deep lakes covering many square miles. The primary purpose of the village tank is to store water for irrigation, but often it is also the only source of water for household use. Moreover, the reservoir that supplies irrigation and drinking water is also the water hole for cattle, the laundry for washing clothes, and the village dump. It may be the spawning ground for fish.

As might be expected, the village reservoir often becomes a breeding ground for disease. Epidemics of malaria and cholera are all too common. Both the British and the succeeding leaders of independent India have attempted to solve the problem of water pollution. However, with so many villages, and with so few Indians educated enough to understand the dangers of pollution, the task has been difficult. Epidemics have been reduced but not eliminated.

In a dry season the reservoirs, like the rivers, often run dry. Failure of one summer monsoon means hard times; failure of two in a row spells disaster. The Deccan and South India, therefore, have experienced many terrible famines because the summer monsoons failed to come.

• CHECK-UP

1. What is the summer monsoon? Why is it important?
2. What are Hindustan's three great river systems? Why are these important?
3. Why are the rivers of peninsular India less dependable as a source of water than those in Hindustan?
4. What is the village "tank"? What are its uses? What problems does it create?

4. The Village is the Core of Indian Life

In studying the history and culture of a people it is all too easy to focus attention upon the great and bustling urban centers. After all, it is generally only the residents of cities — monarchs, statesmen, soldiers, philosophers, and teachers — who get their deeds recorded in history. But in the study of Indian life, one cannot ignore the village. Throughout Indian history the village has been the heart and pulse of life. Despite a modern-day exodus to the city, four out of five Indians still live in villages.

India is a land of villages. Before the partition of the subcontinent, India and Pakistan together had some 450,000 villages. Today the Republic of India alone has some 550,000. India has only about 2900 cities and towns, and less than 150 of these have more than 100,000 people. By way of comparison, the United States has less than half as many people as India but more than twice as many cities and towns. To the vast majority of India's millions, the village is home.

By far the greatest number of India's 550,000 villages are small. Most have fewer than 500 people. The typical village consists of a

INDIAN VILLAGES. These pictures bring out contrasts in village life. They also show why impure water poses a nationwide problem. The cement-lined well is in a Punjabi village. It was built by the government to eliminate disease traced to an earlier polluted well. The pictured canal, in Kerala, is a breeding ground for malaria-carrying mosquitoes. Kerala has water everywhere, but still suffers from a shortage of safe drinking water.

small cluster of huts and cottages. If it has a street at all, the street consists of a rutted lane no better than a cow path. Yet oftentimes a villager's few neighbors are the only people he knows from birth to death. Many Indians live out their lives without traveling more than a few miles from their home village.

Villages differ in appearance. The climate of a region and the availability of building materials have influenced the kind of houses built by the villagers. In the heavily settled regions trees gave way to cultivated land many centuries ago. With no wood for building purposes, peasants in such regions build houses of sun-dried brick. Often in times of flood and heavy rain these houses literally "melt" away.

In northeastern India and in South India, where trees are abundant, housing differs markedly from the mud hut of North India and the northern Deccan. The houses in villages of these regions are lightly constructed, with wood and various kinds of reeds used as building materials. Houses built in this manner are fairly livable during most of the year. At least they are well ventilated, an important consideration in the hot, humid climate of the southern and northeastern parts of India. But they are hardly waterproof. The houses get damp and uncomfortable during the rainy season, and they, too, are often destroyed by flood waters.

Houses in all villages on the subcontinent do have certain characteristics in common. They consist of one or two rooms or, occasionally, three. The floor of the village hut is the bare earth. There is little or no furniture. The family takes its meals sitting on the floor. The bed is a mat or blanket. The possessions of the family — household goods, clothing, farm tools — are stored around the room, suspended on pegs, or hung from the rafters. In a two-room house, the extra room often houses the family's water buffalo or cow.

Most villagers lead a miserable existence. There are few peoples in the world who have such a struggle for existence as Indian villagers. Seven out of ten villagers are poor farmers. They till small plots of land on the outskirts of the villages. The average size for an Indian farm is five acres, but many peasants must be satisfied with an acre or two. Those villagers who do not farm are carpenters, blacksmiths, potters, weavers, or barbers. They earn a living by exchanging their services to farmers for grain.

Indian villagers are unbelievably poor. Many of them eat little except rice, wheat, or jowar. India has many cows, but religious restrictions forbid Hindus to eat beef. Many Indians are hopelessly in debt to money lenders. Often the bills were inherited from parents and, even though children are not required by law to pay their parents' debts, tradition demands that they do so. In many cases a peasant can do no more than pay the interest on the loan.

The Cow in Indian Life

For 3000 years the cow has enjoyed an esteemed place in Indian life. "Sacred" and "holy" are terms often used to describe the animal. Bullocks pull plows and carts, but many cows spend their days wandering the city streets. To the Hindu, the cow is the symbol of motherhood, of fertility, and of life itself. He becomes incensed if a cow is killed. Some parts of India even have *gosadans* — retirement homes for aged cows.

The Indian cow has been regarded as sacred for so long that no one knows for sure just why or when it first came to be venerated. Quite likely this animal received and retained its position because of its usefulness to Indian life. Milk converted into *ghee* (drawn butter) has always been a staple item in Indian meals. Having little wood to use for fuel, Indians burn cow dung in their hearths. The dung that is not collected returns to the soil, providing fertilization. The cow also provides India with a valuable export. Cow hides are shipped from India to many parts of the world.

The cow population of India has multiplied rapidly. India has more cows — they number well over a quarter billion — than any other country in the world. The government of India would like to thin the ranks by a third or more, since excess animals are an economic burden. The food consumed by unneeded cows, argues the government, could be used to feed people. However, the government does not dare to take action. Already it is under fire for refusing to stop Muslims and other non-Hindus from killing cows, even though their actions are necessary if India is to retain its position as an exporter of hides. Were the government to propose the slaughter of cows, India would erupt in protest.

Villages often are isolated from the rest of the country. Because of poverty and inadequate transportation, millions of villagers have never had an opportunity to leave their birthplace. Roads between villages have been little more than dirt paths. The few paved roads on the subcontinent linked the major cities, but even many of these were badly neglected.

Today villages have more contacts with the outside world. New roads are being built, primary schools have been established in most villages, medical clinics are increasing in number. Most villages have at least one radio to keep the inhabitants informed about national and world events. Many villagers are getting jobs in the cities as India becomes more industrialized. They seldom return, but word of city life gets back to the families they leave behind. Despite all these contacts, however, the villager is hardly a part of the modern world.

• CHECK-UP

1. What are the characteristics of a village?
2. How does climate and the availability of building materials affect the type of home a peasant builds?
3. Why was the Indian village long "an island of isolation"? Why is this less true today?

5. Many Races and Languages Are Found on the Indian Subcontinent

Men representing all the major races and several of the language families have settled in the Indian subcontinent at one time or another. For thousands of years migrants from the Middle East, Central Asia, and Southeast Asia have made their way to this part of the world. Over the centuries these peoples have lost any distinguishing physical characteristics they had when they entered the subcontinent. Intermarriage, climate, and dietary factors have modified their features. Racial lines have become so blurred that today the designation "race" is almost meaningless in India.

The major racial type in the subcontinent has two divisions. The great majority of Indians are classified as either Aryans or Dravidians. Although both groups are descended from peoples commonly called Caucasoid, neither fits conveniently into that classification. The Indian peoples are so different from European Caucasoids that some physical anthropologists put them in a special classification. The name suggested for Indians of Caucasoid ancestry, no matter how distant in time, is Indo-Dravidian. Well over 800 million people fall into this category. Hence the Indo-Dravidian "race" must be considered one of the major races of mankind.

The most numerous of the people of Caucasoid ancestry are the Aryans.[5] Several thousand years ago people calling themselves *Aryas* poured into the lightly populated land of India. The Aryas, or Aryans, differed greatly in appearance from peoples already inhabiting the region. They were tall and fair, whereas the people they found were short and dark. The Aryans settled mainly in the Indus and Ganges Valleys. Ultimately, their descendants moved south into the Deccan. Until the Russians pushed across Siberia to reach the Pacific, the Aryans were the farthest extension of the fair-skinned racial types common to Europe and Mediterranean Asia. Most of the Hindu peoples in Hindustan can be classified as Aryans, although they have absorbed strains of many other racial types.

The Aryans largely replaced the early settlers in the Ganges and Indus Valleys. From the collective names of their distinct languages these early settlers have come to be called Dravidians. Though their origins are not well known, it is believed that they had migrated from the Middle East many centuries earlier. While they might well have had Caucasoid features when they arrived, time had brought about great changes in their physical appearance. The tall, fair Aryans described them as short and dark.

Many Dravidians intermarried with the Aryans, adding new strains to the newcomers' racial stock. Most of them, however, fled southward into the Deccan and beyond. Their descendants, short, slight of build, and dark skinned, are today the characteristic inhabitants of South India.

Many people who live in Pakistan do not fit conveniently into either the Dravidian or the Aryan mold. Since the northwest was the gateway for invasion, the region has absorbed settlers from many countries and from many periods of history. Racial lines are difficult to trace throughout the subcontinent, but they are nearly impossible to separate in Pakistan.

Negroid groups are scattered about the Indian subcontinent. Some of the people living in South Asia when the Dravidians arrived were Negroids. Judging from the features of their descendants, they

[5] The term Aryan, as used here, refers to a *people* and not a *race*. The term was grossly distorted by Hitler and his Nazis during the 1930's and 1940's to foster acceptance of their idea of a "super race."

PEOPLES OF INDIA. Over the years racial origins have become blurred in India. Even peoples with distinctive Mongoloid features, such as the northeast Indian family (top, right), exhibit strains of other races. The Rajasthan shepherd, directly above, is Aryan, but he strongly resembles the Dravidian village jeweler beside him. The girl pictured here (top, left) has distinctive Dravidian features. However, the school children in the bottom photo, while living in Dravidian Kerala, exhibit a wide range of racial features.

The Gypsies

Many different peoples, from places north and west, wandered into the Indian subcontinent over the centuries. But India has given to the world some of its most famous wanderers — the Gypsies. The English name for these people — derived from an old but false belief that they were originally Egyptians — has come to mean a "wanderer."

Studies of the language of the Gypsies, known as Romany, have revealed a direct relationship to Sanskrit, the mother language of the Indo-Aryan tongues of North India. The Gypsies, it is now widely believed, lived in ancient times on the Ganges River Plain. Perhaps as long ago as 500 B.C. they began their migrations westward into the Near East, Africa, Europe, and the Americas.

Wherever they have appeared, the Gypsies have become known for their lively music and dances, their fortune telling, and their love of horses and horse-trading. In the twentieth century the Gypsies have begun to give up their nomadic ways and to settle in larger towns and cities.

were more closely related to Negroid peoples who live in isolated parts of Southeast Asia and on various islands of the South Pacific than to the African Negroids. At one time these aboriginal peoples made their homes everywhere in the Indian subcontinent. However, unable to cope with the more aggressive Dravidians and Aryans, they gradually withdrew into the hills and jungles. Here they have lived for centuries, keeping pretty much to themselves. And though they have been strongly influenced by the Hindu village culture, they have succeeded in preserving many of their traditional ways of life.

Mongoloid racial types are present in India. In the Himalayan border region of India are found peoples who strongly resemble the Mongoloids of China, Japan, Korea, and Southeast Asia. They are descended from migrants who entered India from Tibet and southwestern China many centuries ago. Never numerous, these Mongoloid peoples compose only a tiny part of the Indian population.

Signs in English and Bihari at an intersection in Bihar State (right) reflect India's language diversity. English is a useful second language for many Indians. Above, in 1965 angry students demonstrated against a proposed replacement of English by Hindi as the country's official language.

Language differences set the people apart. Racial diversity on the subcontinent is matched by the variety of languages. India, for example, has made Hindi its official national language, but it also recognizes 13 regional languages. Moreover, a hundred dialects are spoken. The languages vary from one another as much as English does from German and Arabic. The difference in dialects is not so great. Many dialects differ from one another only in the manner that the English of Scotland or Ireland differs from that of an American or an Englishman. People speaking different dialects of the same regional language have little difficulty in understanding one another.

Indo-Aryan languages are chiefly spoken. About two-thirds of the Indians and almost all of the people of Pakistan and Bangladesh use languages of the Indo-Aryan group of languages. The Indo-Aryan group is a major division of the Indo-European language family (see sidelight, page 29). In an area beginning with the border region be-tween Turkey and Iran, and spreading across Iran, Afghanistan, and North India, Indo-Aryan languages are spoken by some 400 million people.

The most popular Indo-Aryan language in the subcontinent is Hindi. Spoken by more than 200 million Hindus, it is found primarily in the western and central sections of the Indo-Gangetic Plain. It is an outgrowth of Sanskrit, the most enduring of the languages of the Aryan invaders. A language closely related to Hindi is Urdu, the tongue of some 50 million North Indians and most of the Pakistani people. Many people who speak the one language know the other, and the two languages together are often called Hindustani.

Ranking high in importance among the Indo-Aryan languages of the subcontinent is Bengali. The most famous user of this tongue was Rabindranath Tagore (1861–1941), a writer awarded the Nobel Prize for Literature in 1913. Another major language is Gujarati, the language of western India. This was the tongue of Mahatma Gandhi, India's famous social leader.

Dravidian is the second major language family of India. Ten of the fourteen recognized native languages on the Indian subconti-nent are of the Indo-Aryan group. But more than a fourth of the peoples of India speak one of the four regional languages that are Dravidian in origin. Unlike the Indo-Aryan tongues, a division of the Indo-European family, the Dravidian tongues form a language family of their own. They are spoken only in the Indian subconti-nent and in the adjoining island of Ceylon. But 150 million Indians speak Dravidian languages, making this linguistic group one of the leading language families of the world.[6]

Though there are a few pockets of Dravidian-speaking peoples in the northwest, these languages are primarily encountered in South India. As you read earlier, the Dravidians were living in South Asia when the Indo-Aryan-speaking peoples first made their appearance. The most famous of the Dravidian tongues is Tamil, the main lan-guage of the state of Tamil Nadu (formerly Madras).

---

[6] Actually four language families have an estimated 150 million speakers each. Besides Dravidian, they are the Semitic-Hamitic, Malayo-Polynesian, and sub-Saharan African families. The Indo-European family has well over a billion speakers; the Sino-Tibetan, about 800 million.

Language Families

Over the last half million years, since man first began to form words out of sounds, thousands of languages have evolved. Although many of these have disappeared, linguists — students of language — estimate that between 2500 and 5000 languages are still in use. Some of these are as different from one another as classical music is from jazz. But just as the two schools of music have certain elements in common, so all languages have similar traits. Basically, these are: 1) all languages use sounds; 2) these sounds are made into words; 3) the words are organized in a consistent pattern; and 4) together, the words and their pattern communicate a sense or meaning.

Today's languages are like the divergent branches of a few ancient, giant trees. The trunks of the trees are the parent languages from which branch off numerous language families. These trunks or parent languages, however, are now dead. But the branches or successor languages are very much alive, and each is the parent of new languages.

Today there are at least eleven language families. The most important are the Indo-European and the Sino-Tibetan. Languages stemming from the Indo-European form a broad belt running through Western Europe, the Mediterranean area, the Middle East, and India and Pakistan. Most of the peoples of Asia speak languages from the Sino-Tibetan group, although several other language families also are found in Asia and the nearby islands. A major difference between Indo-European and Sino-Tibetan languages is that in the latter words generally consist of a single syllable with a meaning which varies according to the tone and pitch used by the speaker.

The study of languages tells more than just facts about the languages themselves. You might wish to consult various reference books to learn 1) how linguistics provides clues about the migrations of ancient peoples; 2) how cultures mingled; and 3) how civilizations grew as a result of linguistic influences.

Some tongues are neither Indo-Aryan nor Dravidian. A number of Indian dialects and languages are unrelated to either of the two major language groups. English is widely understood by the educated classes, since it was the language of government during the British period and was taught in government and missionary schools. Jawaharlal Nehru, a founding father of the modern Republic of India, spoke Hindi but felt more at ease when conversing in English! English has an especially wide acceptance among the Dravidian speakers of South India, where it is the second language.

In the northern border areas Sino-Tibetan dialects are spoken. They are also spoken in isolated sections of the hilly country to the northeast. These dialects came over the mountain wall with immigrants from Tibet and China. Tribal peoples in various parts of the subcontinent converse in dialects which are faintly similar to tongues heard in Southeast Asia and the Pacific. Linguists also place most of these dialects in the Sino-Tibetan language family.

Language variety has obstructed political efficiency. Historically, the linguistic diversity of the subcontinent has raised many grave political problems. For centuries it was a contributing factor in the fragmentation of India into hundreds of realms. Indians speaking a particular dialect more readily accepted a ruler who talked as they did rather than one who did not. Though not the only factor hindering political unification, the linguistic diversity nevertheless was an important one. Also, the diversity contributed much to the division of India into traditional "realms." Based on strong regional ties, these realms resisted every effort to alter them. For example, at one time the British divided Bengal into two provinces because it was too large to be governed efficiently. But the people of Bengal were united both linguistically and culturally, and they objected strenuously to the British action. To settle the seething discontent the British were forced to reunite Bengal.

The modern Republic of India finds the diversity of languages particularly troublesome. It has hindered the construction of a truly national state and an effective central government. Officials in the national capital have difficulty in making their wishes known to members of the National Assembly and to administrators in the provinces. Attempts to standardize the nation's schools have been hindered by the unwillingness of the various regions to accept a common language. However, considering the strong regional attachments to the various languages, it is unlikely that a single national language will ever meet the approval of all Indians.

- CHECK-UP
    1. Who were the Aryans? the Dravidians? What other racial types are present in India?
    2. What are the two major language families in India? Why is English important?
    3. How has the diversity of languages posed many problems for India?

Summing Up

India has been a major center of civilization in Asia for well over 4000 years. Its way of life evolved mainly within the subcontinent, but it also has been influenced by developments beyond India's frontiers. Events in the lands beyond the mountain wall in the north have had especially critical effects.

Until modern times, India was not a country in the usually accepted sense of the term. Rather, it was a composite of many countries. North India, with its fertile soil and great rivers, always has been the heartland of the subcontinent. The vast Thar Desert and the low Vindhya Hills effectively prevented the march of armies, customs, and ideas from North India into the Deccan, the great interior plateau. The extreme southern portion of India developed a way of life all its own.

Since agriculture has been the mainstay of the Indian economy since ancient times, the availability of water for farming has been of crucial importance. Areas which have been too heavily dependent upon the wet monsoon have periodically suffered from droughts and floods. In North India the water supply of rivers has year after year spelled the difference between rich and slim harvests.

Ever since ancient times four out of five Indians have lived in villages. These villages are similar in many ways. Most of them are tiny, housing in all villages is barely adequate, most villagers are poor, and most villages have been isolated from the outside world. Also, the villages are alike in that all have been slow to change.

The human diversity of India is revealed in its racial and linguistic composition. Over the centuries men of several different races have settled in the subcontinent, bringing with them a multitude of languages. In the course of time racial divisions have become greatly blurred, but the language differences have become even more pronounced. Many major languages and numerous dialects, representing several different language families, are spoken by the people of the subcontinent. The lack of a common language has hindered political efficiency in India in the past and has posed a paramount problem to the independent India of today.

. . . .

CHAPTER REVIEW

Can You Identify?

Himalayas	Deccan	Thar Desert
Hindustan	Ghats	Vindhya Hills
Khyber Pass	"tank"	Indo-Gangetic Plain
the Punjab	Aryans	Dravidians
Pakistan	monsoon	language family

What Do You Think?

1. Early invaders of India, using overland routes, were more often absorbed than repelled. Why?

2. More than half of the Indian people live on one fifth of the subcontinent's total area — the northern plain. Why is this so?

3. In India, a country plagued by a great number of spoken languages, English is widely understood. Why has not the Indian government adopted English as a national language?

4. For centuries, race has not weighed heavily in Indian attitudes towards mankind. Why, do you think, is this so?

5. "To know the village is to know India." What is the basis for this statement?

Extending and Applying Your Knowledge

1. In *India's Ex-Untouchables* (Day, 1965), Harold Isaacs includes a series of interviews with underprivileged Indians in which they discuss their condition and problems. *Blossoms in the Dust* (Praeger, 1962) by Kusum Nair describes the author's travels in rural India and what she learned. Read these or similar books to get a better understanding of the problem confronting India's poor people.

2. Americans find it difficult to understand why most Indians, even in a time of famine, are opposed to the slaughter of their "sacred cows." To understand why an Indian reacts as he does to suggestions to reduce the "cow population," read "The Myth of the Sacred Cow," in *Natural History* (March, 1967).

3. For an in-depth study of the Indian subcontinent and its peoples read the first four selections in *India: Selected Readings* (see bibliography, page 218).

2

THE EMERGENCE
OF INDIAN
CIVILIZATION

The study of ancient India presents a number of vexing problems. Many of them stem from the very nature of early Indian civilization. Unlike the Hebrews and Chinese, who faithfully recorded the deeds of their ancestors, the Indians of ancient times were not history-minded. The people of India's earliest known civilization left only fragmentary inscriptions, and these have never been deciphered. The people who conquered this civilization could not write. True, they had a history, but it consisted of fanciful tales of gods and men passed by word of mouth from generation to generation. These tales gained much in the retelling before they were finally recorded. There is not a single written record of ancient India which can be trusted for either factual or chronological accuracy. Or, as a well known scholar has written, "The early history of India resembles a jigsaw puzzle with many missing pieces; some parts of the picture are fairly clear; others may be reconstructed with the aid of a controlled imagination; but many gaps remain, and may never be filled."[1]

In the absence of reliable historical records, other sources must be used to reconstruct early Indian civilization. Archaeological excavations have unearthed much evidence about the Harrapan civilization, India's earliest. Used with caution, India's sacred literature can tell us a great deal about the early Aryans, the people who conquered the Harappans. Priests of the Buddhist and Jainist religions wrote many religious and philosophical works. These writings help to fill in the gap between the early Aryan period and the time when fairly accurate

[1] A. L. Basham, *The Wonder That Was India* (London, Sidgwick and Jackson, 1956), p. 45.

history began to be recorded. Finally, a study of the culture of modern India provides more information than one might expect. Indians have never been a people eager to discard old ideas and practices. For this reason legends, traditions, and customs of modern India, if properly analyzed, throw considerable light upon India's remote past. The evidence gleaned from all sources indicates that India is the third oldest center of civilization in the world, being outranked only by Mesopotamia and Egypt.

1. Civilization Struck Early Roots in India

The first center of Indian civilization emerged around 2500 B.C. Based in what is now Pakistan, this Harappan, or Indus, civilization endured for more than a thousand years. It lost its place as a generator of civilization when Aryan invaders from West Asia overran it. The Aryan tribes moved eastward onto the Ganges Plain. Here, over a period of many centuries, the Aryans developed the Hindu way of life. Constantly enriched and modified, Hindu civilization has lasted to the present day.

Rediscovered cities brought to light the Indus civilization. Until recent times, few people suspected that Indian civilization began in the Indus Valley. For centuries the center of Indian life had been the Ganges Valley, and much of the Indus region was barren wasteland. In the 1920's, however, archaeological excavations were begun in parts of the Punjab and Sind. To the amazement of nearly everyone, the archaeologists uncovered a number of forgotten cities and towns. Moreover, the excavations proved that the civilization served by the cities extended north and south for at least a thousand miles. No other civilization of its time covered that much ground.

The most important cities discovered by the archaeologists were Harappa and Mohenjo Daro (moh-*hen'*joh *dah'*roh). No other cities of antiquity were as well planned. Avenues and streets crossed in an orderly pattern. A special district of large, elaborate buildings lay on the western outskirts of each city. Probably, these buildings were the palaces of rulers, government offices, and temples. The eastern part of each city was composed of smaller buildings. Evidently this section had been set aside for the homes and working quarters of the common people. Each city was dominated by a powerful palace-fortress. Obviously designed for defense against rebellion and invasion, each fortress was built on a high elevation of earth and baked bricks. Since the fortresses rose high above the surrounding plain, lookouts could easily spot all approaching invaders.

The houses in Harappa and Mohenjo Daro probably were the finest of their times. Each city had many two-story buildings, something unusual for that day. The buildings had staircases and were divided into a number of rooms. The better homes had inner courtyards, facilities for bathing, and drainage systems. (No other ancient people devised a system of indoor "plumbing" until the Romans did so some 2000 years later.) Outside the houses, paved drainage channels carried waste along streets and alleys and out of the city. Not only was the Indus civilization the largest of its time, but it also was one of the most advanced.

The ruins of Harappa and Mohenjo Daro indicate that each city was rebuilt many times. The nearby rivers often flooded, destroying large sections of the two cities and covering them with silt. Yet when a section was rebuilt it always followed the original "master plan."

Little is known about the origins of the Harappan people. The origins of the Harappan people, and how they lived, can never be known for certain. Probably they were descendants of long-time inhabitants of the region. There is some evidence that they progressed from a Stone Age culture to an advanced civilization over a period of several thousand years. It is likely, too, that the Harappans were closely related to peoples who at an early time had built advanced agricultural communities in the hilly region west of the Indus Valley. There is even some evidence that the Harappan people had made contacts with the centers of civilized life in Mesopotamia. Items found in excavations have decorations that closely resemble Mesopotamian art, indicating that some "borrowing" of ideas did occur. However, the resemblances are few. The Harappan civilization must stand as an independently developed, not a borrowed, way of life.

The Harappans had a system of writing. Clay cylinder seals inscribed with writing have been found in numerous parts of Pakistan. Unfortunately the four hundred or so symbols used in this Harappan system have defied every effort at translation. The symbols resemble no other early system of writing used in the ancient world. Even if this baffling early Indian script is deciphered, it probably will shed little light upon Harappan life. No seals uncovered so far contain more than a few characters. Archaeologists need fairly lengthy passages, or at least a few connected sentences, to make any valid judgments about the people who wrote them.

Archaeological Methods

The idea of uncovering the secrets of a hidden civilization is intriguing. Preceding every momentous discovery, however, are many hours of painstaking work. Archaeology is a science concerned with reconstructing a cultural picture by excavating and studying artifacts, or man-made objects. In addition to knowing how to use a shovel, the archaeologist must draw from a broad range of facts and ideas. An understanding of the social sciences is essential, for the purpose of archaeology is to contribute to the history of man and society. Useful also is a knowledge of art and foreign languages. Scientific ability, particularly in the field of geology, is required. Often, too, the archaeologist draws from the knowledge of experts in fields such as paleontology, chemistry, biology, and climatology.

There is always a reason why a particular area is picked for study. Often aerial photographs of a region reveal unnatural physical conditions which indicate a buried village or town. Often, too, a ridge or mound on the landscape indicates the same thing. After choosing a site for study, the archaeologist examines the surface itself, looking for artifacts which will give him a clue as to what lies below. Then he draws a detailed contour map, for archaeology depends on stratigraphy, the determination of time sequence by dating earth layers. The simple fact that the bottom layer is always the oldest is basic to archaeological studies. Next, the archaeologist divides the area into squares, and only then does the slow and careful process of digging begin. Under the supervision of the archaeologist trenches are dug, one layer at a time. Artifacts are carefully unearthed and classified. The archaeologist dates the artifacts as accurately as possible, then attempts to reach some conclusions from his findings.

The archaeological process began relatively late in India. No excavations were started before the twentieth century. Digging at Harappa and Mohenjo Daro began in 1924. Though not yet completed, the excavations at these two cities have opened up a whole new chapter in Indian history.

THE HARAPPAN CIVILIZATION. Until 1924, when excavations were begun at Harappa and Mohenjo Daro, archaeologists only suspected that the subcontinent's oldest cities arose in the Indus Valley. To learn more about the early civilization, the Pakistani government has encouraged the exploration of these ancient ruins. At left is a part of Mohenjo Daro.

Pointing to the importance of religion in Harappan life are the statuette of a bearded priest (left) and the seals showing a seated god (above, left) and a bull, the symbol of fertility.

Using two-wheeled carts drawn by oxen, peasants brought cotton, grain, and other goods to the Harappan cities. Grain was stored in large granaries; much of the cotton was loaded onto river boats which carried it to more distant markets. At the right is an artist's version of the busy wharf at Mohenjo Daro.

Little is known about the religious life of the Harappans. Students of Indian history believe that religion played an important role in the lives of the Harappans. They point out that reluctance to change is a characteristic of a conservative, priest-dominated society, and that the Harappan practice of rebuilding on old foundations shows a reluctance to change. Also, many objects of a religious nature have been uncovered at Harappa and Mohenjo Daro. Some of these objects represent the awesome powers of life and creation, a favorite theme in early religions. For example, the bull, a symbol of fertility in many societies, was portrayed in many Harappan figurines. Moreover, statuettes resembling Shiva (*shee'*vuh), a major Hindu deity of later times, have been found in Harappan ruins. It is quite possible that some of the ideas found in modern Hinduism originated in the Harappan civilization.

The Indus Valley had a complex economy. By using a controlled imagination, one can reconstruct the economy of the Harappan civilization. Many occupations were represented. Most of the people, however, were peasants who lived in the outlying villages. This pattern is characteristic of the subcontinent to this day. The Harappan farmers raised crops of wheat and barley. These crops not only provided a livelihood but were used to pay taxes. The peasants also cultivated cotton — the first farmers in history to do so. Present-day farmers in the Indus Valley continue to raise wheat, barley, and cotton.

Judging from the sophisticated level of its urban life, the Harappan civilization included highly skilled artisans and craftsmen. Cities such

TIMETABLE	Early History of North India
2500–1500 B.C.	Indus Valley Civilization
1500–500 B.C.	Aryan Invasions Vedic Age
563 B.C.	Traditional date of Gautama Buddha's birth
326 B.C.	Invasion of Alexander the Great
324 B.C.	Founding of Maurya Dynasty
269–232 B.C.	Reign of Ashoka

as Harappa and Mohenjo Daro could not have been built, much less maintained, without the services of carpenters, masons, plasterers, potters, and metal workers. Jewelry and other articles fashioned from copper, bronze and precious stones have been found. The workmanship exhibited in them points to the existence of talented Harappan artisans. And evidently children in the Harappan state were far from neglected. Dozens of cleverly molded toy animals, baby rattles, and miniature wagons and carts have been uncovered in various excavations.

Trade was evidently an important part of Harappan life. Not only was there trade between the various cities and towns, but it extended far beyond the borders of India. Small engraved Harappan seals have been found in Mesopotamia. But judging from excavations in both Mesopotamia and the Indus Valley, neither civilization transferred much of its culture to the other through trade.

Harappan civilization gradually declined. No civilization can stand still; it either improves or deteriorates. Seemingly Harappan rulers tried to maintain a static society, and as a consequence the Harappan civilization entered a long period of decline. Archaeologists who have studied Harappa and Mohenjo Daro have noticed that in the upper layers of these cities, each layer exhibits workmanship which is somewhat inferior to the one before. Evidently each generation was less careful than the preceding one. Fine craftsmanship became a lost art, irrigation ditches filled with silt, flood damage was left unrepaired, and fortifications were neglected. Moreover, nomadic peoples from West Asia were settling among the Harappans. The new arrivals had little appreciation for the cultural advances which the Harappans had made. All these factors tended to weaken the Indus Valley civilization.

Aryan invaders destroyed the Indus civilization. The newcomers to the Indus Valley were the Aryans. As you will recall from Chapter One, these early Aryans were the ancestors of most of the Hindus of present-day North India. While the Harappan civilization was developing the Aryans were living a nomadic life on the great grasslands which extend from Central Europe into West Asia. But perhaps 3500 years ago, or about the time the Harappan civilization began to decline, the Aryans began to move out of their traditional pasturelands. Why, no one knows. Perhaps climatic changes, food shortages, or "family quarrels" forced some tribes to seek new homes. At any rate, Aryan tribes began to press against the frontiers of civilized life.

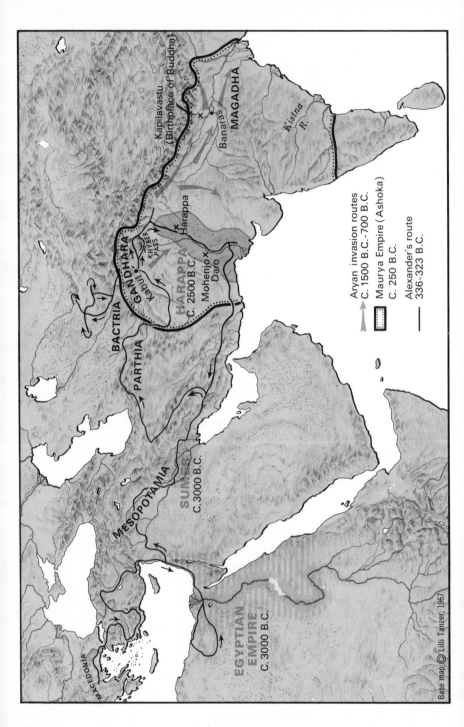

Kapilavastu
(Birthplace of Buddha)

MAGADHA

Banaras ×

Kistna R.

Harappa
×

KHYBER PASS

GANDHARA

Kabul

HARAPPA
C. 2500 B.C.

Mohenjo Daro ×

BACTRIA

PARTHIA

Aryan invasion routes
C. 1500 B.C.–700 B.C.

Maurya Empire (Ashoka)
C. 250 B.C.

Alexander's route
336–323 B.C.

SUMER
C. 3000 B.C.

MESOPOTAMIA

EGYPTIAN
EMPIRE
C. 3000 B.C.

MACEDONIA

Base map © Lilli Tanzer, 1967

Many of them settled in present-day Iran and Afghanistan; others crossed the mountain passes into northwest India.

What had begun as a trickle became a wave. By 1500 B.C. the cities and towns in the Indus Valley were under constant attack by Aryan invaders. The Aryans were fierce warriors who fought from horse-drawn chariots. Since the Harappan state already was in a state of decline, its defenders were no match for the hardy tribesmen. Harappa and Mohenjo Daro were sacked and burned and the last vestiges of the Indus civilization were destroyed.

Early Aryan life is dimly outlined in the Vedas. The period of Aryan expansion in India is known as the Vedic Age. It lasted from about 1500 B.C. to 500 B.C. The term is derived from *Veda*, the name applied to each of the four collections of Aryan legends, myths, battle hymns, and religious beliefs. The oldest of the four collections, the *Rig Veda*, provides glimpses into the life and migrations of the early Aryans. The work is largely religious poetry and has little historical worth. However, in the absence of other sources of information about early Aryan life, students of Indian culture have had to turn to it for light.

The *Rig Veda* reveals the Aryans as a fierce tribal people who depended largely on their cattle for a living. Traditionally they lived in small groups which rarely came together except to wage war. They seemed to thoroughly enjoy fighting, and their favorite pastimes were gambling and boasting about their martial deeds. Since they were reluctant to settle down in cities and towns they were not attracted by the Harappan way of life. After pillaging the communities in the Indus Valley many of the Aryan tribes moved eastward onto the Ganges River Plain. Centuries of struggle followed as the peoples living on the Plain sought to repel the invaders. Eventually, however, the Aryans achieved a position of leadership.

THE DAWN OF CIVILIZATION. Pictured on the map are three of the early "cradles" of civilization. (A fourth center was China.) The original Harappan civilization was destroyed when Aryan tribesmen forced their way into northwest India. These Aryans then moved eastward onto the Ganges Plain. By the time Alexander the Great invaded India (page 53), the Harappan civilization was forgotten. But Alexander, too, was soon forgotten. During the Maurya Empire, seventy-five years later, his name was not even known in India.

Evidently the Aryans established numerous small kingdoms in the Ganges Valley, but they were unable to subdue completely the people already living there. The *Rig Veda* mentions a bewildering number of principalities, many of which were ruled by monarchs with non-Aryan names. The *Rig Veda* seems to indicate that North India was divided into a host of small states which constantly were at war with each other. We can be certain of little more. The material in the *Rig Veda* was passed down by word of mouth for many centuries before finally being recorded. By the time it was set down in writing the imagination of earlier generations had transformed actual events and places into myth and legend.

• CHECK-UP

1. How have we learned about Harappan civilization? Where did it emerge? When?
2. In what respects were Harappan cities different from other early cities? What conclusions have been drawn from these differences?
3. What conclusions can we draw about Harappan ways of living: crops, taxes, crafts, commerce, religion?
4. Who were the Aryans? Why were they able to destroy Harappan civilization? What is the *Rig Veda*? What does it tell us about the Aryans?

2. Hinduism Gives Meaning and Purpose to Indian Life

During the Vedic Age the foundations were laid for Hinduism, a way of life that Indians have followed since shortly before the Christian era. Based on the religion of the invading Aryan tribesmen, Hinduism has absorbed many new ideas and customs over the centuries. If an Aryan of the Vedic Age could come back to life in the twentieth century, he would be puzzled by many of the practices and beliefs of modern Indians. But he would also recognize much that was familiar, for many of the basic ideas, customs, and attitudes of the Vedic religion were carried into Hinduism. These have persisted even into modern times.

The Vedas formed the core of the Aryan religion. Hinduism has no single sacred book such as the Bible or the Koran, the holy book of Muslims. It has several works, the oldest of which is the Vedic literature: the tales, songs, and ceremonial instructions which the Aryans developed before and during their settlement in the Indian subcontinent. The largest part of this literature is contained in the four Vedas: the *Rig Veda*, the oldest religious book in the world which is still held sacred; the *Sama Veda*, a collection of hymns; the *Yajur Veda*, a manual used by priests in the performance of their religious duties; and the *Atharva Veda*, a book of magical spells and incantations. The *Rig Veda* probably was put together between 1500 and 900 B.C. The other Vedas were compiled later, probably during the closing years of the Vedic Age. All of them, however, were passed on by word of mouth from one generation to the next for many centuries before being written down. In the Vedas may be found the roots of basic Hindu beliefs and ideas. Today the Vedas are generally studied only by scholars and priests. However, many of the rites and ceremonies of the *Yajur Veda* have been conducted year after year to the present day.

Epics are a major part of Hindu tradition. More familiar than the Vedas to most Hindus are the *Epics*, tales of early Aryan heroes. Like the Vedas, the Epics were passed on by word of mouth for many generations before being recorded. The longest of the two Epics is the *Mahabharata* (muh-*hah'buh'*ruh-tuh),[2] a poetical work consisting of some 100,000 couplets, and the longest poem in the world. It is basically the story of a great civil war in the region where now is located the city of Delhi. Its most famous portion is the lovely *Bhagavad Gita* (*bah'*guh-vud *gee'*tuh).[3] (See sidelight, page 45.) The second of the two great Epics, the *Ramayana* (rah-*mah'*yuh-nuh'), tells the story of Rama, a heroic Aryan king of Vedic times. It relates the adventures of Rama as he undertakes to rescue his wife Sita, who had been kidnapped by a devil-king of Ceylon.

Originally the tales in the Epics were told to preserve the memory of the deeds of famous Aryan warriors. However, as the stories were passed down from generation to generation they began to take on religious significance. Many of the basic beliefs of modern Hinduism became embodied in the tales. The Epics are also important to Hindu art and culture, for they have furnished many generations of Indian

---

[2] *Mahabharata* is a two-word compound. "Maha" means "great"; note the word maharajah, a "great prince." "Bharat" is the name of a legendary state of the Vedic Age. It has been adopted as the official name of the Republic of India.

[3] *Bhagavad Gita* is translated as "The Song of God" or "Song of the Lord." Generally, the title is shortened to "Gita."

artists and writers with endless inspirations for sculpture, paintings, stories, poems, and plays. Moreover the tales told in the Epics, no matter how fanciful, take the place of history for Hindus.

The caste system of India had its beginnings in Vedic times. The system of caste, one of the most persistent features of the Hindu way of life, reflects the conditions of society during the Vedic Age. At that time life in India was far less complex than it became in later times. First in Aryan society were the *Brahmins*,[4] the priests of the Aryan religion. They had attained their rank after centuries of challenge for first place from the *Kshatriya* (kuh-*sheh*'tree-yuh), the rulers and warriors. Ranking third in the Aryan class system were the *Vaishya*, or peasants. Later this class developed into a class of merchants and townspeople. The *Shudra*, or serfs, occupied the bottom rung on the class ladder. They included the conquered peoples who chose to remain in North India, as well as any Aryans who married into the ranks of the conquered peoples. The Shudras were farm laborers.

Gradually the four classes, or *varnas*, of Aryan times became the four main castes of the Indian social system. However, as Hindu civilization advanced, the caste system became increasingly complex. As new economic activities and skills developed, the four main castes were subdivided time and again. Caste lines came to be formed along occupational rather than social lines. Today the Indian subcontinent has more than 2300 different castes and subcastes. Every Hindu is a member of both his occupational caste and the varna into which his most remote ancestor was born.

Reformers and government leaders have tried for centuries to lessen caste distinctions, but caste is still the most important single factor in Hindu life. Forbidden to leave the hereditary caste, Hindus remain members of it during their entire lives. To a large extent caste determines what is permissible for an individual and what is forbidden, especially in rural areas. A Hindu's occupation, whom he can marry, what he can eat, and how he behaves toward others are matters ordained by caste customs and traditions.

Untouchables are outside the pale of Hindu society. India has a large group of unfortunate people to whom all the undesirable and "unclean" tasks are assigned. Variously called Untouchables, outcastes, pariahs, *Harijans*, or Scheduled Castes, these people form one

---

[4] *Brahmin* refers to the Brahmin caste. Also important in Indian thought is *Brahma*, the mythological creator, and *Brahman*, the indescribable Supreme Principle of Life which fills all space and time. The Aryan religion came to be called *Brahmanism*.

The Bhagavad Gita

The long and lovely *Bhagavad Gita* is part of one of the eighteen books in the *Mahabharata*. The *Gita* itself has eighteen chapters, but represents less than one per cent of the entire work. It is a dialogue involving four speakers. In the *Gita* Arjuna, a hero of the early Aryan age, is faced with the necessity of fighting a civil war in order to regain the kingdom which belonged to him and his brothers. Among those opposing him are many of his friends, relatives, and former teachers. Rather than see loved ones on both sides killed, Arjuna decides not to fight.

Driving Arjuna's war-chariot is Krishna, an incarnation of Vishnu the Preserver, one of the principal gods of Hinduism. When Arjuna informs Krishna of his decision, a long discussion between the two heroes follows. In it Krishna urges Arjuna to change his mind:

> Your words are wise, Arjuna, but your sorrow is for nothing. The truly wise mourn neither for the living nor for the dead. There never was a time when I did not exist, nor you, nor any of these kings. Nor is there any future in which we shall cease to be. . . . Even if you consider this from the standpoint of your own caste-duty, you ought not to hesitate; for, to a warrior, there is nothing nobler than a righteous war. . . . But if you refuse to fight this righteous war, you will be turning aside from your duty. . . . Your enemies will slander your courage. . . . What could be harder to bear than that? . . . Realize that pleasure and pain, gain and loss, victory and defeat, are all one and the same: then go into battle. Do this and you cannot commit any sin.[5]

The *Gita* is not a historical treatise, and no attempt is made to ascertain the outcome of the battle. Perhaps such a battle never occurred. Rather, the poem is a religious and philosophical work which reveals deep-seated beliefs. In the lines just quoted one finds the principles of rebirth; the importance of caste; and the rightness of violence in a righteous cause. Other parts of the *Gita* contain most of the doctrines which have become a part of Hinduism. To read the *Gita* is to study the inner workings of the Hindu mind.

[5] Adapted from Swami Prabhavananda and Christopher Isherwood, translators, *The Bhagavad Gita* (Mentor, 1967), pp. 36–39.

of the largest groups in India. Because they are outside the caste system, they lead a miserable existence. Members of the three highest varnas and of the higher subcastes of Shudras are forbidden by caste law to associate with them. Despite national laws to the contrary, the Untouchable often cannot use the village well or even enter a village except to do appointed tasks — such things as sweeping the street, cleaning the latrines, or disposing of dead animals. Every moment of the day the Untouchable is constantly reminded, through words or actions, of his low position in Indian life.

Indians are Untouchables for a variety of reasons. Certain groups of Shudras are excluded from the caste system because their traditional occupations are regarded as unclean. The tanners are a group which fall into this category. Some Untouchables are descendants of Hindus who were expelled from their castes for violations of caste regulations. Still others are descendants of invaders of the subcontinent, such as the Muslims. Over the centuries, as the ranks of Untouchables grew larger, a caste system of Untouchables developed. This system, too, has its ranks, traditions, and restrictions.

Since World War II the lot of the Untouchable has shown improvement. Mahatma Gandhi, the great Indian leader of pre-independence days, did much to bring this about. Gandhi, pleading that the Untouchables be accepted as human beings, adopted them as his fellow men, and violated the caste restriction barring association with them. It was he who gave them the name "Harijan," which means "Children of God." His example was an important factor in the passage of post-World War II laws which prohibit discrimination against Untouchables.

The improved status of the Untouchable is most noticeable in the large cities. Away from the small rural village where outcaste families are known, Untouchables lose their identity. In the masses of India's cities there is no way to tell an Untouchable from a Brahmin, for both are likely to wear Western-type clothing/ or lightweight Indian garb. Caste Hindus and outcastes work side by side in factories and offices. But in general the plight of the Untouchables, especially in rural India, is improving but slowly.

The caste system was justified by several cardinal beliefs. The Vedic and Epic literature contains many principles which have helped to maintain the caste system. One of these is the idea of *karma*, the belief that the status of a Hindu in any span of life has been determined by his behavior in a previous existence. Linked inseparably to karma is the idea of *samsara*, or transmigration of the soul. Because of samsara, eternity for each living creature — including gods and, according to some sects, even plants — consists of the repeated passing of the soul from one life to the next. At the base of both ideas is the belief that life and the world is *maya* — an illusion of reality, somewhat like a mirage in the desert, which no one really understands.

The basic beliefs of Hinduism give a certain spirit of futility to Indian life. The Hindu believes that he gets what he deserves; whatever happens, he is simply being repaid for behavior in his previous lives. This means that, if he is born a peasant, he should be guided by his *dharma* (duty, law, obligation) and accept his lot in life. But while it is true that Hindus generally accept life as it is, it must not be assumed that they never protest against misery, poverty, and oppression. Hinduism allows rebellion for a righteous cause. The history of India has many chapters full of violence and bloodshed caused by unwise or incompetent rulers. But, while causing political changes, Hindu rebels have never sought to change the existing social order.

Hinduism is a broad, inclusive, hard-to-define faith. The religion of the Aryans cannot rightly be called Hinduism. Hinduism as we know it today grew out of Aryan Brahmanism, but it also absorbed ideas from other sects. Much that is accepted in present-day Hinduism has come from descendants of the very people whom the Aryans had overcome. Wandering preachers and hymn singers from cults originating in the Dravidian South did as much as anyone to make Hinduism the main faith throughout the subcontinent. Before Hinduism was to emerge as the leading faith in India, Buddhism, another religion which grew out of Aryan Brahmanism, was to enjoy a long period of dominance. And Buddhism, in turn, was to contribute much to Hinduism as we know it today.

Perhaps the strength of Hinduism lies in its ability to understand and meet the tremendously different spiritual and philosophical needs of its multitude of followers. Unlike Judaism, Christianity, and Islam, Hinduism has no basic creed to which all its followers subscribe. Its essential beliefs range from simple superstition to the highest philosophical truths. Each believer finds his specific elements of faith within this broad range of ideas; no Hindu is expected to understand more than he is capable of understanding. As long as he identifies himself with the Hindu faith, accepts as sacred works the Vedic literature, and accepts the requirements of the caste system, he is assured of a place in Hindu society.

● CHECK-UP

1. What is the relation of the Vedas to Hinduism? the Epics?
2. What were the four original castes? Why are there more castes today? What is the significance of the caste system? Who are the Untouchables?
3. Explain the terms karma, samsara, maya, dharma. How do these help to maintain the caste system?
4. Why is Hinduism a popular religion?

3. Buddhism Arose in India but Met with Little Initial Success

By the end of the Vedic Age there were signs of growing dissatisfaction with Vedic society and religion. Many Indians objected to the increasing rigidity of the caste system and the great power wielded by the Brahmins. Moreover, some Indians were upset because the Brahmins appeared more interested in religious rites and ceremonies than in teaching respect for Aryan tradition.

During the period of mounting unrest many Indians denied themselves material comforts in order to free their minds for religious contemplation. Two such men developed doctrines which greatly affected the emerging Hindu faith. One was Mahavira (muh-hah-*vee'*ruh), the founder of Jainism (see sidelight, page 50). The other was Siddhartha Gautama (sid-*dahr'*tuh *gow'*tuh-muh), otherwise known as the Buddha. The faith that eventually evolved from the Buddha's teachings became one of the major faiths of the world.

Gautama's first protest was against his own way of living. The founder of Buddhism, probably born in 563 B.C., was the son and heir of the ruler of the Shakyas, a people who lived at the foothills of the Himalayas. Gautama's birthplace (map, page 40) is in the present-day nation of Nepal. Destined for the throne, Gautama was reared in comfort and luxury. According to tradition, he was shielded from the sight of the ugly and wretched things of life. While a young man, he married and became the father of two children. Nothing, it seems, was further from his thoughts than the serious problems of life.

Tradition states that one day Gautama left the palace grounds. In quick order he received several emotional jolts: he observed hunger, sickness, and death. He began to brood about what he had seen, wondering why men should experience such sorrow and suffering. Unable to find a satisfactory answer, he decided to go out into the world for help. At the age of 29 he left his wife and children, gave up his inheritance, and began wandering from place to place seeking an answer to his question. For six years neither instruction, study, nor the life of a hermit was of any avail. Then one day as Gautama, deep in contemplation, sat under a tree, he received in a sudden flash of insight the answer to the mystery and meaning of life and its suffering. At that moment he became the Buddha, the "Enlightened One."

The Buddha's beliefs were based upon Four Noble Truths. According to tradition, the Buddha first presented the truths of his Enlightenment to five monks in the Deer Park in the city of Banaras. The Buddha is credited with disclosing to them Four Noble Truths around which his beliefs were centered. These truths not only singled out the cause of man's suffering but also revealed the way of deliverance.

The first truth was that suffering is a part of existence. The Buddha maintained that mere existence meant pain and sorrow for man. In his sermon to the five monks, he is supposed to have revealed this first truth in the following words:

> O monks, I will tell you the truth about suffering. Suffering is birth, suffering is old age, suffering is sickness, suffering is death. You are bound to that which you hate: suffering; you are separated from that which you love: suffering; you do not obtain that which you desire: suffering. To cling to bodies, to sensations, to forms, to impressions, to perceptions: suffering, suffering, suffering.[6]

The second truth concerned the origin of suffering. The Buddha upheld the essentials of Brahmin philosophy. His explanation for human misery took into account the doctrine of karma and the cycle of rebirth. The Buddha detected the basic cause for the unhappiness of man as constant yearning and desire. People become attached to things they must sooner or later lose. They want things they can never have. In explaining this second truth, the Buddha supposedly said:

> O monks, I will tell you the truth about the origin of suffering. The thirst for existence leads from rebirth to rebirth; lust and pleasure follow. Power alone can satisfy lust. The thirst for power, the thirst for pleasure, the thirst for existence; there, O monks, is the origin of suffering.

[6] This quotation and the succeeding ones dealing with the Buddha's Enlightenment are taken from A. Ferdinand Herold (Paul C. Blum, translator), *The Life of Buddha* (Rutland, Vermont, Charles C. Tuttle, 1954), pp. 119–120.

Jainism

It is difficult, and often impossible, to trace a particular idea from Indian thought to a single source. Many basic religious ideas arose from Vedic tradition and are a part of all Indian sects. Hinduism, Buddhism, Jainism, and the hundreds of small sects all recognize the probability of a common source for all religions. Indian sects seldom compete for followers, as do many Christian sects. Indeed, Buddhism, Jainism, and the other Indian sects often are recognized as a part of Hinduism.

Jainist tradition claims that Jainism has always existed. The universe is cyclical, composed of periods of improvement and decline. In each cycle Jainism is revealed through a series of 24 prophets. The latest of these was Mahavira (540 B.C.?–468 B.C.?), the son of a Kshatriya ruler. In many ways the story of Mahavira parallels that of the Buddha, who lived about the same time. Like the Buddha, Mahavira's life was climaxed by an enlightenment. Buddha, however, had attained perfection by following an eight-fold path. Mahavira's way was a three-fold path — right faith, right knowledge, and right conduct.

Jainism as systematized by Mahavira has several distinctive features. It neither admits nor denies the existence of gods, claiming that human perfection is the ultimate end of life. Perfection comes through karma (page 46) and is determined by the present life. Ahimsa, the practice of respecting life in every form, often is traced to Jainism. Jainists say that even rocks and insects are involved in the process of karma; they, too, have souls. Strict Jainists sweep the path before them to avoid killing living things.

Jainists regard farming as a disturbance of nature. For this reason most of them are merchants. Now few in number, the Jainists believe the world is in the "decline" phase of the latest cycle of the universe. They look forward to the beginning of the next cycle and the subsequent improvement in life.

The third truth told what man must do to find peace. To find lasting peace, the Buddha taught, man must snuff out the yearning within himself. To the five monks, he said:

> O monks, I will tell you the truth about the suppression of suffering. Quench your thirst by annihilating desire. Drive away desire. Forgo desire. Free yourselves of desire. Be ignorant of desire.

The Buddha's fourth truth revealed the path to permanent peace. To begin his sermon to the five monks, the Buddha had warned them to avoid the two extremes of living: a life devoted solely to pleasure and a life deprived of everything.[7] He himself, the Buddha is credited with claiming, had discovered a middle path which required eight practices — right faith, right resolve, right speech, right action, right living, right effort, right thought, right meditation. Now, as his fourth point, the Buddha told the monks that man could find permanent peace by walking this Noble Eightfold Path:

> O monks, I will tell you the truth about the path that leads to the extinction of suffering. It is the sacred path, the Noble Eightfold Path. . . .

The Buddha taught that attainment of perfect peace was not easy. The Buddha believed that a man would have to experience numerous rebirths before his inner desires were overcome. Not all men, however, would succeed in achieving this victory over self. Those who did not succeed would never be able to remove themselves from the treadmill of repeated rebirths. But for those who succeeded in extinguishing their attachment to the things of this world the final reward would be the attainment of *nirvana*. This was a state in which man, freed from the cycle of rebirth, became one with the Universe. Nirvana would be supreme bliss, for the individual self and soul would have disappeared completely. To conclude his sermon to the monks, the Buddha told them:

> O monks, now that I have a complete understanding of these four truths, I know that . . . I have attained the supreme rank of Buddha [a word that means "to become enlightened" or "to be wise"]. I am forever set free: for me there will be no new birth.

---

[7] It should be noted that the Buddha had experienced both extremes; the life of a rich prince and the life of the ascetic, a person who stripped himself of everything in the hopes of finding answers to the problems of life.

At first, the teachings of the Buddha failed to gain acceptance. Gautama did not reject the principal ideas of the emerging faith of Hinduism, but because of his position on two matters his own message could not be approved by Brahmins. In the first place, the Buddha ignored the rites and ceremonies traditionally performed by the Brahminical priesthood. In this simple but effective way he expressed his view that such religious practices were useless. Secondly, he indirectly attacked the caste system by saying that "enlightenment" could come to anyone at any time, not just after one had climbed through the caste system in a succession of lives.

When the Buddha died about 483 B.C., only a small number of people counted themselves as his followers. But the disciples of the Buddha kept his gospel alive, founding monasteries throughout North India where his teachings could be studied. Yet it was not until explosive political changes took place in the subcontinent that Buddhism surged forward to a leading position in Indian life. These changes, which began in the third century B.C., are treated in the next section.

- CHECK-UP
  1. Who was Gautama? What problems troubled him?
  2. What were the Four Noble Truths? What eight practices led to the middle path, i.e. the extinction of suffering?
  3. What is nirvana?

4. Buddhism Swept Through India During the Maurya Age

By the time Buddha was born the numerous tribal governments in North India had evolved into kingdoms and republics. Perhaps the most important of these was Magadha, a kingdom in the lower Ganges Plain. Blessed with rich soil, a busy river trade, iron for metal working and export, elephants for use in war, and forests where timber could be obtained, Magadha grew in power. About 324 B.C. Chandragupta Maurya (*chun'*druh-*goop'*tuh *mow'*ree-uh) came to the throne. In the next century and a half he and his successors built a great empire in North India. This empire, possibly India's first, was the instrument by which Buddhism became the dominant religion.

India was invaded by the Persians and Greeks. The rise of Magadha in the Ganges Plain was paralleled by important developments in the northwest. Some time before 530 B.C. Cyrus, the great ruler of the Persian Empire, crossed the Hindu Kush mountains and pushed into the Indus Plain. After making the region his twentieth satrapy (province), Cyrus exacted promises of tribute from the various Indian kings. This satrapy of Gandhara (gun-*dahr'*uh) was the furthest outpost of Cyrus's empire, and neither he nor his successors tried to rule it directly. They were content to receive tribute and, occasionally, a levy of soldiers.

Shortly before Chandragupta came to power another famous conqueror entered the Indus Plain. After conquering the Persian Empire, Alexander the Great invaded India in 326 B.C. Victorious in the Indus Valley, Alexander made plans to conquer the Ganges Plain as well. However, his troops were weary of war and refused to go further. After making arrangements for the government of his conquests Alexander withdrew from India. The brilliant young leader died on his return journey.

Alexander's empire did not survive his death. In time several of his generals established kingdoms of their own. India became part of the domain of Seleucus, an empire which included Syria, Babylonia, and Alexander's eastern provinces. Although the glory of their deeds was long remembered in the West, Alexander and his generals were soon forgotten in the subcontinent. Indeed their names do not even appear in Indian records of the period.

The Maurya Empire was established soon after Alexander's invasion. Although Alexander never reached the borders of Magadha, his conquests are inseparably linked with the rise of that kingdom to power. For one thing, Alexander had overthrown the small republics and kingdoms in the northwest. His departure, therefore, left a political vacuum, of which Chandragupta Maurya was quick to take advantage. Chandragupta quickly included these states in his empire. Also, it was because of Alexander's conquests that we have a reliable description of the Maurya Empire. Much that we know about it is derived from the account of Megasthenes (meh-*gas'*theh-neez), an ambassador from the kingdom founded by Seleucus. Megasthenes lived for some years at the court of the Maurya emperor. His account states that the Maurya Empire was efficiently administered, that the will of the ruler was carried out by a large staff of officials, and that a

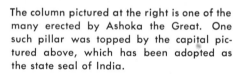

The column pictured at the right is one of the many erected by Ashoka the Great. One such pillar was topped by the capital pictured above, which has been adopted as the state seal of India.

network of police and spies maintained security within the realm. Megasthenes also wrote glowing accounts of the prosperous economy, the efficient tax system, and the Indian way of life.

Ashoka became a champion of Buddhism. Buddhism became firmly grounded in India because of the support of Ashoka (uh-*shoh'*-kuh), the grandson of Chandragupta Maurya. Although the exact dates of Ashoka's reign are not known, he seems to have been in power from 269 to 232 B.C. Ashoka, seeking to take over the kingdoms in the northern Deccan, began his reign as a conqueror. Despite great successes the casualties were staggering. According to Buddhist tradition, Ashoka surveyed the battlefield after one of his victories; then, appalled by the frightful carnage, vowed to abandon war and devote his life to promoting peace. Needing guidance to achieve this goal, he turned to Buddhism.

Ashoka adopted the teachings of Buddhism as the underlying policies of his reign. He exhorted officials and subjects to be just and considerate in their conduct. Punishment for many types of crime was made less severe. Ashoka's compassion extended even to the animal kingdom, for the slaughter of animals was discouraged, even for food. Ashoka had his humane commands inscribed on stately stone pillars that were erected throughout the empire. Many of them are still standing, and they are the source of much of our information about the Maurya Empire.

Ashoka's conversion to Buddhism benefited both him and the religion. The teachings of Buddhism reduced unrest and the threat of rebellion, making it easier for the emperor to build a strong, centralized empire. And thanks to Ashoka's patronage, Buddhism became widely known and accepted. Soon the faith began to spread over the mountain wall into Central and East Asia and across the seas into Ceylon and Southeast Asia.

Because Ashoka's successors lacked his greatness, the last Maurya king was overthrown barely fifty years after his death. By that time the empire already was greatly diminished in size. The empire of the Shungas (*shoong'*ghas) replaced the Maurya Empire. The Shungas ruled a large kingdom in the Ganges Valley, and were accepted as overlords by the lesser kingdoms bordering on their domain. But the Shunga Empire was nowhere near as powerful as the Maurya Empire. Many of the old Maurya lands became independent kingdoms, and the highly centralized empire of Ashoka soon was only a memory.

Changes crept into Buddhism after Ashoka's death. The destruction of the Maurya Empire did not halt the growth of Buddhism. The religion continued to spread throughout the Indian subcontinent and into many other lands in Asia. As it did so it came in contact with many other cults and sects. In India many of these sects had been absorbed into Hinduism, and Buddhism became more and more like this emerging faith.

By the early centuries of the Christian era two distinct Buddhist movements had come into being. Buddhists who adhered to the earlier teachings of the faith formed the Southern School, popularly called Hinayana (*heen'*uh-*yahn'*uh) Buddhism.[8] Hinayana means "Lesser Vehicle." According to followers of the Southern School, the "vehicle" transporting worthy souls to nirvana has room for some but not for all. The second movement became known as the Northern

[8] Its adherents term it "Therevada" Buddhism.

School, or Mahayana (mah-huh-*yahn'*uh) Buddhism. It reflected strong influences from sects in North India and, possibly, even Christianity. Mahayana means "Greater Vehicle." According to this school, the "vehicle" conveying deserving souls to nirvana has room for all.

Northern Buddhism showed a great departure from original Buddhist thinking. For one thing, it transformed the founder of the faith, Gautama, into an all-powerful, all-knowing, and all-seeing deity. He was placed at the summit of a host of lesser deities. A second change was in the nature of nirvana. To the Northern School Buddhist, nirvana was no longer the state of extinction of the soul and "Oneness with the Universe." Instead, it was a paradise of the afterworld where eternal bliss was enjoyed by the faithful.

The popularity of Buddhism was reflected in architecture and art. As Buddhism became widespread, distinctive styles in architecture and art emerged. Temples and other places of worship were built in a similar style. Perhaps the most notable Buddhist structure was the artificial mound, later a building, called a stupa (*stoo'*pah). It was originally designed as a shrine for the deposit of relics of the Buddha. When Buddhism spread to China, Korea, and Japan, the stupa inspired the development of the pagoda, a structure which has ever since been characteristic of the landscape in East Asia.

The transformation of the Buddha into a deity had an effect upon art. Those who placed their faith in him wished to be inspired by his symbolic presence. Statues of the Buddha were cut from stone, cast in metal, and carved from wood. The artists and craftsmen, perhaps having no strong tradition of their own to draw upon, turned to the sculptured work of Westerners for models. Through contacts with the Roman Empire, they acquired ideas and techniques of sculpture from the classical Graeco-Roman tradition. As a result, the early statues of the Buddha reveal pronounced Hellenistic (Grecian) and Roman influences. The posture of these statues, the face and body, and even the clothing betray foreign cultural origins.

Buddhism lost ground in the land of its birth. The teachings of the Buddha won millions of converts in many lands. Advocating gentleness and mercy, stressing good moral behavior, and offering hope after death to millions of men, Buddhism proved especially attractive to the poor and unfortunate. In India, for example, the teachings of the Buddha met with widest acceptance among the Shudras and Untouchables, while the upper three varnas preferred Hinduism. Without a

BUDDHIST SCULPTURE. The most famous of India's stupas, that at Sanchi (left), has been called "the crowning achievement of North Indian sculpture." The mound is simple, but the gateways are adorned with some of India's finest sculpture. The architrave in the foreground is an example of the elaborate decorations around entrances.

For reasons which are not entirely clear the Buddha was not portrayed in early stupas. Rather, he was symbolized by a wheel, a tree, footprints, or an empty throne. The earliest Buddhas were sculptured after Roman influences had affected Indian artistry. The Buddha above is definitely Western in style. Later Buddhas, such as the one at the left, were more Asian in pose and appearance.

doubt, Buddhism has been one of the most potent civilizing and
"equalizing" forces the world has known.

For a variety of reasons, some of which will be treated in Chapter
Three, Buddhism declined in the homeland of its founder. Over a
period of 1500 years Hinduism and other religions were to capture
the loyalties of most Indians. Today less than 1 per cent of the people of India are followers of Buddhism.

● CHECK-UP

    1. How did Alexander's conquests prepare the way for the Maurya Em-
       pire? Why was it a success?

    2. Why is Ashoka remembered as a great ruler?

    3. How did Buddhism change after Ashoka's death? To what groups
       did it appeal?

    4. How did the spread of Buddhism influence architecture and art?

Summing Up

The foundations of Indian civilization were laid in the Indus River
region. The most important cities, Harappa and Mohenjo Daro, were
the most skillfully designed cities in the ancient world. Little is
known about the government, social organization, and religion of
the cities or the region they served, but such evidence as has been
found suggests that the Harappan people had advanced far beyond the
stage of village agricultural communities. The Harappan civilization
began to crumble about 1500 B.C. under the impact of Aryan invaders
from beyond the mountain wall.

The Aryan tribes, after overwhelming northwestern India, advanced eastward onto the Ganges River Plain. There they achieved
supremacy after many centuries of struggle. The Aryans preserved
the memories of their conquests, their ideas about man and life, and
their rituals and ceremonies in the Vedas. By the end of the Vedic
period (ca. 500 B.C.) the Aryans had developed the main characteristics of what came to be the Hindu way of life.

The domination of the Brahmins (Vedic priests) aroused increasing
dissatisfaction and opposition. For many centuries the principal alternative to the Brahmin scheme of things was posed by the Buddhist
movement. Ignoring the Brahminical caste system and the sanctity
of its rites, the Buddhists emphasized knowledge, ethics, and compassion as the right ways for man. Thanks to the patronage of the
great Emperor Ashoka of the Maurya dynasty, Buddhism began to

spread. After the death of Ashoka, however, many changes crept into Buddhism. It survived and grew stronger in many parts of Asia, but in India it almost disappeared.

. . . .

CHAPTER REVIEW

Can You Identify?

Harappan civilization	Buddhism	stupa
Four Noble Truths	Jainism	Ashoka
Maurya Empire	Gautama	karma
cylinder seals	Vedas	samsara
caste system	Epics	maya
Brahmanism	nirvana	dharma
Hinduism	ahimsa	

What Do You Think?

1. Why, do you think, were the Harappans conservative?

2. Can the same factors contribute to the rise of an empire and to its decline? Consider the case of the Maurya Empire.

3. What would be the likely effect on a society of an acceptance of the doctrines of karma and samsara?

4. Mahayana Buddhism gained more followers than Hinayana Buddhism. Why, do you think, was this so?

5. Hindus can be rebellious at times but never revolutionary. Why? Bring out the exact meaning of the two terms.

6. Do you think that getting what you want "would eliminate suffering"? Why, or why not? What was the Buddha's view?

Extending and Applying Your Knowledge

1. For more on the *Mahabharata* and the *Ramayana*, the great epics of Hinduism, read the excerpts entitled "The Lord's Song" and "The Kidnapping of Sita" in *India: Selected Readings*.

2. Those interested in learning more about Buddhism and Hinduism will enjoy *Three Ways of Asian Wisdom* (Simon and Schuster, 1966). This book, written by Nancy Wilson Ross, is a readable, accurate survey of Hinduism, Buddhism, and Zen.

3. A thorough treatment of India before the coming of the Muslims is found in *The Wonder That Was India* by Arthur L. Basham. Grove Press issued a paperback edition in 1959. There are chapters on pre-history, the nature of the state and the social order, religion and literature.

3

INDIA: TO THE RISE OF ISLAM

The genius of the Indian people lay in social rather than political organization. By the end of the Maurya dynasty the basic characteristics of the caste system and Hinduism, its underlying philosophy, had taken form. Buddhism also had arisen, providing inspiration for a rich heritage of religious thought and artistic accomplishment. But the task of devising efficient methods of political administration for great empires and kingdoms remained incomplete. Although several large kingdoms and at least one empire, the Gupta, did arise, none was able to unite the subcontinent into a political whole. For almost 2000 years after Maurya times India remained politically fragmented.

Despite its political ups and downs, India saw a flourishing of creative arts after Maurya times. Within the subcontinent scholars, artists, and craftsmen consolidated the achievements of their ancestors and made major contributions on their own. For the first thousand years after Maurya times India shared the riches of its civilization with peoples beyond its borders, for during that period trade between India and other parts of the world showed a marked increase. Along with trade, Indians brought to other lands their rich cultural achievements and, in many cases, Hinduism and Buddhism. It is worthy of note, too, that the spread of Indian civilization was accomplished not by force of arms but through peaceful means. In Chapter Four we shall see that the opposite was true in the case of the spread of Islam.

As to political organization, the Indian people relied primarily on custom, tradition, and pure chance. The heritage of the past was such an important part of Indian life that religion and tradition determined politics. In stating that the people of India failed to achieve political unity, one should also point out that, up to this point in time, few peoples had done so. And while not establishing a stable, unified political system, the Indian people did develop social institutions which have given direction to life until the present day.

1. An Era of Invasions Was Marked by the Spread of Indian Culture

Even at the height of the Mauryan Empire invaders were pouring into India through the mountain passes in the northwest. As the Maurya Empire grew weaker these invasions increased. By the time the empire came to an end (about 183 B.C.), one wave of "barbarians" after another was rolling across the frontier of northwest India. This era of invasions lasted from about 200 B.C. to 300 A.D. To trace the history of India during this period is difficult. The chief written records are the sacred writings of Buddhist and Jainist priests, and these documents treat history as incidental to religion. But these documents and other scanty evidence reveal several important developments: 1) Buddhism became a worldwide religion; 2) the Deccan and South India began to assume an important role in the subcontinent; and 3) trade opened the door for increased Indian contacts with the West and with Southeast Asia.

TIMETABLE	History of North India, 200 B.C.–1200 A.D.
200 B.C.–300 A.D.	Age of Invasions
320–550 A.D.	Empire of the Imperial Gupta Gupta Golden Age
540–606	Period of invasions and fragmentation
606–647	Harsha's empire
647–1200	Ascendancy of princely states Muslim invasions

Northwest India became a highway for invaders. For 500 years (200 B.C.–300 A.D.) northwest India was largely controlled by invaders. The road to the subcontinent was pointed out by Greeks from Bactria and Parthia, two regions to the northwest of India (see map, pages 64–65). These Greeks were descended from colonists settled there by Persian generals and by Alexander the Great. Although some of the Bactrian and Parthian kingdoms which arose in northwest India survived for several hundred years, most were soon overthrown by nomadic tribesmen from Central Asia. These invaders, the Shakas, had destroyed the Bactrian states before entering India. But in the first century A.D. the Shakas fell before the might of yet other nomadic invaders, the Kushanas of Central Asia. For the remainder of this "barbarian" period in Indian history the Kushanas controlled most of the northwest.

The Kushanas are important in Indian history because of their role in spreading Buddhism. Like other non-Indian invaders, the Kushanas were excluded from the caste system and Hinduism. Some of them adopted Jainism, but more became Buddhists. Carrying Buddhism along the caravan routes into Central Asia and China, the Kushanas helped to make their adopted faith the religion of millions. Kanishka, the most famous of the Kushana monarchs, was especially active in promoting Buddhism. Not only did he encourage missionary efforts in other lands but he called the conference which led to the division of Buddhism into Northern and Southern Schools (see pages 55–56).

In time the post-Maurya invaders lost their identity in India. As was true of earlier would-be conquerors, they found it difficult to resist assimilation by the culturally more advanced Indians. They intermarried with Indians and adopted Indian customs, and eventually they virtually disappeared as separate cultural groups.

The barbarian invasions coincided with the emergence of southern India. Until this period of barbarian invasions India south of the Vindhyas figured but little in the history of the subcontinent. To be sure, Hindu culture was penetrating the area, and the emerging faith was incorporating the region's gods and absorbing its people into the caste system. But little is known of the history of the Deccan and South India before the invasions.

The Deccan came into prominence in the subcontinent during the reign of the Andhra dynasty. These rulers established a power base in the northwestern part of that great plateau. Occasional references to the Andhras in various North Indian sources suggest that they had been important since Maurya times. In the first and second centuries A.D. the Andhra dynasty built an empire that controlled a large part of the Deccan from coast to coast. This empire was loosely knit, and it did not last very long. However, through marriage alliances and military campaigns the Andhras established close contacts with the peoples of the north. Thus the Deccan became the connecting link between Hindustan and South India.

South India began to move into the mainstream of Indian history in the last century B.C. The shadowy historical records of the time tell of battles among the Cholas, Pandyas, and Keralas, three peoples who spoke languages belonging to the Dravidian group. They lived in the region comprising modern Andhra Pradesh, Madras, Mysore, and Kerala (see map, page 176). For many centuries to come this region was called Tamil country after the principal Dravidian language in use there. With the empire of the Andhras serving as a connecting link, the peoples of Tamil country were beginning to absorb Hindu culture. Later they synthesized the Hindu traditions of the Aryans with their own Dravidian folklore to produce some of India's finest poetry, epics, and music. More will be said about this Tamil Culture in Section Two.

India's trade expanded by leaps and bounds. The period from 200 B.C. to 300 A.D. was marked by a great expansion of Indian trade. The Greek kingdoms in northwest India kept in touch with West Asia and the Mediterranean world, and important overland trade routes developed to link the regions. The Shakas and Kushanas encouraged trade between India and their former homes in Central Asia, and this trade was also extended into China. In the Deccan and South India commerce increased as traders from Arabia and the Mediterranean world opened sea routes from the Roman Empire.

The Arabs were the first to become involved in sea trade with the Indian subcontinent. At a very early period they learned to make use of the summer monsoon winds[1] to drive their ships across the Arabian Sea. Since the monsoon winds reversed in the winter, the Arabs would load their cargoes and wait for the winds to bring them home. During the first century B.C. other sailors from the West came to understand the usefulness of monsoons. Sea trade flourished, and peninsular India, long overshadowed by the states to the north, began to play a prominent role in the affairs of the subcontinent.

[1] The word "monsoon" is derived from the Arabic *mauzim*, meaning "season."

CROSSROADS OF EMPIRE. India has always occupied a strategic position in trade between East and West. The Kushana Empire, of which North India was a part, sat astride the main overland trade routes between the Roman and Chinese Empires. At a later period, as overland routes became less popular, South India and the Andhra Empire became a link in the ocean trade between the Western World and East and Southeast Asia. But India did not serve just as a link in East-West trade. It also exported its own goods, both by land and by sea, both West and East.

Chief among India's contributions were its two great religions, Hinduism and Buddhism. Their impact was especially felt in Southeast Asia. An undeveloped region at the time India's trade was blossoming, it looked to the subcontinent for guidance. Signs of Indian influence are seen everywhere. Pictured on the opposite page, and keyed to the map, are a Buddhist temple in Burma (left); temple dancers in Thailand performing a Hindu dance (right); and Java's Borobudur (bottom), a Hindu-Buddhist temple which ranks as one of the world's architectural marvels.

KUSHANA
EMPIRE
(C. 150 A.D.)

GUPTA EMPIRE
(C. 395 A.D.)

Main trade
routes

The Indian goods exported over the sea routes to the West usually ended up in the Roman Empire. For many centuries the pattern of this trade varied little. The peoples of the Mediterranean world continued to demand the same kinds of Indian goods. Spices, perfumes, precious stones, fine textiles, carved ivory, and iron ore were brought to the Roman Empire. The rare birds and animals of the subcontinent — peacocks, parrots, monkeys, tigers, and elephants — were also wanted by fun-seeking Romans. Because the Indians demanded few Western goods in return, their chief import for centuries was gold.

Trade prepared the way for Hinduism in Southeast Asia. India's contacts with Southeast Asia developed as a direct result of her trade with the Roman Empire. At the time the lands and islands of Southeast Asia were largely unsettled and undeveloped. However, they produced spices, a commodity much in demand in the Roman world. Indian traders voyaged to Malaya, Cambodia, Java, Sumatra, and Borneo to get spices for export to Rome. Many of them settled in Southeast Asian lands. The penetration of Southeast Asia by Indians was facilitated by the Southeast Asian peoples themselves, particularly those in the East Indies. Being sea-farers, they assumed much of the initiative in opening the sea routes between their island homes and the Indian subcontinent.

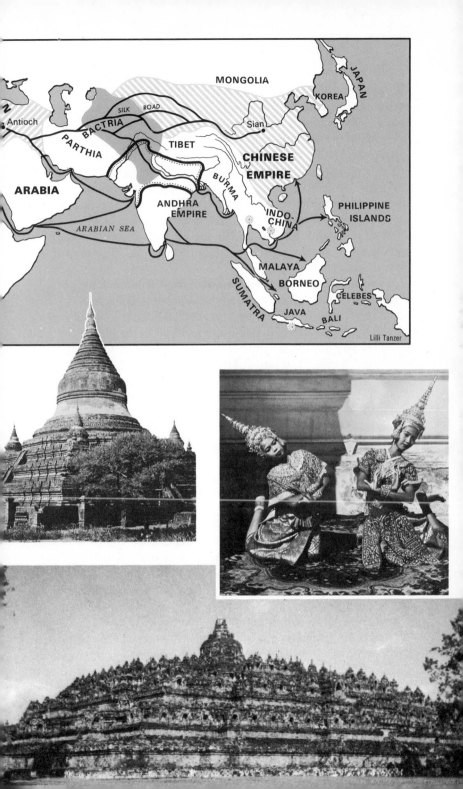

MONGOLIA
JAPAN
KOREA
SILK ROAD
Sian
Antioch
BACTRIA
PARTHIA
TIBET
CHINESE
EMPIRE
BURMA
ARABIA
ANDHRA
EMPIRE
INDO-
CHINA
PHILIPPINE
ISLANDS
ARABIAN SEA
MALAYA
SUMATRA
BORNEO
CELEBES
JAVA
BALI

Lilli Tanzer

The first kingdoms in the history of Southeast Asia developed during the early centuries of the Christian era. Some Southeast Asian princes invited high-caste Hindus to join their courts as counselors. The cultured and knowledgeable Hindus were deeply respected. Many of them spent their lives in the service of these foreign governments and attained lofty rank. Some married women belonging to the local aristocracy and a few made brides of the daughters of ruling families. Hinduized descendants of these unions were in an excellent position to influence the culture of the upper classes and to modify prevailing patterns of government. Thus the upper classes in Southeast Asian lands were Hinduized, although Hindu manners, customs, and ideas did not penetrate deeply into the ways of the common people.

Hinduism left lasting marks on Southeast Asian culture. The influence of Hindu culture gradually waned in the lands to the east of India as other faiths and cultures became prominent. Thus the appeal of Hinduism was offset by Buddhism and by Confucianism, the great moral philosophy from China. At a later time Islam swept like a whirlwind through the East Indies, Malaya, and the southern Philippines. To this day the peoples of these lands follow the teachings of Mohammed. The last cultural invasion of Southeast Asia occurred in recent centuries with the arrival of Westerners and their way of life. Islam has continued to be the most popular religion, but Christianity has made notable inroads in many areas, particularly the Philippines and Indonesia.

Despite the influence of other religions, the early impact of Hinduism was too strong to be erased. Hindu practices and customs have endured in Southeast Asia. The dances of Siam (Thailand), the drama of Indonesia, and the traditional literature of several Southeast Asian lands are testimony to India's lasting cultural contributions. As for Hinduism as a faith, it struck permanent roots mainly on the Indonesian island of Bali. Strongly modified by local customs and traditions, it has pervaded the way of life of the island's inhabitants to this day.

Buddhism left a strong imprint on Southeast Asia. As in the case of Hinduism, trade brought Buddhism to Southeast Asia. During the early centuries of the Christian era Buddhism became the main religion of China. As trade increased between China and India, the sea route between the two countries was used more and more. Overland caravan routes simply were too slow and difficult. And since this sea route touched ports in Southeast Asia, Buddhist monks settled in the area, erected temples, established monasteries, and won converts to their faith.

Buddhism began to lose its hold upon the peoples of India after the period of barbarian invasions, but the faith flourished in the lands to which it had been transplanted. Besides China, the lands of Tibet, Mongolia, Korea, and Japan were brought into the Buddhist fold. In Southeast Asia the religion took root in the region now composing Burma, Thailand, Cambodia, Laos, and Vietnam.

Indian culture is reflected in Southeast Asian architecture. The remarkable success of Hinduism and Buddhism in Southeast Asia is borne out by imposing monuments found there. One of these, the Borobodur (bohr-oh-boo-*door'*), is in central Java. Completed in the eighth, or possibly the ninth, century A.D., the Borobodur is a large hill encased by terraces of carved stone. Engraved on the walls of each level are stories and legends from the history and lore of Buddhism. Perhaps as much as ten years of work by armies of laborers and craftsmen were required to build this noble memorial. After Buddhism declined in the East Indies, the Borobodur unfortunately was neglected for many centuries. In modern times, however, it was restored by the Dutch rulers of the archipelago.

Even more imposing are the ruins of magnificent cities and temples built by the Khmer (*kmer*) people, the ancestors of the Cambodians. These magnificent edifices were erected between the ninth and thirteenth centuries, when the empire of the Khmers included much of the Southeast Asian mainland. However, after the downfall of the Khmer Empire the beautiful buildings were neglected. In time they were forgotten. The modern world was unaware of their existence until 1858, when French explorers discovered them.

After the initial discovery, many other expeditions penetrated the jungles of Cambodia in search of lost cities. The most impressive finds were the ruins of Angkor Thom (*ang'*kohr *tahm'*) and Angkor Wat (*waht*). These ruins of temples and palaces in ancient cities clearly reflect the heavy impact of Hindu civilization upon the Khmers. So too do the countless stone statues, representing both Hindu and Buddhist gods, and the stories chiseled on great stone slabs. Patiently restored by the French, Angkor Thom and Angkor Wat have become known as the "Eighth Wonder of the World." They tell an amazing, though incomplete, story of the influence of Indian culture on life in Southeast Asia.

Angkor Thom is pictured at left as it looked when discovered in 1858.

The photo at right, of Angkor Wat, shows the care taken in its restoration.

● CHECK-UP

1. What important developments took place in India during the period of barbarian invasions? Why are the Kushanas considered the most important of these invaders?

2. How did Arab traders reach India? What goods did the Romans want from India? How did they pay for them? Why?

3. What brought Indian traders to Southeast Asia? Why did high-caste Hindus come? Why were the upper classes in Southeast Asia "Hinduized"?

4. How did Buddhism reach Southeast Asia? Where was it most firmly established?

2. Hinduism Grew Stronger During and After the Gupta Age

As we have seen in Chapter Two, Hinduism had no founder, no set dogma, no single deity which all its adherents worshiped. The fact that millions of villagers were unwilling to abandon the gods and religious customs of their ancestors did not prevent them from becoming Hindus. Hinduism readily found a place for such gods and customs. For several centuries, while Hinduism was spreading throughout the subcontinent, Buddhism provided strong competition. The Buddhists not only had won a large following but had built a great many temples and monasteries. But beginning about the fourth century, a time when great political changes were occurring throughout the subcontinent, Buddhism began to wither in India. Hinduism then assumed the dominant position in Indian life that it still holds today.

The founding of the Gupta dynasty opened a stable age for North India. At the beginning of the fourth century, after centuries of mauling at the hands of barbarians, North India entered into a period of peace. The ruler who was to bring unity to Hindustan was king of one of the hundreds of small kingdoms on the Indian subcontinent. How this ruler, Chandragupta I, became so powerful, is not known. His rise was sudden and unexpected. As the founder of the Imperial Gupta dynasty, he laid the cornerstone for one of the greatest of the Hindu empires.[2]

The empire of the Imperial Gupta endured for more than two centuries. At its peak all of North India and large parts of the Deccan were under its sway. For the first time since the days of the Mauryas the frontier regions were fairly secure against barbarian invaders. Law and order were enforced within the realm, and imperial officials sought to promote the welfare of the people. The Gupta rulers abolished the oppressive policies of the monarchs they displaced and eased the heavy taxes paid by the people. All of northern India benefited from the enlightened rule of the Gupta.

Conditions during and after the Gupta period have been described by Chinese Buddhist pilgrims who visited India in search of scriptural materials. One of the most renowned of these travelers was Fa-Hsien (*fah'*shee-*en'*), who wandered about the subcontinent during the years 401–411. He described the happy state of life under the Gupta:

> In the Gupta Empire people were numerous and happy; they have not to register their households, or attend to any magistrates and their rules; only those who cultivate the royal land have to pay [a portion of] the gain from it. If they want to go, they go; if they want to stay on, they stay. The king governs without decapitation or [other] corporal punishment. Criminals are simply fined, lightly or heavily, according to the circumstances. Even in case of repeated attempts at wicked rebellion, they only have their right hands cut off. The king's bodyguards and attendants all have salaries.

[2] This dynasty is designated the *Imperial* Gupta to distinguish it from other ruling houses of the same name.

Throughout the whole country the people do not kill any living creature, nor drink intoxicating liquor, nor eat onions or garlic.[3]

As a fervent Buddhist, Fa-Hsien was also pleased by the care given the sick and the poor. He wrote:

The Heads of the Vaishya [third highest varna, see page 44] families establish in the cities houses for dispensing charity and medicines. All the poor and destitute in the country, orphans, widowers, and childless men, maimed people and cripples, and all who are diseased, go to those houses, and are provided with every kind of help, and doctors examine their diseases. They get the food and medicines which their cases require, and are made to feel at ease; and when they are better, they go away of themselves.[4]

Fa-Hsien undoubtedly exaggerated the facts, but even so we can conclude that no land was more socially enlightened than India under the Gupta.

The fall of the Gupta was followed by political turmoil. The Gupta regime began to crumble in the middle of the fifth century. Pressures along the frontier became too great for the imperial forces to resist. The last of the Gupta rulers held out for another half century, then the dynasty disappeared. From time to time other substantial kingdoms came into being in the subcontinent. In the Ganges Valley the mightiest of these was founded by a prince named Harsha. During the years 605–647 he ruled an empire that equalled the Gupta in brilliance and power. But for the most part, the six centuries that followed the passing of the Guptas were characterized by chaos and strife.

A significant development during this period of turmoil was the increasing importance of the southern kingdoms. For the first time rulers of states south of the Vindhya Hills felt strong enough to invade the northern region. One king even defeated the mighty Harsha in battle. Although various kingdoms controlled large sections of the Deccan and South India for many decades, none was as stable, prosperous, or well-governed as the Gupta Empire. Many centuries passed before the Guptas were surpassed as empire-builders, and when this happened, conquerors from abroad were responsible. Never again was a Hindu dynasty to exercise as great power as had the Guptas.

---

[3] James Legge, translator, *A Record of Buddhistic Kingdoms*, by Fa-Hsien (New York, Paragon Book Reprint Corp. and Dover Publications, 1965), p. 43.
[4] *A Record of Buddhistic Kingdoms*, p. 79.

The Tamil Culture

While the Gupta empire was rising and falling in the north, South India was developing its own way of living. Named Tamil after the predominant language in the south, the culture endured from the first century A.D. until the fourteenth century. However, it did not develop entirely free of northern influence. Over the centuries Buddhism, Jainism, and Hinduism all were carried south, and each left its distinctive marks upon South India.

Hinduism had the greatest impact. It became the religion of prestige, and caste divisions became important. The upper classes eagerly accepted the religion, but the common people resented this Aryan intrusion upon traditional Dravidian ways. Especially disliked was the Brahminical order of worship, which emphasized sacrifice. The common people turned to a personal, devotion-centered worship of Vishnu and Shiva. Hinduism in its present form owes much to these people, for modern Hinduism stresses devotion to deities rather than sacrifice.

The Tamil culture left lasting contributions in the fields of literature and art. The early poetry and epics of the Tamil people were crude, but later they became expressive and free flowing. The art of the Tamil culture is best seen in the beautiful Hindu temples in the south. Some temples were free standing; others were built in caves. Sometimes an entire temple was carved from a huge rock. The art work within these temples included magnificent murals denoting Indian religion and life.

In the fourteenth century Muslims from the north intruded upon the Tamil culture. This occurrence, together with the steadily increasing contacts between north and south, brought to an end the distinctive civilization of South India. During its long lifetime, however, it had synthesized the Aryan and Dravidian traditions, producing a single tradition which was uniquely Indian.

Political disorder was offset by new triumphs of Hinduism. Probably the most important developments in the new era of turmoil were of a religious nature. Since the Guptas had not openly favored Buddhism, as had the earlier barbarian rulers, Hindu princes in North India gave increased support to their religion. In the Deccan and South India princes had openly supported Hinduism since before Gupta times, for they did not have to answer to Buddhist overlords. In these central and southern regions Hinduism had attracted the finest minds; Dravidian scholars especially had refined and enlarged upon Hindu doctrines. Indeed they gave these doctrines the form in which they exist today. During the centuries of turmoil Hindu scholars and holy men traveled throughout the subcontinent, spreading the "word" wherever they went. Imposing temples were constructed, especially in the Deccan and South India, and throughout India official backing was given Hindu rites and festivals.

Hinduism laid great stress upon devotion to deities. Hinduism, as it evolved during and after Gupta times, singled out and popularized three divinities: Brahma, Vishnu, and Shiva. Their primacy has not been appreciably challenged since.

Brahma, deemed the Creator, had enjoyed a following since remote times. Though always honored by Hindus, he rarely has deeply stirred their spirit. On the whole, he has been considered too lofty and remote to be approached by mortal men.

Vishnu has been adored by countless generations as the Preserver of Life. In Hindu art Vishnu is usually depicted with four arms, symbolizing his all-embracing power. His followers teach that he has gone through nine major rebirths. Vishnu's first incarnation was as a fish which prevented the destruction of mankind by rescuing the first man from a universal flood. Rama, the hero of the Ramayana Epic (page 43), was the seventh incarnation, while the Buddha was the ninth and most recent. The tenth rebirth is yet to come. It will be in the form of Kalkin, a man carrying a flaming sword and mounted on a white horse. Kalkin will punish the wicked, reward the good, and establish a new age of gold.

Shiva, the Destroyer, is often portrayed in art and sculpture with a necklace of skulls around his neck. Devotees of Shiva, however, do not view him as the "Grim Reaper"; in Hinduism there can be no life without death, no creation without destruction, no rebirth without the passing of the former life. Shiva is looked upon as a necessary part of the process of birth and life.

THE HINDU "TRINITY." There are comparatively few statues of Brahma (top, left), one of Hinduism's "trinity." Here his four heads signify the four directions, an indication of the all-seeing nature of the deity. Shiva (top, right) is best known in the West as Lord of the Dance. In Hindu thought the light reflected from his limbs as he dances forms the universe. Both Shiva and Vishnu (bottom, right), the most enduring of the three gods, appear in Indian sculpture in a variety of forms.

73

By the seventh century most Hindus belonged to one of two main sects. One stressed Vishnu as the high or only God while the other preferred Shiva. To the Hindu there was, and is, no contradiction in having two high gods, each of which is regarded by some as the only God. The Vaishnavite believes that Shiva is a lesser form of Vishnu, while the Shivaite holds that Vishnu is a secondary expression of Shiva. Historically, the followers of Vishnu have always been the more numerous; Shivaites are concentrated mostly in South India and the northern mountain regions.

The development of Hinduism paralleled the rise and fall of Buddhism. The roots of Hinduism were established long before the Buddha was born, and they were growing into a faith during the centuries that Buddhism was sweeping across Asia. Because Hinduism was broad and tolerant, it accepted many of the teachings of the Buddha — even finding a place for the Buddha himself in its theology (page 72). In India, Buddhists were quite willing to compromise with the beliefs and customs of Hinduism, even making use of Brahmin priests on occasion. Indian Buddhism eventually became so much like Hinduism that it was regarded as a sect of Hinduism. Like many other "offshoots" of a major faith, Buddhism then entered into a state of steady decline.

The final blow to Buddhism in India was delivered by the Muslims. Pushing into northwest India from the eighth century on, they destroyed the great Buddhist monasteries, burned the libraries, and killed the monks. Most of the monks who survived this onslaught fled from India. Already in a state of decline, Buddhism could not stand these fresh blows. Never again was Buddhism to be important in India.

- CHECK-UP
    1. Why is the Gupta remembered as one of the great dynasties of India?
    2. Why did Hinduism make great gains following the fall of the Gupta?
    3. What are the three chief divinities of Hinduism? Characterize each.
    4. Why did Buddhism almost disappear in India?

3. India Experienced a Rich Harvest of Cultural Achievements

In European history, the period known as the Renaissance (1200's–1500's) marked the flowering of the arts and literature and the beginning of modern science. India's Renaissance was the Gupta Age (320–550). Its cultural achievements, like those of Renaissance Europe, were based on the work of earlier generations. We know little about the work of these earlier scholars, artists, and scientists, because few historical records were kept and few artistic accomplishments have survived through the ages. Yet there is sufficient evidence to show that Indians had distinguished themselves in the search for knowledge and in the expression of their artistic talents long before the Gupta came to power. During their Golden Age, Indians carried on where their forgotten predecessors had left off. The work of each generation, in turn, was carried forward by later generations.

Mathematics made great advances in Gupta India. By Gupta times practical mathematical concepts were more highly developed in India than in any other land of antiquity. Transmitted to other parts of Asia as well as to the Western World, these concepts revolutionized arithmetic computation and advanced mathematical studies. One practical tool credited to Indian scholars is Arabic numerals. The idea of zero, one of the most important concepts in mathematics, is another Indian contribution. So is the idea of infinity. Indian philosophers had long been intrigued by this notion, and at some time in the distant past it was applied to mathematics.

Scientific and medical studies were part of the Indian tradition. Learned men in India were greatly interested in the physical and natural world. References in the old Vedic literature indicate that the ancestors of the Hindus studied the movements of the heavenly bodies. Ultimately, enough astronomical knowledge was accumulated to make possible the preparation of a fairly accurate calendar. But since the Indians, like other people of the premodern era, lacked the telescope, their understanding of astronomy remained limited. Indians also explored the fields of physics and chemistry. So-called "atomic theories" were developed by early Indian thinkers, but these were more the product of philosophical speculation than of scientific inquiry. They had greater implications for religious thinkers than for scientists.

By the end of the Gupta period Indians had acquired considerable medical knowledge. They had learned to diagnose and treat many ailments, even though they did not understand their causes. During the Gupta Age Indian surgery was the marvel of its times. Surgeons set broken bones, performed Caesarean sections, and used plastic surgery to repair mutilations. For such work they developed more than a hundred specialized instruments. Also, Indian doctors were aware of an important fact not understood by Western doctors until modern times — that cleanliness can prevent infection.

The Indians developed a wide range of medicines and drugs. As a result of constant experimentation with the properties of plants and herbs, Indians discovered numerous drugs for use in the treatment of disease. One of the most heralded findings of Indian physicians was that the oil of the chaulmoogra tree is effective in treating leprosy. Only in our day has this medicine been replaced by more effective antibiotics.

India's literary heritage reached its peak in the works of Kalidasa. If Indians had produced only the Vedas, they would have assured themselves a respected place in world literature. But in later centuries Indian writers turned out many masterpieces. Unfortunately most of these have not been well received in the West. The Westerner looking at Indian literature might find it overly ornate and seemingly lacking in true feeling.

One author of medieval India who has been widely acclaimed in both East and West is Kalidasa (*kah'*lih-*dah'*suh), the "Shakespeare of India." Kalidasa lived during the reign of Chandragupta II (375–415). He was one of the "Nine Gems" at the court of the Gupta, all outstanding writers who enjoyed the patronage of the imperial rulers. Kalidasa's works reflect the culture of the times. All center around the theme of love, which the writer believed to be the highest and finest emotion of man. The pearl of his achievements is *The Recognition of Sakuntala,* a tender play telling of the meeting, separation, and reunion of a monarch and his beloved wife.

A popular poem written by Kalidasa is the short *Cloud Messenger,* an account of the anguish experienced by an earth-spirit when he is banished from the divine city for a year. Separated from his wife, the spirit uses lovely word-pictures to describe his loneliness:

> I see your body in the sinuous creeper,
>   your gaze in the startled eyes of deer,
> your cheek in the moon, your hair in the plumage
>   of peacocks,
> and in the tiny ripples of the river I see
>   your sidelong glances,
> but alas, my dearest, nowhere do I find
>   your whole likeness.[5]

[5] Quoted in Basham, *The Wonder That Was India,* page 420.

Ancient India produced other outstanding writers. Many of India's best known writers lived during or shortly after the Gupta Age. Dandin (*dun'*din), Subandhu (sub-*un'*doo), and Bana (*bah'*nuh), all of whom lived during the late 500's and early 600's, were masters at the art of writing prose narrative. Dandin's *Tale of the Ten Princes,* an account of the adventures of ten heroes, is valuable for its keen portrayal of life among the common people of India. Subandhu's fame is based on his ornate descriptions rather than excellence of narrative; his one great work, the *Vasavadatta,* has almost no story to tell. Bana gives us much valuable historical material in his *Deeds of Harsa,* an account of the events leading up to Harsha's rise to power.

Outside of Kalidasa, the finest Indian poet was Bhartrihari (*bur'* trih-*huh'*rih), a writer of the seventh century. He wrote many short poems on the subjects of worldly wisdom, love, and the call of the religious life. One of his untitled masterpieces is both amusing and discerning:

> You may boldly take a gem from the jaws of a crocodile,
>   you may swim the ocean with its tossing wreath of waves,
> you may wear an angry serpent like a flower in your hair,
>   but you'll never satisfy a fool who's set in his opinions!
>
> You *may*, if you squeeze hard enough, even get oil from sand,
>   thirsty, you *may* succeed in drinking waters of the mirage,
> perhaps, if you go far enough, you'll find a rabbit's horn,
>   but you'll never satisfy a fool who's set in his opinions.[6]

A type of Indian literature which has influenced Western literature is Indian folklore. It is impossible to trace authorship of Indian folk tales, for the stories arose over a period of many centuries. Many of the stories in *Arabian Nights,* including some of the exploits of Sindbad the Sailor, are based on Indian folklore. The *Panchatantra* (*pun'*-chuh-*tun'*truh), a collection of stories of talking animals, reached the Western World in the sixth century. The story of Reynard the Fox, popular in the folklore of many European countries, owes much to one of the Panchatantra fables.

The importance of religion in Indian life is reflected in art and architecture. Nearly all the art and architecture of ancient India was of a religious nature. By the opening of the Christian era the Indians

[6] Quoted in Basham, *The Wonder That Was India,* page 425.

— both Hindus and Buddhists — had begun to acquire skill in working with stone. For centuries they had maintained temples in caves, and as they became skillful in stonework they created elaborate designs for these temples. India has many cave temples carved out of solid stone. These temples were decorated, both inside and out, with hundreds of beautifully carved stone columns, intricate, highly detailed statues of deities, and delicately chiseled carvings. Bas-reliefs, cut from stone, instructed the faithful in well-known legends and stories from both Vedic and Buddhist tradition.

The zenith of Indian religious art and architecture was reached in the Deccan. The cave temples of Ajanta (uh-*jun′*tuh) and Ellora (eh-*lore′*uh), begun during the second century B.C., were nearly a thousand years in building. A majority of the 61 caves at these two locations were built by Hindus, but many were the work of Buddhists and Jainists. All were hewn out of the solid rock of hillsides. The outside walls are adorned with sculptured figures, columns, and pictorial panels. The interiors are subdivided into many chambers, galleries, corridors, alcoves, and stairways. For sheer grandeur, the temples rival structures built anywhere in the world.

Free-standing temples became the target for invaders. Beginning about the seventh century, kings and wealthy merchants throughout India began to donate large sums of money for the building of magnificent temples. Since these were built from the ground up, rather than carved out of solid rock, they are called free-standing temples. Temple building continued until it was forbidden by Muslim invaders.

Despite the vastness of India, Hindu temples were remarkably uniform in their basic plan. The core of the temple was the shrine where the chief idol was kept. A closed passage joined this shrine to the hall used by the worshipers. The latter was entered from an open porch. Above the shrine rose a great tower, and lesser towers were placed on other parts of the building. A courtyard surrounded the temple, and within the courtyard were a number of shrines for lesser gods. A great wall enclosed the entire courtyard. Styles varied from one part of India to another, and architectural refinements were added over the years, but the basic plan remained unchanged.

Unfortunately many of the great free-standing temples have disappeared. They housed gold and silver idols, and precious metals were used in their construction. As much for plunder as for religious reasons, invading Muslims, beginning in the eleventh century, destroyed the temples and carried away the gold and silver. Few of the

AJANTA. Ajanta, located in a desolate section of the northern Deccan, is the site of 29 of India's most famous cave temples. The illustrations on this page are of temples built there during the seventh century. Typical of Indian architecture of the period are the massive pillars at the entrance of the cave (right). The facade (top, left) is decorated with bas-relief and statues representing scenes from the lives of Hindu and Buddhist heroes and gods. The pictured fresco (top, right) is a representation of the Buddha. It was painted on the wall of a cave.

great temples of North India survived the Muslim invasions. Today the finest examples of temple architecture are found in the Deccan and South India, areas spared the brunt of the Muslim attacks.

• CHECK-UP

1. What contributions were made by Indians to arithmetic? to higher mathematics? to science and medicine?
2. What contributions were made by Indians to literature?
3. How did religion influence Indian art and architecture?
4. Why have few of the free-standing temples in India survived?

4. Post-Gupta India Was Divided into Many Princely States

From the early days of the Harappan state until the rise of the British Indian Empire (Chapter 5), no government succeeded in establishing its rule over all of India. Except for the Mauryas, no dynasty was able to establish even a strongly centralized government over a large area. The Guptas had direct political control over the Ganges Valley, but many kingdoms in the empire simply paid tribute to their overlord. After the fall of the Guptas this fragmentation became greater. Lacking strong central authority, the subcontinent became divided among thousands of princely states.

The Indian economic structure led to the formation of many princely states. According to Indian tradition, the king owned all the land in his kingdom. However, he was free to surrender the right to collect the revenue from these lands. From the seventh century on many kings compensated court officials and military officers with revenue grants instead of salaries. Technically the land remained the property of the king, but in practice the overlord was the real owner. In exchange for the revenue grant, the overlord was expected to give the king a share of the revenue as well as his undivided loyalty. He was also expected to supply the king with soldiers, to use the king's currency, and to glorify the king in monuments, inscriptions, and writings.

Over the centuries this land revenue system became quite complicated. As overlords grew wealthy, they themselves assumed royal titles. They also granted revenue rights to members of their court, thus creating overlords loyal to them. Regardless of the size of his holdings, an overlord eventually came to regard himself as a king.

Because many rulers inherited grants made by several overlords, their loyalties became hopelessly divided. Since rulers were constantly at war with each other, victories and defeats caused many revenue-bearing lands to change hands. By the year 1000 there was a bewildering number of princely states in India. The system of land revenue had become so hopelessly tangled that it was never clear who owned what lands or which ruler owed tribute to whom.

Traditionally, Indian princes lived a life of service and luxury. Despite the confused situation in post-Gupta India, certain generalizations could be applied to every princely state. One concerned the traditional role of the ruler. First and foremost, he was a protector. It was his responsibility to keep out aggressors, to protect life and property, and to preserve traditional customs. Also, he was expected to promote learning and culture. Princes vied with one another to attract the leading writers, artists, musicians, and *pundits* (wise men, or philosophers).

In return for his services as protector and patron, the king expected to live a life of luxury. His palace was as splendid as the kingdom could afford, and it was run by a chamberlain, who directed a large staff of servants. The court of a wealthy prince would include several wives, a harem, and dozens of doctors, poets, musicians, advisers and artists. All persons in the court were supported primarily to satisfy the whims of the ruler.

Despite the splendor of his court the prince did not have unlimited power. More often than not he had to pay tribute to an overlord. The advisers to a ruler traditionally exercised great influence, and it was not at all unusual for a prince to be overthrown by his own advisers. One of the chief checks on the authority of a prince was public opinion. Indians were normally peaceful, but they became belligerent when their rights or religious traditions were violated. Many a thoughtless prince was overthrown by revolt.

The villages had little to do with government officials. Since eight out of ten Indians lived in villages, the villagers were the core of any kingdom. Yet an Indian ruler seldom had political agents in the villages. Instead, a prince would place governors in key cities or towns. Nearly all of the village's contacts with the state were through these governors. Often governorships became hereditary, and these office holders became uncrowned kings. It was not at all unusual for a governor to revolt and establish his own kingdom. Many of the Indian kingdoms of long ago were formed in this way.

Villagers generally looked after all matters of purely local interest. They seldom saw an agent of the king. Said the villagers: "The rains have come! The rice-blades spring! The farmer cares not who is king!" But there were times when even the smallest hamlet did not escape the attention of government officials. One occasion was tax-collecting time, a visit that hardly called for rejoicing. The villagers, generally a poor and wretched lot, could expect no compassion from the king's agents. "Five eggs," the villagers would say, "was all the raja taxed the village; his soldiers took a thousand fowls in pillage."

Another dreaded occasion was the "royal tour." Many kings made occasional tours of their kingdoms to hear local grievances and to punish anyone who had failed in his obligations to the ruler. On such journeys the king would take with him many servants, messengers, and members of his court. Even well-to-do landlords, who usually managed to avoid the payment of taxes, were not eager to entertain a ruler and his entourage. "A raid of elephants," an unlucky host would sigh, "is better than a visit of a raja with a clan."

The villages were governed by local councils. The affairs of each village were conducted by a council of elders. The size of this council varied, but by modern times the *panchayat* (pun-*chye'*yut), or "council of five," had become commonplace. The elders were elected to office, often for a five-year term. Although the village council was composed of elected officials, it was not the preserver of democracy that some Indians have suggested. Councils were usually dominated by the more prosperous villagers and the representatives of the higher castes. In many states, council members had to meet the approval of the raja.

The village council set individual tax assessments, negotiated with the state government the amount to be paid into the state treasury, and often acted as tax collector. It also concerned itself with construction and maintenance of public works, such as the irrigation system, the village tank and wells, and roads. It seldom was called upon to make laws. Villages were governed by custom, tradition, and religious regulations. The council did, however, act as a judge and jury. It ironed out squabbles among the villagers, imposing fines and punishments whenever necessary. It settled disputes among the various castes of the village. The council also decided such ticklish issues as which son would get the best farming plot when the holdings of a feeble or deceased father were divided. Enforcing a decision was seldom a problem. Despite considerable grumbling, villagers generally accepted the judgment of the elders. If the elders could not settle the problem, a state official was called in and his decision was final.

The village councils, or panchayats, continue to be the most important agency on the local level. Modern India has more than 212,000 panchayats, which collectively govern 99 per cent of the entire rural population. In general, they are responsible for agricultural production, local industry, medical care, management of common grazing grounds, and maintenance of village streets, reservoirs, wells, and sanitation and drainage systems. In some places the panchayats also supervise elementary school education, keep the village records, and levy and collect taxes.

Village councils were often supplemented by caste councils. Village elders would not interfere in questions concerning religious obligations. If a Hindu violated the traditions of his caste, his case would be tried before a council consisting of members of his caste. Punishment for religious violations ranged from penance to excommunication (expulsion from the caste). Excommunication was a serious action, for every aspect of a Hindu's life was tied to his caste. A Hindu who received this severe punishment had to leave his home, occupation, and oftentimes even his family. He had to join the ranks of the despised Untouchables, and his only hope for redemption was to be reborn into a caste in his next life.

In the small villages the inhabitants were likely to be members of the same or closely related subcastes. In many cases, a single caste council would serve several villages, and the simplicity of the caste pattern reduced the likelihood of disputes over caste matters. But the limited caste pattern also raised certain difficulties in the village. For one thing, villagers often had to undertake tasks that infringed upon caste regulations, thus raising the possibility of censure by the caste council.

Medium-sized and larger villages included a number of castes and subcastes. But most of the inhabitants of such villages were poor farmers from closely related subcastes. Because the still larger communities also included subcastes of potters, blacksmiths, barbers, and carpenters, the functions of social and economic life were carefully divided. As a result, problems involving religious obligations often arose. If a problem could not be settled by the people involved, it was referred to the caste council.

The concept of a nation was slow in reaching India. Indian villagers had little interest in affairs outside the village. They did have certain regional ties, for a people having common language, customs, and history felt a closer kinship to each other than to neighboring peoples having different traditions. Regional ties were especially strong in South India. But nowhere was there a nationalist spirit. It was not until the mid-1800's that Indians began to think in terms of an Indian nation. Many Indian kings, to be sure, had visions of building a large Indian empire. Some managed to put together fairly extensive kingdoms, but none was able to build an empire such as the Maurya or the Gupta. And no Indian ruler, not even Ashoka or Chandragupta, was able to unite the entire subcontinent.

Many books on Indian history stress the failure of the Indian people to achieve political unification. But should they be blamed for not welding together a nation embracing the entire subcontinent? Few peoples in history have succeeded in organizing a state the size of the Indian subcontinent. Before the expansion of Europe in the sixteenth century only a few peoples — the Romans, Chinese, Arabs, and Ottoman Turks — developed the military and administrative skill to hold and govern an area of continental size. The peoples of India met with no less success in achieving political unity than did their contemporaries in Western Europe. Even today the latter region, which is no more diverse geographically or ethnically than India, is split into 25 nations!

• CHECK-UP

1. Why did the Indian economic system encourage the fragmentation of states?

2. What were the services expected of an Indian prince? What were some of the checks on his power?

3. What were the duties of the village council? of the caste councils?

Summing Up

Soon after the death of Ashoka, the Maurya Empire of North India disintegrated. For the next six hundred years "barbarian" invaders swept over the region. In time, these intruders either were driven out or were absorbed by the numerically stronger and culturally superior Hindus. Meanwhile the Deccan and South India were entering the mainstream of Indian history. Peoples of these regions made important contributions to Hinduism, and traders from the Deccan and

South India brought the West and India closer together through commerce. In the subcontinent as a whole, Buddhism grew weaker, Hinduism became stronger, and contacts with other lands and peoples increased. Southeast Asia was especially influenced by developments within the subcontinent. Through trade, both Buddhism and Hinduism spread into this region and became a part of Southeast Asian culture.

In North India, the period of barbarian invasions came to an end when the Gupta dynasty came to power during the fourth century. The period of comparative peace was short-lived, however, because the later rulers could not contend with the ever-present military pressures on North India's frontiers. By the mid-600's the Guptas were no longer an effective force, and North India entered a period of chaos and political fragmentation. Politically, the Deccan and South India also were fragmented, but culturally the regions showed some progress. South India especially made notable contributions to Hinduism; it also developed the important Tamil Culture. Throughout the subcontinent Buddhism continued to lose ground, and by the eighth century it had nearly disappeared in India. Hinduism had assumed the dominant position which it holds to this day.

The Gupta Age (320–550) has become famous in Indian history as a Golden Age of culture. Indian scholars, writers, and artists of this period distinguished themselves by advancing knowledge and by producing masterpieces of literature, art, and architecture. Kalidasa, a writer supported by the Gupta dynasty, was the greatest of the poets and playwrights of the period. The most famous art and architecture, however, have survived in the Deccan and South India. In the Deccan are found the magnificent cave temples at Ajanta and Ellora, while South India has the subcontinent's finest free-standing temples.

An indirect result of the political confusion in India from 200 B.C. on was an increasing reliance on local self-government. With princes constantly at war with each other or with "barbarian" invaders, the villages were free to conduct their own affairs. Village councils, always an important part of Indian life, provided leadership for the peasants. Problems which village councils were unable or unwilling to handle were solved by caste councils. The reliance on local instruments of government continued as each succeeding century saw the failure of the Indian people to unite into a truly national state.

CHAPTER REVIEW

Can You Identify?

Kushanas	Brahma	panchayat
Andhras	Vishnu	Southeast Asia
Khmers	Shiva	Confucianism
Guptas	Kanishka	Angkor Wat
Islam	Borobodur	Angkor Thom
raja	*Panchatantra*	Golden Age

What Do You Think?

1. What were some important results of India's sea-borne trade with the Mediterranean World?

2. Indochina was the name used for many decades for mainland Southeast Asia. Why was this name appropriate?

3. Why has the memory of the Imperial Gupta lived on to the present day in India?

4. Why was the Indian village left comparatively free to run its own affairs?

5. What is the difference between nationalism and the desire of a ruler to build an empire?

Extending and Applying Your Knowledge

1. Explain why the introduction of Arabic numerals and the zero has revolutionized computation. Contrast this system with Roman numerals. Why is the Arabic system better?

2. Read to the class or write a report on the poems of Kalidasa. One source for these is Arthur W. Ryder's *Kalidasa, Translations of Shakuntala, and Other Works*, published by Dutton.

3. For several centuries Western Europe was governed by a system called feudalism. Read about feudalism, then compare the system with the one prevailing in post-Gupta India. How were the two systems similar? How were they different?

4. A good description of the cave temples at Ellora and Ajanta is given in "Glories of Indian Art" in *India: Selected Readings*.

4

ISLAM IN INDIA

From the early eighth century on, the course of Indian history was increasingly influenced by an expanding Islam. The subcontinent reeled under the shock of successive invasions by upholders of the teachings of Mohammed the Prophet, the founder of the Islamic religion. Terrifying as were the assaults, the peoples of India were more lastingly stirred by the formidable challenge of the Islamic civilization which the invaders brought. The intruders from the Middle East founded new kingdoms in northern and, later, central India to which the Islamic faith and way of life were successfully transplanted. Unlike many invaders of the past, these Muslims were so vigorous, spiritually and culturally, that they warded off assimilation by the numerically superior Hindus. Equally important, they were able to lure many Hindus from the faith of their ancestors.

Indian civilization was permanently enriched by Islam and its related culture. Hindu learned men were intrigued by the highly developed Muslim philosophy and literature. Seldom did they abandon their Hindu faith in favor of the Islamic, but they did explore Islam's many novel ideas. New philosophical and religious movements sometimes resulted. Muslim art, architecture, and literature also inspired numerous Hindus. Islamic artistic views and techniques took their place alongside the traditional Hindu. Indian civilization thus became more complex than ever before.

The confrontation of Islam and Hinduism made for many tensions in Indian life. The followers of the two faiths were poles apart on many matters of belief and custom. For centuries these differences

served as irritants in relationships between the two religious communities. These strains were compounded during the sixteenth century, when the Muslim regime of the Mughals dominated much of the
Indian subcontinent. Despite the fact that several Mughal rulers tried
to foster cordial Hindu-Muslim relations, the gulf between adherents
of the two faiths widened. Eventually the Mughal dynasty drew to a
close, but the Hindu-Muslim rivalry continued.

1. Muslim Warriors Opened a New Era of Invasions

Not long after the Gupta Empire disintegrated the entire Middle East
was rocked by the warrior-disciples of Mohammed the Prophet. Burst-
ing out of the Arabian peninsula, in very short order these Arab Muslims overran many neighboring lands. Their initial expeditions against
India were unsuccessful, but by 712 they had taken over the state
of Sind. Soon after the Arab invasions other converts to Islam joined
the struggle for power and riches in India. These Muslims, who were
Afghans and Turks, opened what rightly can be called India's period
of Muslim domination.

Mahmud of Ghazni launched a "holy war" against Hinduism. Between the years 1000 and 1026 galloping horsemen swept across the
plains of North India with disturbing frequency. In battle after battle
savage Afghan and Turkish marauders overwhelmed the armies of the
Hindu princes. These new invaders were the soldiers of Mahmud
(mah-*mood′*), a Turkish chieftain from the kingdom of Ghazni
(*gahz′*nee) in Afghanistan.

Mahmud of Ghazni, a masterful commander of cavalry, was not
interested in territorial conquest. He was undertaking a "holy war"
against the "infidel" Hindus. With the official blessing of the Caliph
of Baghdad, the spiritual leader of the Muslim world, Mahmud
headed 17 devastating expeditions into North India. The fury of his
campaigns was long remembered. He and his Turkish and Afghan
soldiers terrorized Hindu and Buddhist priests, killed many of them,
and tore down hundreds of idols. They also plundered countless
palaces, sacked and destroyed virtually all the Hindu temples in their
path, and scattered those Hindu armies which dared oppose them.

Mahmud expanded the tiny kingdom of Ghazni into a great empire. It fell apart soon after his death in 1030, but his descendants
controlled the Punjab region of India until the late 1100's. More
importantly, Mahmud's conquests had brought the Islamic faith to
India to stay.

Mohammed and the Spread of Islam

Mohammed (570–632), the founder of Islam, did not adopt the belief in a single God until he was a mature adult. As a youth he accepted the many gods in the Arabian pantheon. However, in his travels as a merchant and camel driver, Mohammed came in contact with many Christians and Jews. Gradually he came to believe that their belief in a single God was true. According to Mohammed, he became completely convinced when an angel appeared to him about the year 610. In the vision Mohammed was told to preach the idea of one God throughout the world.

Mohammed began preaching a gospel of one God, whom he called Allah. He told all who would listen about his experience with the angel and of other revelations which Allah supposedly had given him. But his teachings were not accepted in Mecca, his Arabian birthplace and home. So incensed did the people become when he attacked their idols that he was forced to flee to Medina, a nearby town. This flight, called the *Hejira,* took place in the year 622. The people of Medina accepted his teachings and thereafter his gospel, called Islam, spread with amazing speed. Since the Hejira marked a turning point in the history of Islam, this flight is regarded as the beginning of the Muslim era.

At the time of Mohammed's death Islam was limited to the Arabian Peninsula. However, during the next 35 years the fiercely devoted followers of Mohammed spread the new religion into North Africa, Persia, and Central Asia. Within another 35 years Islam had completely encircled the lower half of the Mediterranean Sea and had penetrated India. Throughout the centuries Islam has continued to attract followers. Today it ranks second only to Christianity in total number of believers.

Muhammad Ghori extended Muslim influence in India. In the late 1100's another Turkish chieftan took over the Ghaznawid lands in India. He was Muhammad Ghori (muh-*hahm'*mad goh-*ree'*). Like Mahmud, Muhammad came from a line of Afghan rulers. Between 1175 and 1186 Muhammad conquered all the Indian territory which the Ghazni dynasty had ruled. Then, in 1191, Muhammad began an assault on North Indian kingdoms which even Mahmud had not been able to subdue. In the first campaign the Muslim armies were defeated, but in the following year their great leader returned with a much larger force. After a bitter struggle, the armies of Muhammad came out victorious.

Muhammad had no more intention of staying in India than had Mahmud. He returned to his capital in Afghanistan, giving his generals the task of securing his conquests in India. The generals did a fine job. Within a few years they had extended Muslim rule over most of North India.

TIMETABLE	India During the Muslim Era
712	Arab conquest of Sind
1000–26	Invasions of Mahmud of Ghazni
1175–92	Invasions of Muhammad Ghori
1206–1526	Delhi Sultanate in North India
1221	Invasion of Genghis Khan
1336–1565	Vijayanagar Empire in South India
1398	Invasion of Tamerlane
1498	Arrival of the Portuguese
1519–26	Invasions of Babur
1526–1837	Mughal Empire in India
1526–1658	Mughal Golden Age in India

The Delhi sultans ruled India for more than three centuries. The most trusted of Muhammad's generals, Aybek, made Delhi his headquarters. When Muhammad was assassinated in 1206 Aybek became virtual king of North India. Aybek's rise to power marked the beginning of the Delhi Sultanate, a government of foreign dynasties which

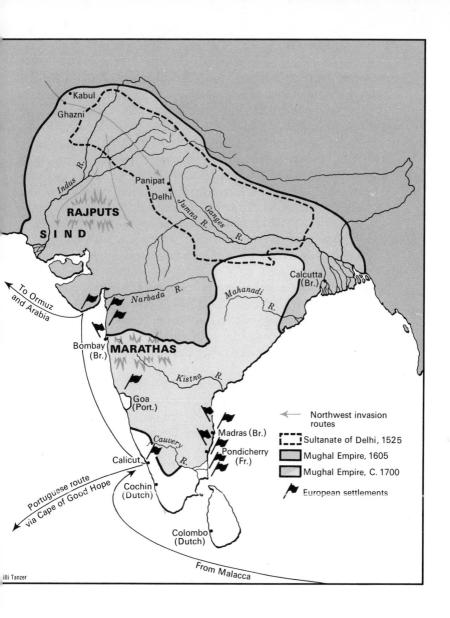

Map labels:
- Kabul
- Ghazni
- Indus R.
- RAJPUTS
- SIND
- Panipat
- Delhi
- Jumna R.
- Ganges R.
- Calcutta (Br.)
- To Ormuz and Arabia
- Narbada R.
- Mahanadi R.
- Bombay (Br.)
- MARATHAS
- Goa (Port.)
- Kistna R.
- Madras (Br.)
- Pondicherry (Fr.)
- Calicut
- Cauvery R.
- Cochin (Dutch)
- Colombo (Dutch)
- Portuguese route via Cape of Good Hope
- From Malacca
- illi Tanzer

Legend:
→ Northwest invasion routes
▪▪ Sultanate of Delhi, 1525
Mughal Empire, 1605
Mughal Empire, C. 1700
⚑ European settlements

PRELUDE TO CONQUEST. An important aspect of India's Muslim era was the formation of the Delhi Sultanate. The Sultanate was replaced by the Mughal Empire, which by the time of Akbar's death (1605) included all of North India and much of the Deccan. Under Aurangzeb the Empire had expanded to include most of the subcontinent. Conquest was never complete, however; some Hindu peoples, such as the Rajputs and Marathas (pages 102–5), were never subdued by the Mughals.

was to rule India for 320 years (1206–1526).[1] During that period 34 monarchs sat upon the throne at Delhi. The average reign was a brief one, for frequently sultans were deposed by their own officers. The three centuries of the Delhi Sultanate was one long, bloody scramble for power. Even members of the royal family, including children of the ruler, helped to plot palace revolts. Often, these rebellions ended in the death of the sultan.

Despite the insecurity of the Delhi throne, some sultans were able and statesmanlike. They supported the construction of public works, promoted trade, and patronized learning and art. Many of the sultans, however, were cruel and debauched. These were feared and despised by Hindu and Muslim alike. The reigns of such rulers were nightmares for the people.

The sultans built a large empire in India. During the 1200's and 1300's armies of the Sultanate fought their way into the Deccan. A few generals even penetrated the southernmost part of the peninsula, an area never before reached by conquerors from North India. For a time the Delhi sultans reigned over the most extensive empire ever put together in South Asia. And wherever the soldiers of the sultans went, they zealously sowed the seeds of their Islamic faith.

The monarchs at Delhi encountered many obstacles in administering their domain. A few rulers of unusual ability were able to maintain a firm grip over this vast empire. But as it swelled in size, the sultans found it impossible to directly govern all their domains. Therefore, they assigned viceroys to administer distant areas and gave them troops to enforce the laws. In some remote areas the sultans left intact the existing governments. After receiving tribute and promises of loyalty and taxes from a ruler in such an area, the sultan would allow the conquered prince to govern as he wished.

The Deccan and South India successfully resisted Islamic penetration. When a Hindu state in the Indo-Gangetic Plain fell to the Muslims, its ruler often was displaced by the Muslim conquerors. Sometimes a North Indian prince was executed. When princes were permitted to retain their thrones they were careful not to antagonize the sultan. Islam thus became a major force in North India. But the Deccan and South India were more remote from Delhi, and the sultans found it difficult to keep a close check on conquered princes in

---

[1] The Delhi Sultanate did not officially begin until 1229, when the Caliph of Baghdad declared Aybek's successor the sultan of India. However, the Sultanate existed in fact as soon as Aybek assumed the throne.

those regions. Moreover, the Hindu princes in the Deccan and South India offered a stubborn resistance to Delhi's efforts at expansion. Eventually the Deccan fell to the Delhi Sultanate, but its Hindu way of life was not substantially changed by the Muslim invaders.

South India was quite successful in resisting the sultans. In 1336 a Hindu kingdom was founded at Vijayanagar (*vij'*uh-yuh-*nug'*er). Strong, wealthy, and vigorous, the new state refused to bow to Muslim power. It built an empire of its own which included that part of the peninsula south of the Kistna River. The kingdom of Vijayanagar actually outlived the Delhi Sultanate, for it did not fall until 1565. In that year several Islamic rulers in the Deccan joined forces to sack the city of Vijayanagar. This attack brought to an end the last important Hindu empire.

The Sultanate was not free from foreign attacks. Despite its Afghan and Turkish origins, the Delhi Sultanate was an Indian state. Whereas Mahmud and Muhammad had governed from Afghanistan, the Delhi sultans had their courts in the subcontinent. As an Indian state, the Sultanate had to cope with traditional Indian problems of security and defense. This meant that every sultan had to guard against invasion across the northwestern frontier. Rulers in Afghanistan constantly were attacking settlements across the border in India. But an even more serious danger lurked behind Afghanistan in Central Asia. This was the homeland of the Mongols, nomadic warriors who had become infamous for their cruelty and ferocity.

The Mongols were of the same racial stock as the Afghan and Turkish rulers of Afghanistan and India. However, kinship did not prevent them from invading and plundering the two lands. The terrible Genghis Khan, founder of the Mongol Empire, led the first Mongol expedition into India in 1221. From that moment until the day the Sultanate fell North India experienced periodic attacks by the Mongol hordes. Fortunately for the sultans, the Mongols did not choose to add India to their huge empire. They came simply for plunder, and directed their expansionist efforts elsewhere. India, Japan, and Southeast Asia were the only major regions of Asia to escape the Mongol yoke.

Destruction in India reached a peak in 1398 when Tamerlane swept into India. Tamerlane was a descendant of Mongols who had settled in Central Asia. Ruthless, merciless, and cunning, Tamerlane had no equal in the conduct of mounted warfare. Rarely was he bested in battle. When he invaded North India he ignored the fact that the region was under Muslim rule, even though he claimed to be a devout Muslim himself. This "Scourge of God" plundered and burned Hindu temples and put to the torch many cities and towns on the Indo-Gangetic Plain.

During the final century of its existence the Delhi Sultanate steadily disintegrated. Its domain was reduced as one subject state after another asserted its independence. The rulers of the restored Hindu states continued wars with each other, which in reality had never stopped. Continuous strife was also the normal pattern in the shrunken domain of the sultans in northwest India. Once again political disunity in the Indian subcontinent encouraged invaders.

The Portuguese established a maritime empire. During the twilight of the Sultanate, southwest India encountered "invaders" who came by sea seeking trade. In 1498 Portuguese ships commanded by Vasco da Gama dropped anchor off Calicut. The arrival of the vessels represented the climax to many years of effort by Portuguese seamen to discover an eastern sea route to Asia. For centuries Islamic peoples — Arabs, Egyptians, and Turks — had a monopoly on Eastern trade with the West, for they controlled the early trade routes. But by sailing around Africa, the Portuguese had bypassed lands under the control of another power. They had broken the Islamic monopoly on the lucrative trade with the East. No longer must the luxury goods of India, Southeast Asia, and East Asia reach Western Europe through middlemen in the Near East. Before long other Portuguese traders followed the new route to the East. In time, too, other Europeans — Spanish, Dutch, French, and English — appeared in the ports of Asia seeking trade and empire.

The Portuguese soon made it clear that they intended to establish a monopoly of their own. Thanks to superior sea power, they succeeded. Between 1509 and 1511 they seized the islands of Ormuz and Malacca and the port of Goa (see map, page 91). Not long afterwards Portuguese ships reached the East Indies and ports in mainland Southeast Asia and South China. In 1542 they entered Japan. Goa became the headquarters of the far-flung Portuguese empire.

At first, the Portuguese were welcomed in India by the local rulers. By the time of the Muslim invasions travel to foreign lands had become an "impure" practice for high-caste Hindus. Trade between India and other lands was conducted largely by Arab and Chinese vessels which regularly called at important ports in the subcontinent.

The Hindu rulers were glad to admit the Portuguese, because this meant an expansion of foreign trade. The opposition to the Portuguese came from Muslim merchants who had left the Near East centuries earlier to reside in the port cities of India. They opposed the Europeans because they were both commercial competitors and Christians. But the Muslims were no match for the ruthless and enterprising newcomers, who gradually extended their commercial activities northward. By the end of the sixteenth century the Indian trade had built many Portuguese fortunes.

- CHECK-UP
  1. Why did the Muslims invade India? What were the results? How was the Delhi Sultanate established?
  2. Why was Sultanate control over the Deccan and South India more shaky than in the north? Why did Muslim invasions continue?
  3. Why did the Portuguese come to India? What were the results?

2. The Mughals Brought Another Golden Age to India

The English word "mogul" means an "important or powerful person." Derived from the Hindi word "mughal," it was introduced into our language by English visitors to India during the seventeenth century. These travelers were awestruck by the splendor of the Mughal regime and impressed by the capability of its Muslim rulers. Though they differed greatly from one another, five of the six Mughal rulers of the 1500's and 1600's left indelible marks upon India. Besides bringing another Golden Age to India, they built an empire that included nearly all of the subcontinent.

Babur brought an end to the Delhi Sultanate. While the Portuguese were building a commercial empire in South India, a Turko-Mongol prince was destroying the political empire of the sultans. The prince was Babur, a descendant of both Genghis Khan and Tamerlane. Babur felt that Tamerlane's conquests had given the family a valid claim to India. This direct descendant of the "Scourge of God" invaded India in 1519. He met with little resistance; the Hindu princes in the northwest had come to ignore Delhi, and now many of them acknowledged Babur's overlordship without a fight. Undoubtedly, they intended to ignore this new invader also.

Babur led three other expeditions into India during the next few years. Although he encountered no serious opposition, he was irritated because North Indian rulers continued to recognize the sultan at Delhi as their nominal ruler. Late in 1525 Babur again invaded India, this time for the purpose of capturing Delhi. He accomplished his goal. In the spring of 1526 Babur met the forces of the Delhi Sultanate at Panipat and defeated them. The sultan himself was killed in the battle. Babur continued unopposed to the capital city. With his capture of Delhi the Sultanate came to an end, and a new and more powerful Indian empire had been started.

Akbar provided a firm foundation for the Mughal Empire. Babur died only a few years after his momentous victories. His son and successor experienced severe military and political defeats and spent most of his adult life as an exile in Persia. It was Babur's fourteen-year-old grandson, Akbar, who took over where Babur had left off. In 1556, at Panipat, the forces of the newly crowned Akbar overcame an Afghan ruler who had occupied much of northwest India. During the rest of Akbar's reign the forces of the Mughal Empire seldom lost a battle. When Akbar died in 1605 the Mughal domains embraced the larger part of the Indo-Gangetic Plain.

Akbar the Great left a lasting imprint upon Indian history. He was a first-rate organizer, an exceptional administrator, and an empire-builder of unusual political vision. More so than all other Muslim rulers before him, he realized the necessity of enlisting the support of the Hindu population in the government of his realm. Akbar included talented Hindus in the administration of his constantly growing empire. By providing them with an opportunity for careers in government, Akbar won their loyal cooperation. This "alliance" between Akbar and the Hindus was a major reason for Akbar's success in controlling his many conquests.

Akbar insured the loyalty of the Hindus by acting boldly to eliminate their grievances. One act which made him popular with Hindus was his elimination of the hated poll taxes. Before his reign Muslim rulers in India (and throughout the Islamic world) had customarily imposed special individual taxes upon "infidels." These head, or poll, taxes underscored the privileged position of the followers of Mohammed. Akbar abolished all special levies upon non-Muslims. This action was bitterly opposed by his Muslim advisers, but Akbar felt that Hindu support was worth a drop in popularity among Muslims.

Akbar sought to create a new religion. Though born a Muslim, Akbar began to doubt that the religion of the Prophet was the only true one. After he became ruler of North India he began to devote much time to the study of other religions. He invited representatives of many beliefs to lecture at his court. Even Jesuit missionaries from the Roman Catholic Church of Europe were given the opportunity to explain their faith. After hearing about all religions, however, Akbar became convinced that none of them was the true faith.

Finally Akbar decided to found a faith which would combine the best teachings from all sects and philosophies. He called his new religion the Divine Faith. But try as he might to promote its acceptance, Akbar made little headway. With his death the Divine Faith quietly disappeared.

Akbar's policies were continued after his death. The first two rulers to follow Akbar wisely decided to follow in his footsteps. Since each of them enjoyed a long reign, Akbar's policies were followed in India for another half century.

Akbar's successors, Jahangir (1605–1628) and Shah Jahan (1628–1658), emulated their illustrious predecessor in many ways. Like Akbar, they extended Mughal power without placing undue strain upon the state's resources. Like Akbar, they were careful to consolidate their conquests and to provide an efficient administration for conquered lands. Like Akbar, too, Jahangir and Shah Jahan enlisted the cooperation of Hindu leaders by granting them favored positions in the Mughal court. The two emperors also followed Akbar's example by promoting friendly relations between Muslims and Hindus.

Jahangir and Shah Jahan were especially careful to preserve the Mughal system of alliances. Babur and Akbar had put together the Mughal Empire by winning allies among the Indian princes. In return for the privilege of managing their own affairs, these allies aided the Mughal dynasty in time of war. Both Jahangir and Shah Jahan grasped this hard fact of Indian politics and warfare. Therefore, they took care to respect the rights of their Hindu allies.

The Mughal emperors were patrons of the arts. Possessors of great wealth, the Mughal monarchs surrounded themselves with every luxury that could be produced by Indian craftsmen or imported from other lands. Moreover, all the Mughal emperors from Babur to Shah Jahan had refined tastes. Each cherished the Persian influences so powerful in the ancestral homeland. Most of them retained Persian artists and architects at their courts. However, the Mughal rulers also supported Hindu artists and architects. Hindu and Persian elements eventually blended into a new Indo-Persian, or Mughal, tradition. Generously supported by the Mughal emperors, this tradition ushered in a new Golden Age for India.

MUGHAL ART. The Mughal school of art was especially famous for portraiture. The painting at left, which was used to illustrate a manuscript, shows Humayan (top, left), the son of Babur; Babur himself (top, right); Jahangir (bottom, left); and Akbar (bottom, right). The small picture (bottom, left) reproduces a miniature portrait of the emperor Shah Jahan. Such paintings, six or seven inches in height, were also used to illustrate books. Below is a painting entitled "Jahangir in the Garden." It is one of the finest examples of the art of seventeenth century India.

The Taj Mahal, perhaps India's most famous structure, is built of white marble on a red sandstone base. Surrounding it are beautiful gardens.

The finest Mughal art was produced during the reign of Jahangir. Akbar had introduced into India the techniques and themes of Persian painting, and these had been combined with traditional Hindu styles. The new Mughal school of art became particularly renowned for its portraits, pictures of animals, and use of color. Unlike Hindu art, which was almost completely religious in nature, Mughal art was secular. The artists of this school aimed at "portraying the somewhat materialistic life of the Court, with its state functions, processions, hunting expeditions, and all the picturesque although barbaric pageantry of an affluent Oriental dynasty."[2]

Of more lasting interest than Mughal art are products of its sister school of architecture. The Mughal emperors were especially interested in the construction of beautiful buildings. Neatly and painstakingly symmetrical, the structures were usually topped by a graceful dome. Slender towers rose at each corner, walls were cut with beautiful open-work tracery, and dome-shaped gateways broke the long expanse of walls. Shimmering white marble and red sandstone were lavishly used. Literally hundreds of magnificent tombs, mosques, palaces, and forts were erected by the great Mughal emperors.

The most famous period of Mughal architecture was the reign of Shah Jahan. Comparatively uninterested in painting, Shah Jahan became the greatest of the Mughal builders. The Taj Mahal, designed by the emperor as a mausoleum for his beloved wife, is one of the most famous buildings in the world.

[2] Quoted in: S. M. Edwards and H. L. O. Garrett, *Mughal Rule in India* (Delhi, reprinted by S. Chand, 1962), p. 215.

Use of the Urdu language was fostered during Mughal times. The appreciation of the Mughal emperors for Persian culture extended to the field of language. They encouraged the adoption of Persian for both writing and speaking, and gradually the language was fused with the Hindi tongue of North India. The result was the creation of a new language known as Urdu (page 28).

The grammar and basic vocabulary of Urdu are drawn from Hindi. The technical words and richer expressions are of Persian origin. Urdu has been spoken by the educated classes of India for several centuries. It also has been embodied in a first-class literature. Today Urdu is one of Pakistan's official languages.

Aurangzeb reversed long-standing Mughal policies. The last of the mighty Mughal emperors, Aurangzeb (1658–1707), chose not to follow the pattern established by his predecessors. But he shared their ambition to enlarge the Mughal Empire. Called the "World Shaker," Aurangzeb was determined to bring the entire subcontinent under his sway. To attain this goal he spent the last half of his reign in the Deccan, leading military operations. By 1690 he was nominal ruler of all of India except the extreme south. However, while extending the empire, Aurangzeb planted the seeds for its downfall.

Aurangzeb made one of his greatest mistakes in trying to enforce Islamic practices and laws. First, he infuriated the Hindu population by reintroducing discriminatory practices such as the poll tax on non-Muslims. He also tried to curb traditional customs and practices which conflicted with Islamic law. Furthermore, he ended many of the privileges which Hindu nobles had enjoyed under earlier Mughal rulers. And because he himself was a strict Muslim, he was puritanical in his habits and outlooks. Scorning luxury and condemning cultural pursuits, he dismissed artists and architects from the royal court. Aurangzeb's strictness not only created ill will but brought to an end the Golden Age of Mughal culture.

Another fatal mistake this Mughal emperor made was quarreling with traditional friends of the Mughal Empire. He aroused the unending hatred of the powerful Sikhs (page 103) by executing their Guru when that leader refused to accept the Islamic faith. He also became involved in wars with the Rajputs (page 102), the most important allies of the Mughal dynasty. One other blunder Aurangzeb made was attempting to overcome the Marathas (page 104), a powerful Hindu people of the Deccan. Although most of Aurangzeb's campaigns in the Deccan were directed against the Marathas, he never conquered them.

Aurangzeb's policies led to the disintegration of the Mughal Empire. Aurangzeb had built a huge empire, but before he died he saw it begin to fall apart. Because of his campaigns in the Deccan, Aurangzeb did not see his capital from 1681 until his death in 1707. His long absence from Delhi caused the Mughal administrative machinery to break down. High government officials became increasingly corrupt and inefficient. Many states became virtually independent. Certain rulers, especially among the Sikhs and Marathas, became more powerful than the emperor himself. But even if Aurangzeb had been served by honest and capable officials, he could not have stopped the empire's decline. The administrative system called for strong leadership from the top, something Aurangzeb refused to supply. Besides, Aurangzeb had drained the treasury to finance his costly wars and had lost the support of most of his Indian allies.

The Peacock Throne

No throne in the world is more famous than the fabled "Peacock Throne" of the Mughal emperors. Built during the reign of Shah Jahan, it was the costliest ever assembled. The back was decorated with two gem-covered peacocks, and the entire throne was covered with rubies, emeralds, diamonds, and pearls. In 1665 a French jeweler estimated its value at six million pounds — more than $16,000,000 in American money!

For many years the throne occupied a recess in the back wall of the Hall of Public Audience at the Mughal palace in Delhi. Then, in 1739, the Persian ruler Nadir Shah invaded Delhi and carried off the throne as a spoil of war. Rumors had it that the throne was stored in the Shah's treasure house at Tehran, but in 1911 a British official proved the stories to be false. Visiting the treasure house, he found that the throne was not there.

Although the Peacock Throne itself has mysteriously disappeared, its name is preserved in a throne still in the possession of the Shah of Iran (Persia). This later Peacock Throne is thought to contain parts of the original throne. Stored in a bank vault, it was last brought out in 1967. In that year Mohammed Reza Pahlavi, the present Shah of Iran, used it for his coronation.

The Mughal Empire did not end with Aurangzeb's death. His descendants occupied the throne at Delhi until 1857. But their domain shrank until it included only the region around the capital city. Finally the empire disappeared altogether.

● CHECK-UP

1. How was the Mughal Empire established? Why was Akbar a great ruler?
2. How did the Mughal emperors promote the arts? How was the Urdu language created?
3. How did Aurangzeb's policies lead to the decline of the Mughal Empire?

3. Various Indian Peoples Resisted Mughal Rule

The Mughals never were masters of all of India. Even at the height of Mughal power many Indian kingdoms and peoples defied every effort to control them. As the Mughal Empire began to fall apart, independence movements became increasingly evident. In Chapter Five we shall read how Europeans filled the power vacuum left by the decline of the Mughal Empire. As they began to gain power it was semi-independent Muslim kingdoms and Rajput, Sikh, and Maratha kings — not the Mughal emperors — who blocked their plans for expansion.

The Rajputs were a powerful force in northwest India. If any one people can be given credit for preventing complete domination of India by the Mughals, that people would be the Rajputs. Their homeland, which by the late 1700's consisted of 36 kingdoms, was called Rajputana (map, page 123). Claiming descent from the Kshatriya of Aryan times (page 44), the Rajputs were proud of their fighting ability. One of their proverbs was "A wall may give way: a Rajput stands fast." Invaders of India who had to force their way through Rajputana found the defenders invincible. Not even the mightiest of the Mughal monarchs was able to conquer this people. The great Akbar gained the loyalty of the Rajputs by granting them special privileges, and they became the mainstay of his system of alliances.

To a great degree, the Rajputs were responsible for preserving Hinduism in northwest India. In the face of the Muslim onslaughts they preserved their Aryan traditions and culture, and their Brahmins tightened caste restrictions to exclude Muslims. By the time Aurangzeb came to power two communities — Hindu and Muslim —

were well established in northwest India, and neither had much use for the other. As we have seen, Aurangzeb's attempts to impose Muslim law on the Rajputs transformed these allies of the Mughal Empire into dangerous enemies.

The Sikhs objected to Mughal rule. Another people of northwest India that caused trouble for the Mughals were the Sikhs. Unlike the Rajputs, the Sikhs had no heritage to unite them; they emerged at the beginning of the Mughal era. While Babur was destroying the Delhi Sultanate, a new religion, Sikhism, was rising in northwest India. The Sikhs were those who adopted the faith.

The founder of Sikhism was Nanak (1469–1539). Born a Hindu, Nanak, as he grew older, began to study the teachings of Mohammed. Unable to find spiritual satisfaction in either Hinduism or Islam, he devised a faith that would rise above the differences in the two religions. From Islam he acquired an unshakable faith in the concept of one God, a distaste for the caste system, and a dislike for religious images. From Hinduism he borrowed the idea of toleration of widely differing points of view. At the center of the faith devised by Nanak was the worship of the principle of "Truth." Eventually the doctrines of Sikhism were set forth in a holy book known as the *Adi Granth*. Recitation of and reflection upon the verses of this book are still the core of Sikhism.

Sikhism became a "third force" in Indian society. The Sikhs, adopting beliefs and customs unlike any in either Hinduism or Islam, aroused the antagonism of Hindu and Muslim alike. For example, the Sikhs condemned the formalism of both of India's major religions. Nanak provided the basis for this condemnation in the *Adi Granth*:

Religion consisteth not in mere words;
He who looketh on all men as equal is religious.
Religion consisteth not in wandering to tombs or places of cremation, or sitting in attitudes of contemplation.
Religion consisteth not in wandering in foreign countries, or in bathing at places of pilgrimage.
Abide pure amidst the impurities of the world;
Thus shalt thou find the way to religion.[3]

[3] Quoted in: R. C. Majumdar *et al.*, *An Advanced History of India* (London, Macmillan, 1946), p. 406.

Inside the Golden Temple at Amritsar, the most sacred shrine of the Sikhs, a preacher addresses believers. Note that the speaker has the distinguishing characteristics of Sikhism: beard, turban, iron bracelet, dagger.

The customs adopted by the Sikhs set them apart from other Indians. All Sikhs adopted the common name of "Singh," meaning "Lion." Men did not cut their hair or shave their faces. Instead, they wore turbans and long beards. Other distinguishing marks of a Sikh were an iron bracelet on the wrist and a dagger at the belt.

The Sikhs became a powerful, militant, and industrious group. They have played an important role in Indian life. By the end of the seventeenth century they had withdrawn into a section of the Indus River Valley, there to establish their own self-sufficient villages. These Sikh communities in the Punjab formed the last region to fall under British rule (page 126).

The Marathas were strong in the Deccan. A third people who actively resisted the Mughals were the Marathas. Living in the region of the Western Ghats, they were looked down upon for many centuries. In the Hindu caste structure they were Shudras, the lowest group. Hard-working peasants, they lived in comparative peace within the Mughal Empire until Aurangzeb came to the throne. Then, because they were persecuted by Muslim zealots, this Hindu people began to think in terms of a nation of their own. From that time on the Marathas were a constant source of harassment and irritation for the Mughal emperors.

The man most responsible for arousing the Marathas was Shivaji (1627–1680). A descendant of Maratha kings and soldiers, he was inspired by his mother to free his people from tyranny. Before he was twenty years old Shivaji began the career which made him the most dangerous of the Mughal Empire's foes. Called the "Mountain Rat of the Deccan" by Aurangzeb, he succeeded in carving an empire out of Muslim lands. His cavalry swept across central India like a swarm of locusts. Shivaji's forces even subdued the Rajputs, and for a time they threatened the Mughal capital at Delhi. Today the Marathas still tell stories of Shivaji's boldness in war, humanity to prisoners, kindness to women and children, and tolerance in matters of religion.

After Shivaji's death his empire disintegrated. However, a confederacy of Maratha chieftains remained, and these rulers dominated much of India until the early 1800's. Unfortunately for the Marathas, their confederacy was loosely knit. Their unwillingness to cooperate with each other and their inability to govern effectively led to their downfall. Taking advantage of these weaknesses, the British finally subdued the Marathas (see page 126).

Important Muslim states outlasted the Mughal Empire. A number of Muslim-controlled states survived the fall of the Mughal Empire. The greatest of these, in terms of size and wealth, began as a Mughal province in the Deccan. This was Hyderabad, the home of the famous cave temples at Ajanta and Ellora (page 78). In 1724 an officer of the imperial government forced the Mughal Emperor to appoint him the first Nizam, or ruler, of Hyderabad. Known as Asaf Jah, this officer made Hyderabad virtually independent of the empire. A Muslim, he prevented the complete submergence of Islam in the south by checking the tide of Maratha power. Although Hyderabad's population was predominantly Hindu, the Muslim Nizams ruled this important kingdom until independent India assumed control of it in 1948.

In South India, the most important post-Mughal kingdom was Mysore. Founded on the ruins of the empire of Vijayanagar (page 93), Mysore is famous as the birthplace of Chandragupta I, founder of the Gupta dynasty. Like Hyderabad, Mysore during the Mughal age was ruled by Muslims although most of the people were Hindu. During the decline of the Mughal Empire Hyder Ali and his successor, Tipu, made the kingdom the chief power in South India. These two sultans resisted the efforts of British leaders to extend

British influence in the region. The death of Tipu in battle with the British (page 126) ended Muslim influence in Mysore. From then on the British controlled Mysore, although officially a Hindu ruler occupied the throne.

● CHECK-UP

1. Who were the Rajputs? the Sikhs? the Marathas? Why was each of these peoples important?
2. What important Muslim states survived in the Deccan? in South India? In what way did each of these come to an end?

4. Islam Became a Vital Force in Indian Life

Few civilizations had as far reaching an influence in India as the Islamic. The beliefs, manners, and customs of Islam were transplanted to the Indian subcontinent over the course of several centuries. As in Africa, Europe, and other parts of Asia, the transmitters of the Islamic way of life were soldiers and merchants. They won converts, either by persuasion or by the threat of the sword, and the converts in turn sought to recruit new followers. Before the close of the Delhi Sultanate Islam had become India's second major religion. By the end of the Mughal Empire, it was a permanent and important Indian institution.

Islam resisted assimilation into the Hindu way of life. Until the soldiers of Mohammed the Prophet arrived in India, most invaders of and immigrants to the subcontinent brought with them ways of life which were less advanced than the Indian way of life. Notable exceptions were the Persians and the Greeks, but few of either group stayed in the subcontinent. Most newcomers could add little or nothing to Indian culture. Often as not, they eventually abandoned their own ways and faith and became "Hinduized." Such was not true of the followers of Islam. By 1000 A.D., when Islam began to penetrate the subcontinent in earnest, Muslims had absorbed much of value from the many highly cultured peoples they had conquered. As we have seen, the Mughals especially were influenced by the advanced Persian culture. Because they had a high culture, and because the Islamic religion forbade compromise with other faiths, the Muslims who entered India rejected the Hindu faith and much of its culture.

The Islamic unwillingness to compromise resulted in a permanent division of India along religious lines. Northwest India, which had borne the brunt of every Muslim attack, became a center of Islamic power. Followers of the Prophet came to this area as soldiers only to remain as permanent settlers. Ultimately their descendants outnumbered the Hindus. Islam also became the religion of most people in northeast India. Islam's insistence that all followers of Mohammed were equal in the sight of Allah induced thousands of Untouchables and low-caste Hindus to accept the new religion. Northeast India had an especially high number of converts. In both northwest and northeast India many Buddhists became Muslims after the marauding Islamic warriors had all but destroyed the Buddhist power structure (see page 74).

The concentration of Muslims in certain regions was of great importance when the subcontinent was partitioned in 1947. The northwest became West Pakistan; the northeast, a thousand miles away, became East Pakistan. (In 1971 East Pakistan broke away and declared itself a separate nation.)

The Muslims delighted in oppressing the Hindu majority. The Hindus of India were accustomed to absorbing rather than repelling invaders who came to their land. Therefore they were not prepared to cope with the Muslims, zealots who refused to be absorbed. On their part, the Muslims set out to establish their faith by force. The wars they waged against the Hindus were religious crusades. From the viewpoint of the Muslims, Hindus were "infidels" (non-believers in the "true" faith of Islam). Infidels in other parts of the world had accepted Islam rather than be killed, but the Hindus refused to "submit to the will of Allah."

The Muslim wars against the Hindus were extraordinarily bitter and furious. The Muslims showed no mercy. They believed that by killing and "sending to hell" the infidel Hindus they could gain favor with Allah. They also believed that death in battle while fighting for Islam would give the fallen one a special place in Paradise. Hence they were fearless in battle. Muslims enjoyed tearing down Hindu holy places and smashing the statues and carvings representing Hindu divinities. The religious zeal of the Muslims laid the groundwork for centuries of fighting, bitterness, and hate between followers of the two great faiths of India.

The customs and social systems of Hinduism and Islam clashed. Even after many centuries of living alongside one another, Hindus and Muslims could not achieve mutual understanding. The Hindu way of life was determined by the traditions of the caste system; the guidelines for Muslims were set forth in the Koran, the holy book of

Islam. The two systems were often in conflict. One serious difference had to do with dietary laws. The Hindu tradition encouraged vegetarianism and veneration of cows, while the Koran allowed any kind of meat to be eaten except pork. Every time a Muslim butchered a cow he provoked the Hindus to fury. Over the centuries many riots and much bloodshed have stemmed from Muslim disregard of Hindu dietary restrictions.

Islam and Hinduism also were poles apart in their attitude toward life. Muslims believe that all men are equal in the sight of God. In the eyes of early Muslims the caste system, with its emphasis on arbitrary and unequal class distinctions, was an affront to Allah. And because Muslims were outside the Hindu caste system, they were consigned to the ranks of the Untouchables.

Other Religions in India

Several "outside" religions were represented in India by the time the Mughal Empire came to an end. Zoroastrianism, a major religion of ancient Persia, became established in the subcontinent during the thirteenth century. At that time groups of Persians came to India to escape the Mongols. They joined smaller communities of their countrymen in India who had fled Persia in earlier centuries to escape persecution at the hands of Arab Muslims. Known as Parsees (the Hindi word for Persians), most of the Zoroastrians settled in Bombay. They have distinguished themselves as businessmen and community leaders in that city.

According to tradition, communities of Christians and Jews have existed in India for nearly 2000 years. St. Thomas, one of the original twelve disciples of Jesus, is credited with introducing Christianity into India soon after Christ's death. The earliest Christian missionaries to India discovered that their religion had preceded them. Tradition also states that Jews entered the subcontinent about the same time. Today about 2 per cent of the Indian people are followers of Christianity.

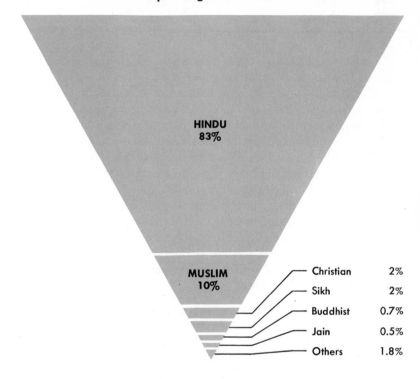

HINDU 83%	
MUSLIM 10%	
Christian	2%
Sikh	2%
Buddhist	0.7%
Jain	0.5%
Others	1.8%

Differing attitude toward intermarriage was another sore point between Hindus and Muslims. The Hindu father arranged the marriages of his children, and almost always found marriage partners for them within his caste. He never approved a child's marriage to a person outside the Hindu faith. Muslim men, on the other hand, were free to choose their own wives. Since the dawn of Islam, when the warriors of the Prophet settled in conquered lands, they married "infidels." They continued this practice in India, much to the dismay of upper class Hindus. However, Muslims did not look with favor upon the marriage of *their* daughters to members of the Hindu community!

Both Hindus and Muslims kept their wives "segregated." In one custom Hindus and Muslims were in agreement. Indian wives, whether Hindu or Muslim, were kept isolated from the outside world. According to Hindu tradition, the woman's place was in the home. Her job was to look after the household and tend to the children. She was free to leave the house only for such necessary chores as drawing water at the well or washing laundry at a nearby stream. At such times she often chatted with women from neighboring households, but she avoided conversation with men.

Like Hindu women, Muslim housewives were expected to confine their activities to home and family. Their religion imposed on them even stricter regulations than were binding on Hindu women. Married Muslim women were obliged to observe *purdah*, the custom of veiling oneself in the presence of all but one's closest relatives. Whenever a Muslim woman left her home she wore a *burka*, a veil which extends from the crown of the head to the ground.

Although purdah is still upheld by the Muslims in India and Pakistan, the custom is gradually dying. Many modern Muslim women have given up the practice. However, in South Asia women draped from head to foot in burkas are a common sight. The custom is a constant reminder that few Muslim women have attained the status enjoyed by Western women.

This picture of the 1967 elections calls attention to the changing role of Indian women. These Muslim wives, though still bound by tradition to wear burkhas, have come to the polls to vote. A few years ago they would not have been allowed to come near the ballot box.

India became a base for the spread of Islam to Southeast Asia.
Not long after the Delhi Sultanate was founded in the subcontinent,
Islam gained a foothold in the East Indian island of Sumatra. No
one knows whether the Muslims who carried the message of Islam
were Arabs or Indians. Probably they were merchants from ports in
South India. From Sumatra Islam was carried to the Malayan Peninsula and to other islands of the Indies. Eventually, Islam became
the faith of most Malayans and Indonesians.

The Spaniards finally arrested the expansion of Islam in Southeast
Asia. Muslim converts had brought the religion into the Sulu Archipelago and the southern Philippines during the fifteenth century.
When the Spaniards arrived in the Philippines in the sixteenth century, Islam already was established. The Spaniards, however, were
successful in converting most of the inhabitants of the central and
northern islands to Christianity. But even today the Moros of Min-
danao, the southernmost of the Philippine Islands, and of the Sulu
Archipelago, count themselves followers of Mohammed.

- CHECK-UP
    1. Why were the Muslims able to resist assimilation by the Hindus? Why
       were they cruel to the Hindu majority?
    2. In what ways were Muslim and Hindu customs similar? How were
       they different?
    3. To what lands did Islam spread from India?

Summing Up

After about 1000 A.D. Hindu civilization was competing with the
ever growing influence of Islam. Mahmud of Ghazni and Muhammad
Ghori, the earliest of the well known Muslim invaders, came principally for plunder. The successors of Muhammad, however, built the
Delhi Sultanate, an Indian-based regime. For several centuries most
of northern and much of central India was dominated by the sultans.
However, the sultans had a difficult time maintaining stability in the
empire and resisting assaults from beyond the Indian frontier. The
most notable of the attackers were Genghis Khan, Tamerlane, and
Babur.

Under Babur's grandson, Akbar the Great, the foundations of the
mighty Mughal Empire were firmly established. Mughal India was
held in high esteem by contemporary peoples of Asia and Europe. It
was the largest and most powerful empire the subcontinent had ever

known. The Mughal rulers took pride not only in their political and military achievements but also in cultural advances. The ambitions of Aurangzeb, however, placed too great a strain upon the realm. Even before his death the Mughal Empire had entered into decline.

During the final years of the Mughal Empire the activities of various Hindu peoples overshadowed Mughal affairs. The most important of these peoples were the Rajputs and Marathas. In addition another force, the Sikhs, began to show some power. After the Mughal emperors themselves had lost their power, the Muslim hold in various parts of the subcontinent was preserved by other Muslim leaders. The most important post-Mughal Muslim states were Hyderabad and Mysore.

The coming of Islam stimulated many changes. The teachings of Mohammed the Prophet found especially fertile ground in the northwest and the northeast. It became the second major religion of India. In the fourteenth and fifteenth centuries zealots used the subcontinent as a base for extending Islam into Southeast Asia. Numerous converts were won in Malaya, the East Indies, and the southern Philippines.

CHAPTER REVIEW

Can You Identify?

Islam	Marathas	purdah
Koran	Tamerlane	Parsees
Urdu	Muhammad Ghori	Mongols
Akbar	Delhi Sultanate	Rajputs
Mohammed	Mughal Empire	Mahmud
Sikhism	Vasco da Gama	Hyderabad
Aurangzeb	Taj Mahal	Mysore

What Do You Think?

1. Earlier invaders of the subcontinent had been absorbed by the Hindus; the Muslims were not. Why?

2. What were the goals of Aybek and Babur in India? Of Genghis Khan and Tamerlane? Why were the goals of the former different from those of the latter?

3. Contrast the policies of Akbar and Aurangzeb. What personal qualities, policies, and goals characterize a great ruler?

4. Why did tensions persist in relations between Hindus and Muslims?

5. What Indian peoples successfully resisted domination by the Mughal emperors? How was this possible?

Extending and Applying Your Knowledge

1. The Mongols under Genghis Khan raided India; under Kublai Khan, they made all of China part of a great Mongol Empire. Read accounts of the Mongols to get a better understanding of these people.

2. Report on some facet of Indian art and the influences which shaped it. See, for example, *India: 5000 Years of Indian Art*, by Herman Goetz. This book contains 60 plates in full color.

3. Read "At the Court of a Mughal Emperor" in *India: Selected Readings*.

5

THE RISE OF THE BRITISH RAJ

"The British Empire," it has been said, "was created in a fit of absent-mindedness." Insofar as the part that became known as the British Indian Empire is concerned, this statement contains more than a grain of truth. The English East India Company laid the foundations for the greatest of all Indian empires. Yet its original interest in India was strictly commercial, and it became involved in Indian affairs only when its commercial interests were threatened. But once the Company recognized that it could not stand aloof from Indian politics, it began to take steps to assure its primacy in the subcontinent.

The very successes of the Company caused the English Parliament to curb the powers of this great commercial corporation. Over a period of many years the British *raj* (rule, or reign) in India was gradually shifted from the East India Company to Parliament, the final step coming after the bloody Sepoy Rebellion of 1857–8. The English East India Company was abolished and the British Crown became sovereign in India. Two decades later India was formally annexed to the British Empire.

During the closing years of the nineteenth century the British undertook to develop their great empire on the subcontinent. Programs to bring about reform and to exploit the great untapped resources of the subcontinent were given top priority. The various changes and developmental programs transformed India into the "jewel of the British Empire." However, nothing Britain did could convince many Indians that the British presence was desirable. Despite the fact that the lot of the peasant was somewhat improved, that industry was developed, and that transportation and communication were expanded, Indians continued to resent the foreign power on their soil.

1. The English East Indian Company Became a Powerful Force in India

On December 31, 1600 Queen Elizabeth I of England granted a charter to the English East India Company. The document gave the Company a monopoly on English trade with the East. In 1613 the Mughal emperor Jahangir gave official approval for a Company trading post at Surat, an Indian town just south of the Vindhya Hills. From these small beginnings the Company built a commercial empire which eventually controlled a large part of India. Exercising powers normally reserved for a national government, the Company provided a firm footing for what became the British Indian Empire.

European-chartered companies competed for the trade of India. While Jahangir, Shah Jahan, and Aurangzeb were extending the Mughal Empire, merchants from European countries were beginning to compete for trade rights in the subcontinent. In the late 1500's Indian commerce was almost exclusively in the hands of the Portuguese (page 94). But in the 1600's the Dutch, English, and French steadily chipped away at the Portuguese commercial monopoly — not only in India, but in many other parts of Asia. Within a generation or two the Portuguese were outstripped by these newcomers.

Calicut was one of the first Indian ports visited by European traders. Below, ships from four different countries are pictured in its harbor.

TIMETABLE	The English in India, 1600–1876
1600	English East India Company chartered
1613	Company trading post at Surat officially established
1744–63	Anglo-French struggle for power in India
1756	"Black Hole of Calcutta" incident
1773	Regulating Act
1784	India Bill
1793	Permanent Settlement in Bengal
1857–8	Sepoy Rebellion
1858	English East India Company abolished
1876	Queen Victoria proclaimed Empress of India

The Dutch, English, and French were better organized than the Portuguese to carry on trade in Asia. The Portuguese enterprise was a royal monopoly which suffered from excessive governmental interference, lack of initiative, and large-scale corruption. Its competitors were private trading companies whose activities were carefully watched by investors in the home countries. These businessmen were interested in profits, not in rewarding political favorites and building an empire.

By 1700 the English and French East India companies had made their respective nations the leading European powers in India. The Dutch still had ports in India, but they were concentrating on trade with the East Indies. The English had established centers of trade and power at Bombay in the west, Madras in the south, and Calcutta in the northeast. The French East India Company had built bases near the English settlements at Madras and Calcutta. Since English and French merchants were in direct competition with each other, a conflict between these two trading companies seemed unavoidable.

Europeans became enmeshed in Indian politics and war. Rivals in business, the English and French companies soon became opponents in war. Southern India had never been completely subdued by the Mughal emperors, and rulers of states in this region constantly were striving for supremacy. Some of them soon saw the Europeans as potential allies in this struggle.

For many years the trading companies tried to avoid direct involvement in Indian rivalries. They much preferred to concentrate on their business interests. In time, however, company officials came to realize that this policy could not be maintained. Indian rulers often requested help from Europeans in military ventures in return for commercial privileges. Moreover, trading posts were sometimes attacked in the princely wars. Consequently French and English officials in India obtained from their directors the right to act as circumstances dictated.

Over a period of years the English trading company received especially broad powers to protect its interests. By the late 1600's it had the right to acquire territory, negotiate treaties, and engage in war. Despite greater restrictions, the French company, too, became a powerful force. It is not surprising, therefore, that the English and French East India companies became involved in Indian affairs and began to supply troops to Indian princes.

Anglo-French rivalry in India was heightened by rivalry in Europe. The rivalry between English and French trading companies in India was part of a larger clash of interests. During the 1700's the parent countries were also confronting each other in Europe and in the New World. To gain military or economic advantage, the English and French governments were willing to encourage fighting in India. Moreover, ambitious leaders of the French and English trading companies were intent on founding empires. Meanwhile Indian princes were eagerly seeking help from one or the other of the companies in their own expansionist schemes. One writer has summarized the importance Indian rulers attached to European aid:

> In the Indian politics of the time all was . . . power politics, and personal ambition; there was no emotional bar, such as patriotism might have provided, against invoking the help of the foreigner. . . . the technical advantages enjoyed by the European would bring victory to whichever side they were given. In the absence of conviction, of national and religious feeling, politics were a matter for lords and their followers; the longest-ranged guns, the quickest-firing musket, the steadiest soldiers would decide the issue. The [European] makeweight had become the balance, the client could become the master.[1]

Of course English and French authorities were equally willing to enter into alliances to advance their own interests.

[1] Vincent A. Smith, *The Oxford History of India,* Percival Speare, ed. (New York, Oxford University Press, 1961), p. 460.

This engraving of eighteenth century Bombay shows the private army of the East India Company at drill. Company officials lived in luxury, leaving hard work to Indian labor.

The English checked the French drive for empire in India. The war of Austrian Succession (1740–1748), which found France and England on opposite sides in Europe, led to the clash of English and French forces in India. The opening move was the capture by the English navy of French ships off the coast of Madras. But it was not long before the French had come back to win many military and diplomatic victories.

Joseph Dupleix (dyoo-*playks'*), governor of the French trading post at Pondicherry, deserves credit for the French successes. A brilliant man, Dupleix had a sixth sense in politics and diplomacy. No Englishman in India could match him in steering a course through the complexities of Indian intrigue or in using Indian princes to further his country's ends. For aiding rulers in dynastic struggles he received major concessions, including control of all lands south of the Kistna River.

With Dupleix as leader, the French won many battles against the English and their Indian allies. But unfortunately for the French, there was only one Dupleix. When incompetent French generals were defeated, Dupleix was blamed for their shortcomings and recalled by his government. His successor signed a treaty with the English which gave up everything that Dupleix had gained.

Robert Clive gained control of Bengal for the English. During the fighting in South India, Robert Clive, a young employee of the English East India Company, left civilian life to become an army officer. He served with distinction, directing many English victories over the French. After his victories in the south Clive was called to the north, for the Company's position in Bengal was being threatened. The Muslim ruler of Bengal and its dependencies died in 1756, and his successor set out to establish control over European-held territories in his realm. His first target was the English post at Calcutta. The new ruler won a quick victory, which was made famous by the "Black Hole of Calcutta" incident. The captured English soldiers were imprisoned in a small room without food or water. Greatly exaggerated accounts of their suffering spread throughout British India, and angry Englishmen demanded retaliation.

Robert Clive, Architect of Empire

Many men helped to build the British Empire in India, but Robert Clive (1725–1774) is remembered as the man who made the initial moves. At the age of nineteen Clive became a clerk for the English East India Company. In 1754 he shifted from the business office to the army. In a short time he demonstrated his military genius by winning important battles in South India and Bengal. These victories laid the foundations of the British Empire in India.

After his military triumphs, Clive was twice appointed governor of Bengal. By the time he returned to England his achievements in India had become legendary. Under his direction, Bengal had become the most profitable of the British trading areas. For his great services he received from the English king the title of Baron Clive of Plassey.

English East India Company officials had many opportunities to enrich themselves illegally, and not all of them could resist the temptation. One such man was Clive. Eventually charges of misconduct were brought against him by Parliament. Distressed by the accusations, Clive took his own life.

Calcutta was recaptured by Clive in January, 1757. By this time news of the Seven Years' War (1756–1763) between England and France had reached India. Despite the protests of Bengal's ruler, Clive attacked and captured the most important French post in Bengal. A few months later he met and defeated the forces of the native ruler at the Battle of Plassey. Clive's victory brought Bengal under Company control. Later Bengal became the base from which the English launched their drive for an empire in India.

The Company adopted traditional methods of tax collection. Like the princes who ruled before the coming of the English East India Company, the latter sought revenue through taxing land and crops. In Bengal it adopted the procedures of the Mughal Empire. Akbar had divided his empire into 12 provinces, a number which had risen to 21 by the time of Aurangzeb. Each province had a *diwan*, or tax collector. In many parts of the empire the diwan did not collect taxes directly from the peasants, but farmed out the responsibility to large landowners in the villages. These men, called *zamindars*, then collected the taxes from the peasants and forwarded the required amount to the diwan.

The zamindars had property rights only in the lands they themselves owned. But as hereditary tax collectors, they were compensated for their work by being permitted to keep about one tenth of the tax money collected. To enrich themselves zamindars often tried to "squeeze" more than a just amount from the peasants. Were they successful the zamindars paid the diwan the sum he demanded and pocketed the rest. It should be recognized, however, that the diwan had to be paid in full even if tax collections fell short of the specified sum.

In 1765 Robert Clive signed a treaty with the Mughal emperor which gave the East India Company the right to collect taxes in Bengal and the neighboring provinces of Bihar and Orissa. For almost thirty years the zamindari system was continued, with the diwans acting as "middlemen" between the zamindars and Company officials. Whereas abuses had been common under the Mughal emperors, they increased sharply after 1765. English officials accepted huge bribes from the diwans, the diwans demanded even larger sums from the zamindars, and the zamindars, in turn, "squeezed" the peasants even more.

The Company's role in India changed in the late 1700's. Years of trading, fighting, and plotting had wrought great changes in the East India Company. From a small trading concern the Company had evolved into a major political and military force with centers of power in the west, the southeast, and the northeast of India. Bengal, with Robert Clive as governor, had become especially powerful and independent. However, almost from the beginning the East India Company had experienced difficulty in administering its realm. One very important reason for the trouble was that the principal holdings were widely separated. The bastions of Company power (Bengal, Bombay, and Madras) formed a huge triangle which covered nearly the entire subcontinent. Within the three points of the triangle were numerous Hindu and Muslim kingdoms, few of which were consistently friendly to the British. Under these conditions one man hardly could be expected to administer efficiently all three regions. Each center had a governor who ruled pretty much as he pleased. With so much independence and so little supervision, governors and other officials both enriched themselves illegally and made agreements with Indian princes which conflicted with British interests.

In 1773 the English government took action to limit the growing power of the Company and to halt the illegal and unwise activities of Company officials. In that year Parliament passed the Regulating Act, a bill which established a Governor-General and Council to supervise the Company's domains in India. The governor of Bengal was to be Governor-General, with authority both to administer his own province and to supervise the actions of the governors at Madras and Bombay. Both the Governor-General and the Council were to be appointed by and accountable to Parliament.

The policies of Hastings assured British primacy in India. Warren Hastings, a career employee of the English East India Company, was the first Governor-General appointed under the Regulating Act. Hastings was told not to expand British control in India; his basic task was to hold the territory already occupied by the Company. Hastings was also to attempt to win respect for English leadership among the hundreds of Indian princes.

Hastings had to overcome many obstacles to achieve these goals. In Bombay the English found themselves on the losing side in a struggle for power among the Marathas, and Hastings had to send troops to that region to maintain the Company's prestige. In the south he had to deal with powerful and ambitious princes who had combined their forces to attack the English. There also the French, who were aiding Britain's American colonies in their war for independence, were attempting to regain territories which they had lost to the English. In the northeast the Company was at war with several native princes. In the words of Hastings, there was "a war actual or impending in every quarter and with every power in Hindustan."

It is a tribute to Hastings' genius that he maintained the Company's position in the face of overwhelming odds. He could count on little help from the English government, for its resources were strained in fighting the American colonies and their European allies. The governors at Madras and Bombay continued to make imprudent agreements with Indian princes, and they were too far away for Hastings to take any action before the damage was done. Indeed, many of his difficulties with the princes were brought about by such agreements. But despite the odds, Hastings preserved the Company's dominant position — an accomplishment which was of great importance for the future of India. It proved beyond a doubt that England had the power to achieve supremacy over the entire subcontinent.

India became increasingly important to England. By Hastings' time India had become a key factor in the British economy. Englishmen who made fortunes in the service of the Company returned to the homeland to spend their wealth. The profits from England's trade with India were a boon. Not only was the country heavily in debt because of the Seven Years' War and the American Revolution, but it was entering a crucial phase of the Industrial Revolution. Money from India helped to pay England's debts and to buy the machines and build the factories needed for industrialization.

India also helped England make its trade with China more profitable. English merchants doing business with the "Middle Kingdom" were hard pressed to pay for cargoes of tea, silk, and porcelain. Because few Western goods appealed to the Chinese, these merchants had to pay their bills in silver bullion. Later opium, a drug made from a plant native to India, came to be in great demand in China. Because the Chinese would both accept opium in trade and pay cash for it, the drain on English-held silver came to an end. The opium trade became a major source of income, with the Company selling the drug to merchants who disposed of it in China.[2]

---

[2] Later the opium trade led to war between Britain and China. In 1839 the Chinese government attempted to wipe out commerce in the dangerous drug. After the Chinese confiscated and destroyed British stocks of opium at a Chinese port, Britain dispatched warships and troops to China. This Opium War raged on and off for three years before the British delivered a decisive blow.

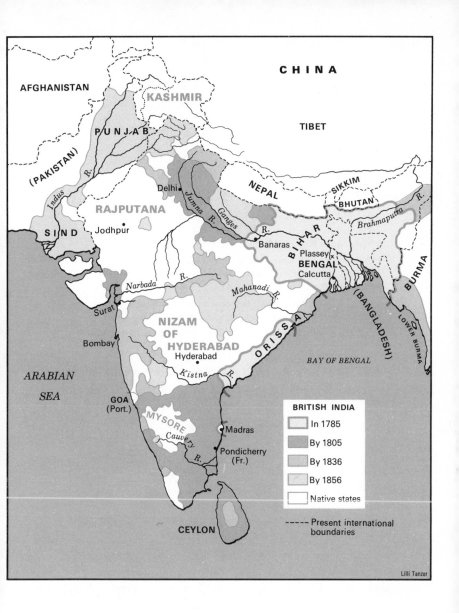

BRITISH INDIA

- In 1785
- By 1805
- By 1836
- By 1856
- Native states

----- Present international boundaries

Lilli Tanzer

THE BRITISH RAJ. When the East India Company established its first trading post at Surat, no one dreamed that 250 years later the British would directly govern three fifths of the subcontinent. Many of the "independent" native states came to owe their continued existence to British support. Other states — notably Hyderabad, Kashmir, and various Rajput kingdoms — stubbornly resisted the British raj. In 1856 these states were still outside the British fold.

123

Because of the growing importance of India, Parliament in 1784 took further steps to safeguard its interests. These were embodied in the India Act, a bill that limited the Company to commercial activities. All civil, military, and financial matters related to British India became the domain of Parliament. The English East India Company, which had shown signs of becoming a "state within a state," thus was stripped of virtually all its powers.

• CHECK-UP

1. Why did the English, French, and Dutch charter companies to trade with India and the East? Why did these outstrip the Portuguese? Where were the chief English trading posts located?

2. Why was there keen rivalry between the English and French companies? Why did they get involved in the intrigues of Indian princes? What was the outcome of the Anglo-French rivalry?

3. How did Parliament limit the role of the Company during the 1700's? Why? What goals were achieved by Hastings?

4. Why did India become increasingly important to England?

2. The British Made Great Changes in India

The India Act of 1784 limited the powers of the East India Company while increasing those of the new Governor-General. Lord Cornwallis, whose surrender at Yorktown had brought an end to fighting in the American Revolution, was appointed Governor-General soon after the India Act went into effect. During his seven years in office Cornwallis introduced a number of important reforms. Although his successors did not ignore reform, they were more concerned about strengthening the British hold on India. By 1850 India was largely a British possession. From 1784 to 1850 everything "English," and much that was "Indian," in India underwent considerable change.

The Indian Civil Service System had its beginnings under Cornwallis. The lack of an adequate civil service made it easier for corrupt or unwise officials to mismanage the Company's affairs. All Company employees were recruited in England. Sent to India with little or no training, most employees knew nothing about Indian ways and had little desire to learn. Because the Company's directors all lived in England, they could provide little supervision. Greedy and dishonest employees at all levels of government were able to carry on illegal trade and to pocket bribes. Many of them were able to retire to England after only a few years of service in India.

The corrupt practices of the Company's employees in India underscored the need for reform. Although Clive and Hastings had brought about considerable improvement in Bengal, the first systematic and widespread reforms were introduced by Cornwallis. Shortly after he came to India, Cornwallis drastically reorganized the administration. Officials engaged in commercial functions were excused from political, judicial, and military responsibilities. This action greatly restricted opportunities for graft. To further reduce temptation, Cornwallis paid his officials substantial salaries. These reforms marked the beginnings of the Indian Civil Service System.

The Governor-Generals who succeeded Cornwallis steadily improved the Indian Civil Service. Prospective officials were carefully screened. Appointees received special training before being posted to India. Occupying key posts in government, the men who made up this new breed of Civil Service employees greatly improved administration throughout British India.

Cornwallis attempted to reform the zamindari system. When Cornwallis became Governor-General he introduced a drastic change in Bengal's tax system. His Permanent Settlement (Assessment) of 1793 recognized the zamindars as the owners of the lands from which they previously had collected taxes. The traditional rights of the cultivators were ignored; they now became tenants paying rent instead of taxes to the zamindars. Moreover, the diwans were stripped of their power, and all revenue collected was paid directly into the Company's treasury at Calcutta.

The Permanent Settlement eliminated many old abuses, but it created a new evil — absentee landlordism. Because many zamindars were unable to make the required tax payments, their lands were confiscated and sold to the highest bidder. Purchasers often were speculators living in the cities. Life, which already had been hard for the peasants, then became even harder. Zamindars might have been unscrupulous tax collectors, but at least they understood the problems confronting the peasants. The new landlords had no interest in the welfare of their tenants. Although the Permanent Settlement had reduced graft, it had also upset a system which had worked effectively for hundreds of years.

The British hold on India was tightened during the early 1800's. The turn of the century saw a reversal in England's attitude toward India. The earliest Governor-Generals had been under orders to preserve but not extend the Company domain. But in 1798 the Earl of

Mornington, a confirmed imperialist, became Governor-General. Convinced that the Company should be supreme in the subcontinent, he abandoned the policy of non-intervention in favor of one of naked imperialism. In 1799 his armies decisively defeated those of Tipu Sultan (page 105), killed the famous leader, and made Mysore a virtual puppet of the Company. A few years later he took from the Marathas important territories which linked the British possessions in Madras and Bengal. Shortly after this action, however, he was recalled from India. His "war loving" policy had enraged the British public, forcing Parliament to ask for his return.

The years 1808–13 saw little military action on the part of the British. Governor-Generals during this period studiously avoided any action which might indicate the British were trying to take over India. But in 1813, with the appointment of the Earl of Moira as Governor-General, the policy of neutrality again was abandoned. By 1826 the Marathas had been completely subjected to British rule and Assam and Lower Burma had been annexed. In addition, a number of smaller Indian states had been forced to surrender many of their sovereign rights to the Company. While formally retaining control of internal affairs, in practice they were subject to frequent British interference.

By 1845 the last obstacle to British paramountcy in India was the Punjab. Here the Sikhs, under the guidance of Ranjit Singh, had brought most of the Indus valley under their control. After that leader's death in 1839, however, the Sikhs were left without capable leadership. In a series of hard-fought wars between 1845 and 1849 the British defeated the Sikhs and annexed the Punjab to their domain. With these victories, the British destroyed the last serious threat to their supremacy in the subcontinent.

What factors enabled the British to score one political or military victory after another? First and foremost was the lack of unity among the Indian princes. Jealous of each other, these rulers were unable to form an effective coalition against the British. A few princes might unite, but then an equal number would join the British side. Both the Marathas and Sikhs might have held off British domination, for both groups were large and had extensive military experience. But seldom could the 12 confederacies of Sikhs or the numerous Maratha princes stop quarreling among themselves long enough to present a united front. Thus Britain's military might coupled with India's lack of unity made possible British control.

Conquest necessitated additional land reforms. Until the Earl of Mornington arrived on the scene, Bengal and the surrounding area was the only region in which the Company collected taxes. In other parts of India revenue came almost entirely from trade. With the development of an imperialistic policy, the Company became the virtual ruler of dozens of small kingdoms. Seemingly, the changed situation provided an opportunity to introduce a uniform method of tax collection. Because customs varied widely from region to region, this was not done.

In South India the Company began to deal directly with the cultivators of the land (the *ryots*, or peasants). After a careful survey of a plot and its productivity, the Company and the ryot agreed on the amount to be paid as an annual tax. These "settlements" usually remained in effect for thirty years. When a term expired, a new settlement was made.

The new method of tax collection, called the *ryotwari* system, was also adopted in Bombay and some parts of the Deccan. In the northwest and in scattered parts of South India, however, Company officials concluded agreements with the village community as a whole. The villagers themselves undertook to determine the tax contribution to be made by each of the local cultivators. These agreements, too, were of a temporary nature, usually for a period of thirty years.

British changes in the traditional methods of land ownership and tax assessment have been both praised and criticized. On the good side, land reforms resulted in lower taxes for many peasants. Moreover, peasants became free to move when conditions in a given locality became intolerable. An unfortunate result of these reforms was an increase in the number of landless peasants. However, this trend cannot be ascribed entirely to British policy. For centuries Indian peasants had been subdividing land inherited from parents. By the time the British came to India many plots simply were too small to support a family.

Indians at first were not admitted to Civil Service. Conquest intensified another problem — this one, in the Indian Civil Service. Cornwallis had introduced the policy of excluding Indians from important positions in government. A man of strong prejudices, he thought most Indians were lazy and unreliable. Consequently even Hindus of outstanding ability were compelled to accept routine jobs if they wished a career in Britain's Indian government. Naturally this policy aroused deep resentment among Indians.

In 1833 the English Parliament passed legislation prohibiting discrimination in the Company's employment practices. No Indian, according to the law, was to be barred from an official position "by reason only of his religion, place of birth, descent, color, or any of them." But for twenty years this law had no effect. Admission to the Civil Service depended on nomination by Company directors. Because the directors lived in England, they knew few Indians.

In 1853 competition for Civil Service positions finally was opened to all. But even then Indian candidates were at a great disadvantage. The examinations tested the candidate's knowledge of Western history and culture and called for the command of the English language. Not until 1864 did an Indian score well enough to qualify for a major post in the Civil Service.

Traditional Indian education was downgraded. British expansion brought changes to Indian education. In traditional India, higher education was limited to classical languages such as Sanskrit, Arabic, and Persian. History, science, and mathematics were not taught. On the elementary level the curriculum consisted of the three R's and religious myths and legends. Of the world outside India, students on both levels learned almost nothing.

The first changes in Indian education had been introduced by Christian missionaries during the eighteenth and early nineteenth centuries. They established schools in India, most of which taught English as well as other subjects usually not taught in Indian schools. The British government itself, at first, did little to change Indian education. But in 1835 Parliament passed a bill limiting the payment of public funds to schools teaching English. Then, in 1854, the government created a nationwide system of schools. These ranged from primary schools to colleges. Indian dialects were to be the language of instruction, but included in the curriculum were the subjects commonly taught in Western schools.

The education bills of 1835 and 1854 had far-reaching effects in India. Not the least of these was that English became widely understood among the educated minority. The new schools became centers for the spread of Western ideas and customs. In them many Indians acquired their first systematic understanding of English history, government, laws, and culture. Because Civil Service examinations were based upon Western knowledge, these schools naturally attracted youth aspiring to careers as government officials. In time, many of these students came to assume positions of leadership.

At this feast of the Thugs, three victims have been beheaded on the raised altar. Another is about to be sacrificed, and still other prisoners await their turn. Behind the altar cultists are holding aloft representations of Kali and the various demigods associated with her.

The English moved slowly towards social reform. In the field of social reform, Governor-Generals usually avoided interfering with customs that were part of India's tradition. The caste system and child marriage, therefore, were allowed to continue. Even when the British felt that customs were of such a nature that they had to be abolished, Governor-Generals were slow in acting. Thus it remained for Lord William Bentinck, who came to office in 1828, to declare suttee and thuggee illegal.

The practice of suttee was closely associated with the Hindu practice of cremating the dead. In parts of North India high-caste widows sometimes showed their respect for a departed husband by giving up their own lives on the funeral pyre. A widow who was reluctant to follow this custom might be compelled to do so by community and family pressure. Bentinck successfully fought to have suttee declared illegal in Bengal. During the next generation it was outlawed in other regions as well.

Bentinck encountered less opposition when he led the fight against thuggee. The thugs were followers of a Hindu cult that believed in offering human sacrifices to the goddess Kali. To obtain their victims thugs resorted to kidnapping, and many travelers thus were seized and sacrificed by members of the cult. The practice of human sacrifice came to an end when Bentinck arrested more than 3000 thugs. Thuggee continued, but sacrificial animals were substituted for human beings.

Slavery had existed in India since ancient times. Though never extensive, it was a feature of prosperous households, where slaves were used to perform domestic tasks. Slave labor was also used in mines and in the craft guilds. In 1843, as part of Britain's policy of ending human bondage in colonial territories, slavery was made illegal in India. As in the case of thuggee, this reform encountered little opposition.

Indian Loan-Words in English

The English borrowed many words from the various local languages spoken in their Indian empire. Many of these loan-words have since become part of the English language. The following terms are a few examples.

Brahmin	a person of the upper class
bungalow	a small cottage typical of Bengal
calico, chintz, khaki, madras	types of cloth originating in India
coolie	a menial laborer
curry	a highly spiced dish of rice
divan	a couch in the court of a ruler
loot	plunder or booty
mogul	a mighty person
pajamas	loose-fitting outer garments
pariah	a person unwelcome in a given society
punch	a beverage originally containing five ingredients (from *panch*, Hindi word for "five")
pundit	a learned man
shawl	a scarf worn over the shoulders
thug	a ruffian or cutthroat

• CHECK-UP

1. What factors made for inefficiency in the Company's administration of its holdings? What reforms were introduced by Cornwallis? How did Indians fare under the Civil Service system?
2. How was the zamindari system modified by Cornwallis? Why? What was the ryotwari system? What advantages and disadvantages stemmed from British changes in traditional methods of land ownership and tax assessment?
3. How was traditional Indian education modified? What were the results? What Indian social customs, though disapproved by the British, were allowed to continue? Which were eliminated?

3. The Sepoy Rebellion Brought India under the Direct Rule of Britain

The growth of British power in India aroused opposition in many quarters. Indian princes, noting the displacement of ruling families in both Hindu and Muslim states, feared that sooner or later they themselves would fall victim to British ambitions. Landlords, badly hurt by programs of agrarian reform, faced economic ruin. Many proud Indians were embittered by the superior attitude of the British, their discriminatory practices, and their interference with age-old religious and social practices. In 1857 these grievances came to a head in the Sepoy Rebellion, a revolt that shook the very foundations of British rule in India.

The security of the East India Company depended heavily on Indian forces. During the early 1800's the armies of the East India Company underwent a slow but significant change. In the 1700's England's military strength in India was based mainly upon European manpower. The Company's comparatively small military units were made up of European mercenaries. In times of crisis, as during the wars with the French (page 118), Company troops were reinforced with soldiers from the British army. But as military requirements increased the Company began to recruit Indian soldiers. Such troops were known as sepoys (*see'*poiz). By 1850 British forces in India numbered almost a quarter of a million men, only one sixth of whom were Europeans.

The sepoys played a major part in many important military campaigns. Led by British officers and trained in the techniques of European warfare, they fought well when their morale was high. But

THE SEPOY REBELLION. The mutiny by Indian troops brought destruction to all parts of the subcontinent. One of the hardest hit towns was Lucknow (above). The British did considerable damage, but the mutineers also destroyed property to keep it out of British hands. After the Rebellion, sepoys who had taken part in the uprising were tried by British military courts and executed (below). Loyal sepoys, such as the soldier at the right, remained in the army.

132

sometimes British officers treated these soldiers unfairly. Not only did they withhold pay or food for petty reasons, but in general they showed less consideration for Indian soldiers than for Europeans. Such treatment lowered morale and made the sepoys unreliable.

"Greased cartridges" set off the Sepoy Rebellion. In 1857 carelessness led to a revolt among the sepoys. Hindu and Muslim troops stationed near Delhi were issued rifle cartridges greased with animal fat. To use these cartridges the soldiers had to bite off the tips. The Hindu troops were incensed, believing that the ammunition had been coated with cow's fat; the Muslims were equally aroused, believing that pig's fat had been used for the purpose. To troops already discontented, a seemingly deliberate disregard for their religious beliefs was sufficient reason for mutiny.

When British officers realized their mistake, they withdrew the greased cartridges. But this action came too late. Many officers were killed by the sepoys. Then the mutinous troops marched to Delhi, the old Mughal capital. There they persuaded the local garrison to join them. After gaining control of the city, they proclaimed the aged and powerless Mughal emperor leader of a movement to overthrow the British raj. Some supporters of the emperor even dreamed of restoring the Mughal Empire to its former glory.

News of the uprising triggered other rebellions. The rulers of some Hindu states in northern and central India joined in the struggle, and many British civilians and soldiers were slain. In some cities besieged English communities repulsed repeated attacks while awaiting relief. Horrible atrocities were committed by the rebels, and these provoked terrible reprisals on the part of the Europeans. The memory of the brutality and viciousness exhibited in these initial stages of the revolt endured long after the Sepoy Rebellion had been suppressed.

The British quickly gained the offensive. British authorities should not have been caught off guard. Dozens of lesser revolts had occurred during the preceding thirty years. Despite early setbacks, however, the British soon were able to contain the revolt. Regular army regiments in India were reinforced with troops from other parts of the British Empire. Furthermore, some units of sepoys (particularly the Sikhs) remained loyal to the English. Both sides suffered heavy losses, but in just fourteen months the Sepoy Rebellion was crushed.

The government of India was overhauled after the Rebellion. The great mutiny of 1857–8 convinced Parliament that the East India Company no longer served a useful purpose. Having steadily reduced the authority of the Company since 1773, the English government now took the final step. In 1858 Parliament abolished the Company and formally annexed its territories in India.

Under the act of 1858 control of Britain's Indian territories was entrusted to a new Secretary of State for India, a member of the British cabinet. This Secretary, though nominally responsible to the Prime Minister and Parliament, in practice had unlimited authority over the government of India. The Governor-General now was given the title of Viceroy, signifying that he was the personal representative of the British monarch. Actually, he was nothing more than the on-the-spot agent of the Secretary of State for India. The days of the strong Governor-General were over.

A satisfactory settlement was reached with the Indian princes. At the end of the Sepoy Rebellion 562 Indian states were still ruled by native princes. They ranged in size from Kashmir and Hyderabad, which were as large as France or Germany, to petty holdings the size of an American town. The states ruled by these princes occupied about two fifths of the subcontinent; the rest of India was under direct British rule.

The East India Company, again and again, had enlarged its holdings at the expense of princely states. But the British government had no intention of following such a policy. Queen Victoria therefore proclaimed that "We desire no extension of our present territorial possessions." However, the British reserved the right to intervene in the administration of any state with a ruler found guilty of mismanagement. Furthermore, the British Crown would control foreign, military, and financial affairs in all the princely states.

Despite these restrictions, the princes fared well. In the final settlement they retained their local authority and received a generous share of the income from their realms. The princes were assured that, as long as they ruled in a competent fashion, they would never have to surrender their domains to the British government. And Britain would see to it that no small state would be taken over by a larger neighbor.

Improved communications and transportation strengthened the British hold on India. The Sepoy Rebellion came at a time when the British government was desperately trying to improve communications between London and India. A letter from London to Bombay or Calcutta had to be carried by steamship to Alexandria, then overland to the Red Sea, and then again by steamship to its destination. Such a journey took many weeks. A canny Governor-General might take advantage of the poor communications to carry out steps not approved by the British government. Many of the incidents that infuriated Indians might have been avoided had there been speedier communications between Europe and India.

The opening of the Suez Canal in 1869 was an important step in improving transportation and communication between India and the home office. It enabled English steamships to make the journey to India without stopping to unload and reload at Suez. The Canal also greatly increased trade between England and the subcontinent. It is little wonder that in 1875 Prime Minister Disraeli seized an opportunity to purchase for England a controlling interest in this waterway.

A tremendous improvement in communications resulted from the completion of a telegraph line between London and India in 1870. British officials in India no longer had a good excuse to make decisions on vital matters without consulting the British capital. Nor did they have to wait for weeks for instructions from home. Direct telegraphic communications enabled the British government to exercise much closer control over Indian affairs.

Communication facilities were improved within India. During the early days of Company rule in India, communications within the subcontinent were very poor. When the British government tightened its hold on India, it had to cope with the problem of improving internal communications.

Even before the Sepoy Rebellion, the British government had made some improvements in India's internal communications. In 1851 it authorized the construction of an Indian telegraph system. In 1854 it introduced an efficient postal service. Work was begun on a railway system, and by 1871 railroads linked all the provinces together and connected outlying regions with the principal ports. Road building was also given a high priority. Dirt roads of Mughal times were paved and new highways were built to connect the major cities.

By 1914 the subcontinent could boast of the best system of roads in Asia. The telegraph and postal systems were in full operation. Railroad trackage had risen to 35,000 miles; by the Second World War this total had reached 43,000. Today, even though thousands of miles of the old British Railway System are in Pakistan, India ranks fourth among the world's nations in total railway mileage.

Irrigation works were expanded under British rule. In an agricultural country like India, irrigation is of vital importance. From the days of the Harappan civilization the construction of canals, dikes, and irrigation ditches had been an important function of the government. Remarkable irrigation systems had been built. The British followed the example of earlier rulers in actively promoting irrigation projects.

The East India Company had undertaken the task of repairing and restoring neglected irrigation systems. But in 1866 the British government began the construction of a number of large canals and several thousand miles of feeder canals. The northwest especially benefited from this British program. In India's Punjab area (much of which is now in Pakistan), more than two million acres of land were reclaimed by irrigation. By the turn of the century the Indian northwest was supporting a population of 800,000 people.

The extension of irrigation has been a major responsibility of the Indian government, both during British rule and after independence. Today about 50 million acres in India and Pakistan, about one fifth of the tillable land, are under irrigation. Together the two countries have nearly 100,000 miles of irrigation canals.

Queen Victoria was proclaimed Empress of India. In 1876 Parliament passed legislation which made Queen Victoria Empress of India. This act marked an important change in the relationship of Britain to the subcontinent. From 1858 until 1876 the British government had treated the Indian states as independent, sovereign governments. By making Queen Victoria Empress of India, Parliament

British India developed the most extensive railroad system in Asia. This picture shows track being laid in East Bengal.

brought the Indian states into the British Empire. The inhabitants of the entire subcontinent became subjects of the British Crown, and the reigning monarch in England became the overlord of the Indian princes. The act of 1876 officially made the British government the paramount power in India, the status it unofficially had enjoyed since the Sepoy Rebellion of 1857–8.

- CHECK-UP

    1. Why did many Indians fear the growth of British power in India? Who were the sepoys? What was the direct cause of their mutiny?
    2. What changes were made in the government of India after the Sepoy Rebellion? What settlement was reached with the princes? What were its advantages to them?
    3. How did improvements in communication and transportation strengthen Britain's hold on India? How were communication and transportation improved in India?
    4. How was the status of India changed when Queen Victoria became Empress of India?

4. India's Value to Great Britain Steadily Mounted

The importance of India in the worldwide British Empire increased steadily in the years after the Sepoy Rebellion. Having won effective control over the entire subcontinent, the British were in a far better position to exploit its resources. It is no wonder that England's determination to hold this imperial prize grew stronger.

The Indian Empire provided employment for thousands of Englishmen. For almost a century after the Sepoy Rebellion many Englishmen enjoyed profitable careers in India. Increasingly, qualified Indians were employed in the clerical and administrative ranks of the Indian Civil Service, but the higher offices were reserved for the British (see pages 127–8). Developmental programs and technical services also were staffed with specialists from the homeland. Few Indians had the engineering, medical, and scientific skills required of the staffs of such programs.

Also, after the Sepoy Rebellion, more British soldiers came to India. Before the mutiny most of the sepoys were high-caste Hindus and Bengali Muslims. The disloyalty of soldiers recruited from these groups caused British officials to rely more upon Sikhs of the Punjab, the tough Gurkhas from Nepal, and Pathan tribesmen from the northwest frontier. Simultaneously they sharply increased the proportion of British regulars in the forces maintained in India. Thousands of British soldiers saw service in India between 1858 and 1947.

Trade was a key link in the Anglo-Indian relationship. British trade with India increased steadily in the second half of the nineteenth century. As Great Britain surged ahead as the "workshop of the world," the products of its factories found a ready market in India. In time the prosperity of English textile mills was heavily dependent upon India, for the subcontinent was a prime market for inexpensive cotton cloth. Moreover, the transport of these goods in British ships meant more profits for Britain's merchant marine.

Foreign countries as well as lands that were part of the British Empire also increased their trade with India. But Great Britain maintained its position as the foremost exporter and importer of goods in the India trade. Between 1870 and 1910 the subcontinent accounted for nearly a fifth of Britain's total overseas commerce.

India provided Britain with other sources of profit. Trade was not the only benefit Britain derived from India. Costly developmental programs required large amounts of capital. To finance such projects bonds were sold in both Great Britain and India. The purchasers of these bonds received handsome interest payments on their investments. The British also invested money in Indian factories, mines, railroads, and plantations. Moreover, British capitalists often loaned money to both the imperial and the princely governments in the subcontinent. Even the Indian Civil Service contributed to the British economy. Each year the number of retiring Civil Service employees increased, and most of these returned to England. The money they received in pensions helped to strengthen the British economy.

The Indian peasant benefited from Britain's imperial rule. The lot of the Indian farmer, for centuries a difficult one, improved at least a little under British rule. This was due largely to technological advances and to increased trade. Sir Reginald Copeland, a specialist on British India, made this statement:

> Now suddenly, owing to the railways and the complementary development of ports, sea-transport, commercial law and practice, and all the machinery of modern business, the products of the [Indian] peasant's labour in his fields or at his craft became saleable and profitable far outside his own locality, not only anywhere in

India but in the world at large. Indian wheat, in particular, was soon selling in the world market, and prices soared from their poor local level to those fixed at Liverpool or Chicago. Other agricultural products shared in the growth of the export trade — rice, oilseeds, cotton, jute, tea. Their higher value meant a little rise in the peasant's standard of living. . . .[3]

Indian industrialists realized the greatest benefits from imperial advances. The peasant might have seen a slight improvement in his way of life, but it was the Indian industrialist who gained most from the relationship between India and Britain. The growth of foreign trade, the founding of new and modern industries, and the expansion of the domestic market provided greater opportunities for Indian businessmen. Notable advances were made in the organization of a modern, native textile industry. The cheap products of British mills had gradually undercut India's most important "cottage" industry — home spinning, for centuries a supplementary source of income for thousands of peasants. Now Indian industrialists opened modern textile plants that could compete with British factories. By the early twentieth century India was a major producer of cotton cloth.

The "heavy" industries — iron and steel — also provided investment opportunities for Indian businessmen. The building of railroads made necessary the tapping of India's rich iron resources. The Tata family of Bombay was a pioneer in the development of India's iron and steel industry. Its mills at Jamshedpur became the greatest in India. They have made India one of Asia's leading producers of iron and steel.

Economic ties with Great Britain stirred up unrest. Many Indian fortunes were built by men who capitalized on the opportunities presented by an expanding economy. Though Indian businessmen grumbled about rising taxes and the lack of tariff protection, they had no serious quarrel with the British raj. Approving its policies and generally optimistic about the future, they were ready to cooperate with the imperial regime.

Many Indians, however, were reluctant to admit that British rule had brought benefits to the Indian people. They were quick to point out that whatever improvements had resulted from the creation of the British Indian Empire were far outweighed by disadvantages.

[3] Sir Reginald Copeland, *Britain and India* (London, Longmans and Green, 1946), pp. 43–44.

They singled out the breakdown of time-honored traditions, the discriminatory policies of the alien rulers, and the continuing "draining away" of India's wealth. Such views, boding trouble for the future, came to a head in the Indian nationalist movement. This movement is the subject of Chapter Six.

- CHECK-UP

  1. What were the chief advantages to Britain of the imperial relationship with India?
  2. In what ways did Indian peasants benefit from Britain's imperial rule? How did Indian industrialists benefit?
  3. What major criticisms were directed at British rule in India?

Summing Up

During the period of Mughal rule European trading companies were becoming increasingly involved in Indian affairs. This was especially true of the French and English East India companies. Their involvement led to wars against each other in India, wars which were both an outgrowth of their participation in Indian affairs and an extension of their countries' conflicts in Europe and America. From these clashes the English East India Company emerged victorious. It then proceeded to lay the foundations for the last and greatest of the empires in India.

In the late 1700's the English Parliament decided that the East India Company was rapidly outliving its usefulness. Parliament therefore began to restrict the Company's powers while increasing those of the English government. As the government's role in the subcontinent increased, social, land, and tax systems underwent changes. Some of the reforms aroused resentment. They contributed much towards a growing dissatisfaction with the British presence in India.

Indian dissatisfaction with Company rule came to a head in the Sepoy Rebellion. The rebels were crushed, but their action brought about a drastic reorganization of the administration of India. The English East India Company was abolished, settlements were made to conciliate the princes, and the British Crown assumed full responsibility for the British presence in India. In 1876 Parliament formally annexed India to the British Empire.

By the time India was annexed to the British Empire it was obvious that the subcontinent was of utmost value to Britain. It supplied employment for thousands of British citizens, provided a market for goods manufactured in British factories, and provided numerous British businessmen with opportunities for profitable investment. Indians, too, benefited from direct British rule, especially those who could afford to develop Indian industry. However, many Indians felt that the disadvantages of being under British rule far outweighed any advantages.

. . . .

CHAPTER REVIEW

Can You Identify?

ryotwari system	Civil Service	Plassey
zamindari system	Suez Canal	Hastings
Permanent Settlement	Calcutta	diwan
"greased cartridges"	Bengal	suttee
Governor-General	Clive	thuggee
Sepoy Rebellion	Dupleix	

What Do You Think?

1. Why did France instead of Holland become England's chief rival?

2. In the 1800's many Indians held that Britain was draining away the wealth of their country. What can be said in defense of the British?

3. Was the zamindari system as reformed by Cornwallis an improvement over the original? Give reasons for your answer.

4. Why was the English Parliament content to let the English East India Company administer India as long as it did?

5. In many histories references are made to the "great wealth of India." Yet most Indians were and are very poor peasants. Why are the two statements not as conflicting as they sound?

Extending and Applying Your Knowledge

1. A sympathetic portrayal of rural life in the Deccan is found in *Indian Village*. S. C. Dube, the author, was an anthropologist who understood both past conditions in India and post-World War II trends.

2. A standard introductory text on 18th and 19th century India is Paul Roberts' *History of British India under the Company and the Crown*, third edition (Oxford Press). Since the early pages deal with the coming of the Europeans in the 17th century, the text parallels the material treated in this chapter.

3. For an interesting account of the reasons and emotions behind the Sepoy Rebellion, read "Flicker of Hate" in *India: Selected Readings*.

6

THE ROAD TO INDEPENDENCE

By welding the many Indian states into an empire, Great Britain brought considerable unity to a land that hardly knew the meaning of the word. One of the outcomes of this unification, however, was the arousal of a nationalistic fervor among the people of India. Britain found itself the object of increasingly stiff demands from Indians for a larger Indian voice in government. By the beginning of the twentieth century Indian political and intellectual leaders were agitating for a national government in which Indians played a responsible role — a type of government which Britain hesitated to grant.

The demand for a responsible Indian voice in government came largely from Indians educated in the Western tradition. They knew about Western ideals of self-government and they could not understand why Britain did not live up to these ideals. The outstanding critic of the British position was Mohandas K. Gandhi. Combining Western ideals, traditions from the Hindu heritage, and the tactics of both ancient and modern politics, Gandhi built Indian nationalism into an explosive force. Ranking next to Gandhi in influence was Jawaharlal Nehru, an early convert to the nationalist cause. Together, Gandhi and Nehru succeeded in changing the goal of Indian nationalism from more Indian participation in government to complete independence for India.

Great Britain was not unwilling to grant broader rights to Indians. However, Parliament moved ever so slowly and hesitantly towards changing the governmental structure of India. Concessions made to appease Indian nationalists generally were too little and too late.

Moreover, the British discovered time and again that every British response to nationalist agitation left some Indians dissatisfied. Eventually the British resigned themselves to a complete withdrawal from the subcontinent.

1. The Indian Nationalist Movement Emerged Before the First World War

In the years following the Sepoy Rebellion a new class of leaders arose among the Indian people. They came from the enlarged middle class: the owners and managers of the new industries, the members of the professions, the intellectuals pursuing careers in education, literature, government, journalism, and religion. These men had little in common with the older generation of Indian leaders, the rulers of Indian states. They were better educated, more Western in their outlook, and more concerned about India as a whole. As this educated middle class became more active in political affairs, the British government had to make more and more concessions in the direction of self-government for India.

India's new leaders were familiar with Western civilization. In the late 1800's a growing number of Indians attended Western-style schools in India. Here they were introduced to ideas and bodies of information largely unknown to their ancestors. Many of these young men went to England for further study. After securing university and professional training, they returned home, where they embarked upon successful careers.

Indians who had been trained in Western-style schools straddled two widely differing worlds: the traditional Indian and the Western. But Western culture did not make the same impression upon all Indians. Some were enthusiastic about it and adopted it wholeheartedly. They admired everything British and condemned anything in Indian life which conflicted with British standards. Their cherished goal was to use the West as a model for changing Indian society. Other Indians, however, were appalled by Western ways. To these, the West seemed to place undue emphasis upon the acquisition of wealth and upon ruthless competition among men. What this second group of Western-educated Indians thought they saw in the culture of the Western World caused them to idealize their Indian heritage and to value it all the more.

Regardless of their attitude toward the West, educated Indians resented the behavior of British officials in India. The European *sahibs* made a mockery of British ideals of liberty and respect for the individual. Legislation and the administration of justice invariably favored the European minority in the subcontinent. Indians were discriminated against and were denied the liberties which the English constitution afforded English citizens. As we have seen, as late as the 1800's high positions in the Indian Civil Service were virtually closed to Indians. Such factors led to the formation of several Indian nationalist organizations.

The Indian National Congress emerged in the 1880's. A retired official of the Indian Civil Service was instrumental in forming India's most important nationalist organization. For it was at the urging of Allan O. Hume, an Englishman, that the Indian National Congress was organized in 1885. The hope of the founders, according to the first chairman, was "to be governed according to the ideas of government prevalent in Europe, and "was in no way incompatible with their thorough loyalty to the British government." Because of the professed loyalty of the organization, the British regime did nothing to discourage its operations.

At this early period in its history the Indian National Congress set modest goals for itself. Leaders did not call for complete self-government (home rule) nor did they clamor for independence. Most members believed that mutually helpful relationships between Britain and India would be fostered in time. Moreover, their demands hardly were revolutionary — they simply asked for more good jobs and more responsibility in government. They were convinced that such goals could be attained within the framework of the existing government.

A vocal minority in the Congress, however, questioned the wisdom of relying upon British promises. These men refused to believe that the imperial homeland intended to relax its grip upon India's government. They were convinced that Britain was interested in the subcontinent only for the sake of profits. To these members, even British reform measures were prompted by selfish motives.

The foremost critic in the Congress was Bal Gangadhar Tilak (1856–1920). A talented writer, this fiery nationalist has been dubbed "the Father of Indian Unrest." Equally dissatisfied with British policies and the moderate views of fellow nationalists, Tilak openly advocated rapid change — by revolution, if necessary. Tilak's

TIMETABLE	The Indian Independence Movement
1885	Indian National Congress organized
1906	Muslim League formed
1909	Morley-Minto Reforms
1914–8	World War I
1917	Montagu's promise of self-rule for India
1918–9	Rowlatt Acts
1919	Amritsar Massacre
	Montagu-Chelmsford Reforms
1927	Simon Commission formed
1930	Gandhi's March to the Sea
1930–2	Round Table Conferences
1935	Government of India Act
1937	First provincial elections held in India
1939–45	World War II
1940	"Two India" proposal by Muslim League
1942	"Quit India" movement against the British
1947	British withdrawal from India

anti-British activities led to his imprisonment. After being released, however, Tilak became even more aggressive in his fight for home rule. In 1906 he and his followers, known as extremists, bolted the Indian National Congress to follow their own political road. Later they returned and helped to swing the Congress into a more aggressive position regarding self-government.

Most Muslims were suspicious of the Indian National Congress. A more serious threat to national unity than Tilak was the large Muslim population of India. Few Muslims could feel comfortable in the Congress. That body appealed largely to teachers, writers, businessmen, and especially lawyers. Muslims were so devoted to preserving the traditional ways of Islam that few of them took advantage of the educational opportunities offered by Western-style schools. Consequently, not many Muslims acquired the education needed to fill governmental posts and to enter modern professions.

The early Muslim "firebrand" in the Hindu-Muslim rivalry was Sayyid Ahmad Khan (1817–1898). Though descended from Mughal officials, the Sayyid had not turned his back upon Western culture. While urging his co-religionists to take pride in their Islamic heritage, he also advocated the study of Western science. To advance his ideas he helped to found Aligarh University, an institution which was to become the foremost seat of Muslim learning in India. But the Sayyid distrusted Hindu institutions. His leadership of the Muslim community was an important influence in keeping small the Muslim membership in the Congress, an organization he associated with the Hindu faith.

Muslim suspicion of the Congress was heightened by the Congress stand that voting rights should be extended to Indians. It seemed obvious to Muslims that Muslim candidates would win few elections because most voters would be Hindus. Muslims became advocates of "communal representation," a plan that would reserve a specified number of political offices for each religious and ethnic community. To protect its interests and to further this idea, the Islamic minority formed the Muslim League in 1906. In time, Mohammad Ali Jinnah, a Western-educated lawyer, emerged as the undisputed leader of the League. He remained so until his death in 1948.

Nationalist fervor was aroused by the partition of Bengal. Shortly before the organization of the Muslim League the British took a step which greatly upset the people of India. This was the partition of Bengal in 1905. Because of its great area and large population, Bengal had been a difficult province to administer. The partition created an East Bengal of 31 million people and a West Bengal of 47 million. Undoubtedly this action facilitated administration, but it also provoked a fierce and unexpected reaction on the part of Hindus.

The furor arose because the British had completely ignored social divisions in making the partition. Hindus were upset because they became a minority in East Bengal, which was predominantly Muslim. Bengalese in West Bengal were unhappy because, with the addition of Bihar and Orissa to the new province of West Bengal, they became a minority in their own land. Throughout India an outcry arose for reunification of Bengal. By ignoring these protests, the British caused the nationalist movement to gather momentum.

The British made concessions to quiet the nationalists. In 1909 Parliament enacted the Morley-Minto Reforms, a program designed to quiet the rising discontent of educated Indians. The Reforms

These pictures of Jinnah (left) and Gandhi show that both men were influenced by the Western way of life. In time Gandhi renounced Western ways for the simple life and dress of the Indian peasant.

opened numerous high positions to qualified Indians, but they stopped short of giving them any degree of control of the government. Most Congressmen realized that the Reforms barely touched on the many grievances they had forwarded to Parliament. But at least, said the moderates, the program was a step in the right direction.

In 1911 the British took further steps to appease the Indians. During the visit of King George V to India several important announcements were made. Among these was the decision to reunite Bengal. The British also revealed their plan to move the capital of India from Calcutta to Delhi, the old capital of the Mughal Empire and a city rich in Indian tradition. Both moves were popular with the nationalists.

Gandhi became a champion of equal rights for Indians. During the early years of the nationalist movement, the man most commonly associated with Indian independence, Mohandas K. Gandhi, was fighting for the rights of Indian nationals in South Africa. Born in western India, Gandhi was a Vaishya (page 44) and a son of the prime minister of a small state. At the age of nineteen, he went to London to study law. After completing his studies Gandhi returned to India. Soon he began the practice of law in Bombay.

In 1893 the young lawyer went to South Africa, a part of the British Empire to which many Indians had migrated. Local authorities had adopted various measures not only to restrict the immigration of Asians but also to limit the citizenship rights of those already in the country. Gandhi devoted his time and talent to defending Indians in court, often receiving little or no compensation for his efforts. Soon he became a leader in the movement to insure fair treatment for Indians. It was in South Africa that Gandhi formulated his theory of using civil disobedience and passive resistance as weapons to fight discrimination and injustice. For his activities he was imprisoned three times.

When Gandhi returned to India in 1914, his reputation as a foe of discrimination was well established. However, at first Gandhi kept in the background of the Indian nationalist movement. England was fighting for existence in the First World War, and Gandhi wisely decided to refrain from divisive nationalist activity for the duration of the conflict.

- CHECK-UP

    1. Why did many Indians attend Western-style schools? What were the results?
    2. What problems stemmed from distrust of the English? Why were Hindus and Muslims jealous of each other?
    3. What were the Morley-Minto Reforms? Why were they enacted?
    4. How did Gandhi first become a champion of equal rights for Indians?

2. The First World War Marked a Significant Change in Indian Nationalism

India, as part of the British Empire, was drawn into the First World War. In a sense, she responded loyally. Thousands of Indian volunteers took part in crucial campaigns in Europe and the Middle East. The factories of India became a vital source of supplies for the Allied cause. Wealthy Indians, especially the rulers of princely states, responded generously to the appeal for war bonds. Yet, India was restless, and as the war progressed this became increasingly obvious. By the time it ended Indians no longer were seeking *more* responsibility in government. Under the leadership of Mahatma Gandhi,[1] they were demanding *complete* responsibility.

---

[1] Mahatma, meaning "great soul," was the title given Gandhi by the poet Rabindranath Tagore in 1915.

Nationalists became increasingly cool towards the British raj.
Despite their apparent support of the British war effort, Indians had
not rejected nationalism. They expected and even demanded concessions for services rendered. However, to Indian requests for
change, the British always gave the same response — "After the war."
Under the circumstances Indian nationalists became increasingly impatient with British rule.

The war also diminished India's respect for its imperial ruler.
British power seemed less awesome as Indians came to realize that
England was but one of a number of powerful nations. Indians also
lost respect for Western culture in general. How could the culture
of the West be superior to theirs, Indians asked, if it led to such a
bloody war? After seeing their requests rejected and having lost their
respect for their ruler, Indians thought even more about their nationalistic goals.

The British lost the support of India's Muslim minority. For years
the fear of losing their identity in the huge population of India had
kept Muslims loyal to the British raj. But during the First World
War Muslims became increasingly upset by policies of their British
masters. The British government was playing a leading role in the
destruction of Turkey, long the leading Muslim state. An attack on
Turkey was also an attack on the Caliph, the spiritual leader of the
Muslim world. Many Muslims in India and elsewhere began to consider the war a British conspiracy against their religion.

The increasing militancy of the nationalist cause, together with
growing disenchantment with British rule on the part of Muslims,
combined to bring the Muslims into the Hindu-dominated nationalist movement. The firebrand Tilak, who had been imprisoned for his
active resistance to British rule, emerged from prison to find a favorable climate for his brand of nationalism. Soon he had gained control
of the Congress Party. In 1916, under Tilak's leadership, the Congress took a step calculated to attract Muslims to the nationalist
cause. It declared itself in favor of "communal representation" (page
146), long a goal of Muslim leaders. The strategy worked. Soon
Hindus and Muslims were presenting a united front in demanding
complete self-rule.

India's faith in Britain was rudely shaken. A promise made by
Britain near the end of the war seemed to indicate that Britain was
ready to meet the demands of the nationalists. On August 20, 1917,
Edwin Montagu, the Secretary of State for India, made an important

announcement. He stated that England would take steps towards the "increasing association of Indians in every branch of Indian administration, and the gradual development of self-governing institutions, with a view to the progressive realization of responsible government in British India as an integral part of the Empire." Clearly, this was a promise of self-rule for India.

Unfortunately, the first postwar acts of the British government brought further repression. During the war militant nationalists had resorted to acts of violence to register their protest against the policies of the British raj. With such acts in mind, the British government passed the two Rowlatt Acts in 1918 and 1919. These measures empowered British authorities to arrest and try in secret Indians accused of political crimes. Thus the accused were denied legal counsel and trial by jury. To Indians educated in English-controlled schools, the Rowlatt Acts were a clear violation of rights guaranteed under the English judicial system.

Anglo-Indian relations grew increasingly tense. The Rowlatt Acts aroused great indignation in the already impatient nationalist camp. At the urging of Mahatma Gandhi Indians began staging *hartals,* one-day strikes in which all activity ceased. Throughout Indian history the hartal had been a favorite non-violent method of registering dissatisfaction. But in this case the hartal led to riots, which in turn provoked repressive measures by British troops. In consequence the antagonism between Indians and the British was heightened.

The most serious incident occurred at Amritsar, a town in the province of Punjab. Though forbidden to do so, hundreds of Indians had gathered in a wall-enclosed park to listen to political speeches. Suddenly a unit of English soldiers appeared. The soldiers fired repeated volleys into the unarmed crowd, killing almost 400 Indians and wounding more than 1200. Later, General Dyer, who had ordered the action, was censured by an investigating committee and ordered back to England. But the House of Lords officially approved his action and even established a fund in his behalf. The Amritsar incident caused many Indians to lose whatever faith they had in English justice.

The Montagu-Chelmsford Reforms gave Indians a voice in government. To the credit of the British, they were attempting to fulfill their wartime promise even while taking repressive action. In 1919 the British announced the Montagu-Chelmsford Reforms, a program designed to provide a larger role for Indians in the adminis-

This enclosure was the site of one of the most tragic events in the history of British India — the Amritsar Massacre. Hundreds of Indians were killed or wounded when the British troops fired into a crowd gathered for a meeting to protest British policies.

tration of their country. The Reforms did not limit English control over Indian affairs. The Viceroy in Delhi continued to have the last word in matters affecting India as a whole. But three Indians were to serve on the Viceroy's advisory council of seven members, and a two-house legislature was to be established. In both houses more members were to be elected by Indians than were to be appointed by the English government. Indians thus were to be placed in positions of influence. Moreover, they were provided a forum where they might express their grievances.

The Reforms also provided for changes at the provincial level. The governor of each province, who was appointed by the Crown, was to be responsible for law and order and matters involving revenue. A unicameral (one-house) legislature was to be established in each province. A majority of the members in each legislature was to be elected by the eligible voters. These legislatures were assigned responsibility for such "nation-building" affairs as education, public health, and local self-government. But just as the Viceroy was to have the last word at the national level, the governor was given final authority at the provincial level.

The Reforms went into effect in 1921. From the point of view of the British, they were a major concession. That Indians were not satisfied with the Reforms is an indication of the great change that had taken place in their attitude since the beginning of the First World War. The Indian nationalist now regarded himself as an equal of the Britisher. He believed that self-rule was a right, not a favor to be granted by others. In the political climate of the new nationalism, even a major concession was almost an insult. Consequently, the institution of the Reforms did little to quiet unrest.

The upsurge of nationalism brought Gandhi to the fore. Before 1918 Gandhi had shared the hope of moderate nationalist leaders that at the end of World War I Britain would extend generous rights of self-government to India. But disillusioned by the Rowlatt Acts and outraged by the Amritsar Massacre, Gandhi had lost patience with Britain. The "beneficent institutions of the British Government," he concluded, "are like the fabled snake with a brilliant jewel on its head, but which has fangs full of poison. . . ."

Gandhi's goal for India became *swaraj*, self-rule free of all foreign control. Even while the Montagu-Chelmsford Reforms were being discussed he rejected them as piecemeal concessions. Without waiting to judge their effectiveness Gandhi began his campaign to achieve swaraj. But he did not advocate terror and force, as had more militant nationalist leaders such as Tilak. Gandhi firmly believed in *ahimsa*, the Indian doctrine of non-injury to living creatures. His program, therefore, called for a non-violent non-cooperation campaign against the British.

In 1920 Gandhi called for a peaceful boycott of governmental agencies and services. Students responded to his call by staying out of classes in government schools. Many voters refused to vote when elections were called to implement the Montagu-Chelmsford Reforms.

Gandhi's ashram was always filled with Indians seeking advice or inspiration. Sometimes they waited for days as Gandhi sat wordlessly at his spinning wheel, thinking about the problems of his native land.

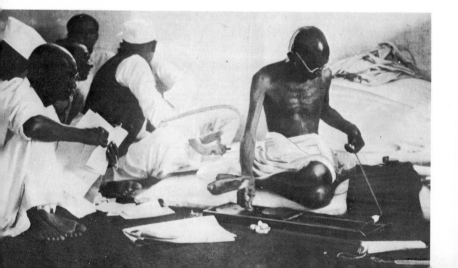

Some Indians even resigned from the Civil Service. The unrest created by the boycott led to riots in some parts of India. Gandhi was blamed for these disorders, arrested, and sentenced to six years in prison.

After serving two years of his sentence, Gandhi was released. Since aggressive leaders were in control of the Congress, Gandhi made no attempt to force his non-violent program upon the nationalist movement. Instead he retired to his *ashram*, or religious retreat. To the ashram came admirers not only from all over India but from all parts of the world. While waiting for the right moment to make his move, Gandhi expounded his ideas to a group of devoted disciples. He also wrote many articles setting forth his ideas. These writings permanently established Gandhi as the leader of the Indian nationalist movement.

In 1924 Gandhi began another boycott, this one against British goods. He urged Indians not to use English-manufactured textiles. Instead Gandhi sought to popularize homemade Indian cloth. Visitors to the ashram understandably were impressed by the sight of Gandhi using a traditional Indian spinning wheel while leading a discussion of lofty philosophical and spiritual questions. Gandhi's example in spinning yarn for his own needs was followed by tens of thousands of his countrymen, including members of the wealthy classes. The spinning wheel became the symbol of the struggle for independence and was emblazoned upon the Congress Party flag.

● CHECK-UP

1. What effect did World War I have on tensions between Indian nationalists and Britain?
2. What were the Montagu-Chelmsford Reforms? Did they accomplish their purpose? Why, or why not?
3. How did Gandhi become a leader of the opposition to British rule? Describe his tactics.

3. Nationalists Shifted Their Goal from Self-Government to Independence

A new class of Indian leaders had arisen after the Sepoy Rebellion; another arose after the First World War. As stubborn as their predecessors, the new leaders sought other goals than those pursued by the older generation. Just as nationalist demands at an earlier period had changed from more responsibility in government to complete responsibility, they now evolved into demands for independence. Bombarded with criticisms and protests, the British continued to wrestle with the problem of formulating an acceptable system of government for India. It seemed to the British that no program could satisfy this highly vocal generation of nationalist leaders.

Nehru became active in the Indian nationalist movement. Beginning in the late 1920's, the burden of leadership in the nationalist movement fell increasingly on the shoulders of Jawaharlal Nehru (juh-*wah'*hur-lahl *nay'*roo). Born in 1889, Nehru was the son of a prosperous lawyer. The Nehru family was Brahmin and traced its ancestry to the province of Kashmir in the far north of India. Jawaharlal was raised in the lap of luxury and, like his father, studied law in England.

For many years Nehru was not notably moved by the nationalist movement. Though he joined the Congress in 1916, he did not give his undivided attention to political affairs until after the massacre at Amritsar. How Nehru discovered what came to be the central purpose in his life has been dramatically recounted in his autobiography:

. . . Gandhiji [Gandhi] took the leadership in his first all-India agitation. He started the *Satyagraha Sabha*, the members of which were pledged to disobey the Rowlatt Act, if it was applied to them, as well as other objectionable laws to be specified from time to time. In other words, they were to court jail openly and deliberately.

When I first read about this proposal in the newspapers, my reaction was one of tremendous relief. Here at last was a way out of the tangle, a method of action which was straight and open and possibly effective. I was afire with enthusiasm and wanted to join the *Satyagraha Sabha* immediately. I hardly thought of the consequences — law-breaking, jail-going, etc., and if I thought of them I did not care.[2]

Nehru and Gandhi were divided over important issues. Despite his admiration for Gandhi's movement, Nehru did not always go along with that leader's views. Gandhi would not accept an elective post in any nationalist organization because he wanted to be free to work outside an organization whenever the occasion so demanded. Nehru provided the political leadership that Gandhi shunned, eventually serving four terms as president of the Indian

[2] Jawaharlal Nehru, *Toward Freedom* (Boston: Beacon Press, 1958), p. 48.

Jawaharlal Nehru joined the Indian National Congress at age 27, but did not become active in the body until he was nearing 40. This picture, taken in 1927, shows him about the time he was becoming a leader in the independence movement.

National Congress. Gandhi and Nehru also took different positions on the question of independence. By the late 1920's both leaders were advocating independence for India, but Gandhi would have been satisfied with dominion status. (A dominion was a self-governing member of the British Commonwealth linked to the United Kingdom and to other dominions by allegiance to the British Crown.) Nehru wished to sever all political ties with Britain. Gandhi eventually accepted complete independence as the goal. He also gave his full support to Nehru — an important factor in the rise of the latter to a position of permanent leadership.

Nehru and Gandhi also differed over social and economic problems. In 1927 Nehru visited Russia to see the experiments in socialism that were taking place in that country. He returned to India with the conviction that his country could solve its many problems only by turning to socialism. Gandhi's ideas, though frequently startling, could hardly be called socialistic. In his autobiography, Nehru described Gandhi's outlook:

India's salvation [according to Gandhi] consists . . . in unlearning what she has learned during the last fifty years. The railways, telegraphs, hospitals, lawyers, doctors, and suchlike have all to go; and the so-called upper classes have to learn consciously, religiously, and deliberately the simple peasant life, knowing it to be a life giving true happiness.

155

Nehru then showed how his own philosophy differed from that of Gandhi:

> Personally, I dislike the praise of poverty and suffering. I do not think they are at all desirable, and they ought to be abolished. . . . Nor do I appreciate in the least the idealization of the 'simple peasant life.' I have almost a horror of it, and instead of submitting to it myself I want to drag . . . the peasantry from it, not to urbanization, but to the spread of urban cultural facilities to rural areas. Far from . . . giving me true happiness, it [the life of a peasant] would be almost as bad as imprisonment for me. What is there in "The Man with the Hoe" to idealize over? Crushed and exploited for innumerable generations, he is only little removed from the animals who keep him company.[3]

The appointment of the Simon Commission angered the Indian National Congress. Nehru's leadership came to the fore when Parliament appointed a commission to evaluate the Montagu-Chelmsford Reforms. The Act of 1919, which called for the Reforms, also provided for a review of the program after 10 years. As a gesture of goodwill toward India, Parliament decided to hold the review in 1927, two years early. A commission of Parliament members headed by Sir John Simon came to India to examine the situation. But to its surprise, instead of finding a grateful India, the Commission met outraged Indians on every hand. Offended because no Indians had been asked to serve, both the National Congress and the Indian Legislative Assembly boycotted the Commission. Wherever they went in India, Sir Simon and his fellow members of Parliament encountered hostile demonstrations and lack of cooperation.

The seriousness of Parliament's mistake soon became evident. At the urging of Nehru and other "young radicals," the Indian National Congress issued a demand for independence. To work out the details the Congress proposed a round-table conference involving British and Indian leaders. Thoroughly alarmed, the British government agreed to call the conference and announced that the "attainment of Dominion status" was its goal for India. Few nationalists, however, believed that the British were sincere.

After the Congress pronouncement Gandhi, who recently had been inactive in the Congress, rejoined the group to lead the opposition to British rule. To dramatize Indian discontent he organized the Civil

[3] *Toward Freedom*, p. 314.

Disobedience Movement, a plan to have Indians openly, but peacefully, defy British regulations. As his first target Gandhi chose the British monopoly on the manufacture of salt. For many years the Indians had resented the fact that they had to pay a tax on all salt produced in the country. In 1930 Gandhi marched 60 miles to the sea. There on the beach he distilled salt from the water and used it.

Gandhi's march started a widespread demonstration against British policies. Protest marches, hartals, and riots occurred all over India. At least 100,000 Indians, including Gandhi himself, were arrested and jailed. The response proved to the British that the Indian problem was getting out of hand.

The Round-Table Conferences did little to quiet discontent. Between 1930 and 1932 Parliament held the promised round-table discussions. The recommendations of the Simon Commission were discussed by members of Parliament and Indian leaders at three conferences held in London. Hoping to include every interest group in India, the British government invited representatives of the Indian National Congress, the various Hindu castes, the Untouchables, the Muslims, and the princely states, as well as leaders from India's industrial community.

The Round-Table Conferences were complete failures. Claiming that the British called in the many groups simply to confuse the issue, the Indian National Congress boycotted the meetings. Gandhi attended the second Conference as the sole Congress delegate, but his presence did nothing to bring about an agreement. He demanded that the Congress should dominate whatever new system of government was devised. The Muslims, however, refused to budge from their demand for communal representation. Only if they had a guaranteed number of seats in government, they reasoned, could they protect their interests. The various princes objected to any plan which might limit their powers or threaten their privileged position in the subcontinent. If the British learned anything from the three Round-Table Conferences, it was that they could never satisfy all parties.

The Hindu-Muslim cleavage widened during the thirties. Muslim distrust of the Hindu majority had never disappeared despite the wartime pledge of the Congress to support communal representation. During and after the Round-Table Conferences the views expressed by Hindu political leaders did nothing to allay this suspicion. Beginning in the early thirties, therefore, Muslim nationalists advanced

THE INDEPENDENCE MOVEMENT. The Round-Table Conferences of 1930–32 were held at a time when civil disobedience was rife in India. In Gandhi's famous March to the Sea (above), thousands of Indians joined in a protest against the salt tax. After the March, nationalists supported Gandhi's program by staging hartals (page 150). In the picture below, Indians are pondering whether to defy a hartal by walking over the outstretched bodies and reporting to work. British officials stand by to maintain order.

proposal after proposal to insure that Muslim rights would not be trampled upon by either the British or the Hindus. Many of their suggestions went further than earlier demands for separate electorates.

Sir Mohammed Iqbal, a widely respected scholar, was one of the most vocal Muslim nationalists of this era. Iqbal was known far and wide as a poet. Some of his most often quoted lines breathed the fire of Muslim nationalism and openly condemned Western imperialism. In 1930, in his presidential address before the Muslim League, this leader called for the establishment of an autonomous Muslim state in the Indian Northwest. Though Iqbal did not go so far as to advocate a separate nation for Muslims, other followers of Islam soon began to champion that idea.

The Government of India Act laid the basis for political change. Despite the discouraging outcome of the Round-Table Conferences and the continuing antagonism between Hindus and Muslims, Parliament passed the Government of India Act in 1935. The new plan of government was based largely upon the report of the Simon Commission. The underlying principle was to establish a partnership between the Indians and the British government which eventually would lead to dominion status for the subcontinent.

Under the Government of India Act the eleven provinces would elect their own governments. These would be subject to British intervention only in time of emergency. At the national level there was to be a two-house legislature. This body, while having extensive powers, was to be kept in check by the British Viceroy. Muslims and other minority groups were to have more than their proportionate share of seats in the legislature. The princely states were given the option of joining or not joining the new federation.

The Congress Party threatened to dominate the new political system. The leaders of the Indian National Congress were not happy with the political system worked out by the British government. It failed to give India complete independence and it did not insure a Congress monopoly on government. Neither were the Muslims satisfied. Despite the fact that they received the communal representation they had asked for, they discovered that in only a few small provinces would the plan insure them effective control. And since the Indian princes were reluctant to join the proposed federation, the federal provisions of the Act could not be put into effect. (The British government did follow through with its plan to appoint Indians to the Council of Ministers.) Despite these problems, elections to fill seats in the provincial legislatures were scheduled for 1937. After much discussion both the Congress and the Muslim League decided to participate.

The Congress scored a great victory in the provincial elections, winning a majority of the seats in six provinces and a plurality in three others. This outcome seemed to justify Muslim fears of Hindu domination. Congress Party[4] ministries were formed in eight of the provinces. By refusing to include non-members of the Congress Party in these ministries and deciding not to participate in coalition ministries in provinces where no party had a majority, the Congress Party further aroused the resentment of the Muslim League. Mohammad Ali Jinnah (page 146), who had hoped to work with the Congress Party in establishing cooperative governments, now began to attack the Congress with all his might. From this time until the British withdrew in 1947, neither the Muslim League nor the Congress Party would make a concession to the other. This stubbornness made it clear that the two organizations could never work together in a united India.

The British spent the years between 1937 and the outbreak of World War II attempting to bring the princely states into the new federation. The princes, however, held back, fearing that in the proposed federation they would lose their special privileges. The Congress ministries in the provinces made a good record during their short period in office, 1937–1939. Indeed, through its High Command or central committee, the Congress Party already was well on its way to control of India.

- CHECK-UP

  1. How did the goals Nehru had for India differ from those of Gandhi?
  2. Why did the appointment of the Simon Commission anger the Congress? How did Gandhi dramatize Indian discontent?
  3. What efforts were made by Britain to do something about the Simon Commission's report? What were the results? Why did differences between Hindus and Muslims widen during the 1930's?
  4. What recommendations were made in the Government of India Act? What came of them?

[4] The Indian National Congress of prewar days became the Indian Congress Party when it began competing in elections.

4. World War II Changed the Political Situation in India

Despite its flaws, the Government of India Act brought about an improvement in Anglo-Indian relations. But this calm was broken in 1939. When Britain declared war on Nazi Germany the Viceroy of India, without consulting the Council of Ministers, proclaimed India to be in a state of war. Members of the Indian Congress Party were incensed because the Council had been ignored. They fully realized also that during the war Britain would be in no mood to act on self-government for India. Perhaps unwisely, the Congress Party resolved to press its demand for Indian independence and refused to cooperate in the war effort unless the demand was granted. Throughout the war, therefore, Britain had to contend not only with Nazi and Japanese aggressors, but also with uncooperative, impatient Indian nationalists.

Why did the Congress Party refuse to cooperate in the British war effort? With the exception of the powerful Indian Congress Party, all Indian political parties, including the Muslim League, expressed their willingness to help the British in their fight for survival. But the Congress Party, in a resolution written mainly by Nehru, made clear its position:

> If this war is to defend the status quo, imperialist possessions, colonies, vested interests and privileges, then India can have nothing to do with it. If, however, the issue is democracy and a world order based on democracy, then India is intensely interested in it. And if Great Britain fights for the maintenance and extension of democracy then she must necessarily end imperialism in her own possessions, establish full democracy in India, and the Indian people must have the right of self-determination — and must guide their own policy. . . .[5]

This declaration by Congress leaders placed them at loggerheads with their imperial rulers. Nehru and his colleagues were determined to withhold all support for Britain's war effort unless their demands for an independent and undivided India were met immediately. The British government thought it unwise to make this change during wartime. They feared that confusion and strife would be the outcome at the very time when harmony and cooperation were especially

[5] Quoted in: Frank Moraes, *Jawaharlal Nehru; A Biography* (New York, Macmillan, 1957), p. 277.

needed. Locked in the struggle with Hitler, Britain stressed the urgency of getting on with the war. But instead of cooperating, the Congress Party instructed its members to resign their posts in the provincial ministries.

The Muslims sought to exploit the breach between the Congress Party and Britain. The Muslim League, headed by Mohammad Ali Jinnah, took comfort from the growing friction between England and the Congress Party. It regarded the withdrawal of Congress Party members from political office as a golden opportunity to further Muslim interests. At its meeting in March, 1940, the Muslim League issued a momentous declaration. It called for the division of India into two parts, one part to be an independent nation for the Muslims. The idea of a nation called Pakistan, informally discussed for years, thus became a stated goal.[6] Since the Muslim League remained loyal to Britain, its leaders were hopeful that Britain would listen to their request. And since the Congress Party was out of favor with the British government, League leaders thought that Britain might favor the Muslim League in any postwar settlement of the Indian problem.

Britain made an effort to win the support of the Congress. In the summer of 1940 Hitler's armies overran much of Western Europe. It seemed that nothing short of a miracle could save Britain from defeat. In the summer and fall, therefore, the English government tried to gain the support of the Congress Party. Again, as in World War I, all promises were to be fulfilled "after the war." These long-range promises failed to satisfy Nehru and other Congress Party leaders. The British attempt to reach an agreement with the Party thus ended in failure.

Gandhi revealed his displeasure with British unwillingness to act by launching another campaign of non-violent non-cooperation. Many Indian nationalists were imprisoned for taking part in the campaign. Nehru and Gandhi were among the nationalist leaders who were jailed, but they refused to budge from their position.

Japan's attack once again forced Britain to the wall. The Royal Navy and Air Force saved Britain from an invasion by Nazi armies. Then, when England was reeling from night raids by Nazi airplanes,

[6] The origin of the word "Pakistan" is in dispute. A widely accepted view is that the name was "invented" by a group of Muslim students at Oxford University in 1933. Supposedly the word was derived as follows: P — Punjab: A — Afghans (Pathans); K — Kashmir; S — Sind; "-stan" — Persian for country. The original idea called for a self-governing state within India which would consist of the Punjab, Kashmir, and Sind.

Hitler decided to attack the Soviet Union before he had overcome the stubborn British resistance. With the Nazi forces divided between eastern and western fronts the pressure upon the British Isles was greatly relaxed. But in December, 1941, England had to face another powerful enemy. While Japan was striking American bases in Hawaii and the Philippines, it was opening another front against British holdings in Southeast Asia.

The winter of 1941–2 was a long nightmare for the British in Asia. Japanese troops quickly overran Malaya, then continued their advance to overwhelm the British naval base at Singapore. Next they pushed into Burma and again defeated British defenders. Difficult terrain, long supply lines, and spirited opposition, however, prevented the Japanese from invading India. Faced with a hostile Japan at the very door of India, Great Britain needed India's full cooperation. To secure it, Britain initiated an effort to appease all parties in the subcontinent.

The Cripps Mission was Britain's final effort to break the wartime impasse. In March, 1942, Sir Stafford Cripps was sent to India to seek a settlement with India's political leaders. He made what the British government considered to be a generous offer. The Cripps Mission proposed dominion status for India, to be given at the end of the war. Moreover, each province and state could choose between joining a union of Indian states or becoming a separate dominion. The British also offered to renegotiate treaties with the Indian princes and to take all necessary steps to protect the interests of minority groups such as the Muslims. In addition to these long-range promises, the British were willing to grant immediately one important concession — the filling of all posts on the Viceroy's Council of Ministers with Indians. By so doing they would give Indians a larger role in the administration of their land. With respect to the war itself, the British insisted upon retaining complete control.

The Cripps Mission ended in failure. At first it seemed that Congress Party leaders would accept the plan, but then Gandhi brought his influence to bear. He objected to the Cripps program because it did not give India immediate control over its own affairs. Gandhi wanted the Council of Ministers to be a policy-making body, not an advisory board which could be ignored by the Viceroy. Remembering disappointments during the First World War, most nationalist leaders went along with Gandhi. No one in the nationalist movement wanted to risk a second round of failure.

A "Quit-India" campaign was launched by Gandhi. After the Congress Party had rejected the terms proposed by the Cripps Mission, Gandhi started a drive to win immediate independence. He told British officials that he would direct another campaign of non-cooperation if Britain did not immediately withdraw from India. Nehru and most other Congress leaders backed Gandhi's plan. The British were understandably angered and, before the "Quit-India" movement could gain momentum, they arrested Gandhi, Nehru, and 60,000 of their followers. Gandhi and most other nationalists were released before the conclusion of peace, but Nehru was among hundreds of Indians who spent the rest of the war in jail.

During his long period of "enforced leisure," Nehru wrote many letters to his daughter Indira, later to become independent India's third Prime Minister. In them he evaluated the long history and the rich culture of the Indian people. Eventually these letters were published in book form as *The Discovery of India*. Though unacceptable to historians as a record of the past, the book is an interesting presentation of Nehru's own view of Indian history. It is also an excellent mirror reflecting the emotions and influences which compelled Indians to revolt against their British masters.

India furthered the British war effort. Despite lack of support from the Indian Congress Party, Britain found India valuable in its struggle for victory. Early in the war, Indian troops were used to reinforce British and imperial units in North Africa, Singapore, and Hong Kong. Indian industrialists adapted their factories to meet the demands of military production, and soon military supplies from India were flowing to the various war fronts. Indian shipbuilders built naval vessels, and their shipyards were used for repairing British ships damaged in battle. A general lack of enthusiasm for war in India did not prevent Britain from utilizing the resources of its great colony.

India also provided an important base for military operations. Without it, the British war effort in Asia would have been severely handicapped. The subcontinent, also, was important to the military activities of the United States. American troops were trained in India for the recapture of Burma, while American officers trained Chinese troops on Indian soil. From northeast India, moreover, supplies were transported into blockaded China. This aid enabled Chiang Kai-shek, the Chinese leader, to hold out against Japan until that country finally surrendered.

The British moved fast to grant independence to India. As the Second World War drew to a close, it became clear that Britain could not hope to retain its prewar empire. British holdings everywhere were showing signs of nationalist restiveness. Moreover, the British were too exhausted from the war to resist independence movements. Viewing the situation realistically, Britain resigned itself to granting independence to its possessions. High on the list of priorities was India, a land where millions of people were anxiously awaiting the fulfillment of British wartime promises.

Independence for India was speeded by the Labour Party's victory over Prime Minister Winston Churchill and the Conservatives in the British election of 1945. Churchill, an outspoken defender of Great Britain's imperial policies, only a short time before had stated that he had not become "His Majesty's First Minister in order to preside over the liquidation of the British Empire." The Labour Party was more willing to allow the various peoples under the British flag to go their independent ways.

Like the Conservatives, the Labourites soon found themselves at a loss for a formula for the transfer of power in India that would be acceptable to all Indians. For months the road to independence was blocked by differences between the Congress Party and the Muslim League. Each organization, realizing that a turning point in the history of India was at hand, sought the maximum advantage. Various plans were put forward by the British, but none met the approval of both Hindus and Muslims. While the discussions were going on, restive nationalists of all persuasions began to take matters in their own hands. Riots and demonstrations occurred daily in various parts of the subcontinent. Finally the British decided they could wait no longer for the bickering groups to harmonize their differences. In February, 1947, Britain announced that it would withdraw from India, and a few months later proclaimed its plan for creating the two nations of India and Pakistan.

- CHECK-UP
    1. With the outbreak of World War II, what stand was taken by the Congress Party? by the Muslim League?
    2. What suggestions were made by the Cripps Mission? How were these received? How did India aid Britain?
    3. What contributions did India make to Britain's war effort? How did Indian leaders hamper it?

August 15, Independence Day, is India's most important holiday. Here Nehru is pictured speaking to an overflow crowd in Delhi on Independence Day, 1960.

5. India and Pakistan Became Nations Under the Most Trying of Circumstances

On August 15, 1947, Britain officially withdrew from the subcontinent. Two new nations, India and Pakistan, had been born. Ordinarily the birth of a new nation is an occasion for rejoicing, but such was not the case when India and Pakistan achieved nationhood. Even as independence was being proclaimed unprecedented waves of violence and bloodshed were sweeping over large areas of the subcontinent.

Partition of India was accomplished in great haste. British and Indian leaders had spent years in fruitless negotiation, but once the fact of independence was agreed upon the British wasted no time in withdrawing from India. Six months after Britain had announced its intentions it turned over all its properties and powers in the subcontinent to Indian and Pakistani officials. A Viceroy remained for a time, but he was merely an adviser. As of midnight of August 14, 1947, India and Pakistan were free to chart their own courses.

Under a plan worked out beforehand, the provinces and princely states rapidly aligned themselves with one or the other country after Britain had withdrawn. Outwardly simple, the plan called for each

India's first Independence Day was not a time for rejoicing. Whole villages lay in ruins because of conflicts that had erupted between Hindus and Muslims. Refugee camps were crowded with Hindus who had fled from Muslim Pakistan. Conditions in Pakistan were equally bleak.

province under direct British rule to join the country with the religion that was accepted by most of its residents. Thus provinces inhabited mainly by Hindus became part of India, while those with largely Muslim populations joined Pakistan. The princes were expected to surrender their states to the country of their choice. Almost all the rulers respected the religious views of their subjects in arranging the transfer.

The partition led to violence in the Punjab and Bengal. The speed of the partition did not insure that it was painless. Partition caused suffering for millions of Indians. This was particularly true of Hindus, Muslims, and Sikhs in the heavily populated provinces of the Punjab and Bengal.

At the time of partition, large numbers of both Hindus and Muslims lived in the Punjab and Bengal. For this reason, British officials had divided each province between India and Pakistan. The portion of the Punjab where Muslims were in the majority became part of West Pakistan, while the Muslim part of Bengal went to East Pakistan. During the negotiations preceding the division long-smouldering religious hatreds burst into flame; Bengal and the Punjab were torn by massacres, looting, and burning. Muslims attacked Hindus living in Muslim areas and Hindus persecuted Muslims living in their regions. The Sikhs, whose land had been divided between India and West Pakistan, joined Hindus in mistreating Muslims. In turn, Sikhs were the victims of Muslim reprisals. Before the disorders ended, at least 500,000 Hindus, Muslims, and Sikhs had been killed. Some 5,500,000 Hindus and Sikhs had fled from Pakistan into India, and even more Muslims had moved from India to Pakistan.

Some princes rejected the plan of partition. By offering generous settlements and exerting economic and political pressure, the Indian and Pakistani governments persuaded all but two princes to surrender their independence. One holdout was the Maharaja of Kashmir, ruler of a large state on the Indo-Pakistani border. Although Kashmir was 70 per cent Muslim, the Hindu Maharaja would not transfer his holdings to Pakistan. And he also was reluctant to join India. Only when Kashmir was invaded by Pathan tribesmen from Pakistan did he agree to cooperate with Indian officials. At his request Indian troops entered Kashmir. In return for their services the Maharaja agreed to join the Indian federation. However, the action of the Maharaja did not fix the status of Kashmir. For years Kashmir was to be a sore spot between India and Pakistan.

The Nizam of Hyderabad ruled a state with a population 85 per cent Hindu. And since it was completely surrounded by India, there really was no alternative to union with that country. When the proud and stubborn Nizam refused to yield, India took over his state by force. In 1956 Hyderabad was partitioned along linguistic lines among Deccan states.

The other holdout was the Nizam of Hyderabad. A Muslim, the Nizam rejected the idea that Hyderabad should join India even though most of the inhabitants were Hindus. Like the Maharaja of Kashmir, the Nizam refused to join either country. The infuriated Indians settled the issue by force. In 1948 an Indian army occupied Hyderabad, pensioned off the ruler, and made the state a part of the Republic of India.

Partition disrupted government services. In addition to causing the conflicts just described, partition brought chaos to many services developed under British rule. The British had provided extensive transportation, communications, and irrigation systems, all of which had to be divided. This division of services, property, and assets led to endless haggling and disputes.

Perhaps the most serious problems concerned the British-built irrigation and railroad systems. Most of the thousands of miles of irrigation canals built by the British were in the Punjab, a province divided between India and Pakistan. Partition left sources of water in one country and many of the "feeder" canals in another. The railroad system, which was the best in Asia, had been built long before partition became an issue. Since Pakistan and India were far from friendly with each other, neither country was willing to accept joint operation of the irrigation and railroad networks. The problem of dividing railroad and irrigation systems plagued Indian and Pakistani officials for many years. Though a division was finally made, the efficiency of both systems was badly impaired.

Partition also disrupted such government services as mail delivery, health services, schools, and law enforcement. The assets of and responsibility for these services had to be divided between India and Pakistan. Many months passed before satisfactory arrangements could be made. The inconvenience and delay further increased discontent among people in both countries.

The assassination of Gandhi capped the turmoil. No Indian was more distressed by the disorders and violence accompanying partition than Gandhi. During the mass upheavals the aged leader pleaded for humane behavior by both Hindus and Muslims, but his pleas fell on deaf ears. Then, in January, 1948, Gandhi was shot to death by a fellow Hindu. Disturbed by the consideration Gandhi had shown for Muslims, this Hindu fanatic charged that the saintly Gandhi had been a traitor to his religion. Gandhi's death was mourned throughout the subcontinent, by Hindu and Muslim alike. A tearful Nehru expressed the shock and sorrow of the millions of Indians. "A light," he said, "has gone out of our lives."

● CHECK-UP

1. Why did the partition of India lead to violence? What happened in Kashmir and Hyderabad? Explain.
2. How did partition affect government services?

Summing Up

A new type of political leader emerged in India in the years after the Sepoy Rebellion. Often educated in English universities and familiar with the English tradition of political rights, this leader wanted a greater share in the government of his own land. The Indian National Congress, founded in 1885, was designed to help him achieve this objective. But before it succeeded, this pioneer nationalist group was badly split by political differences. Moreover, in addition to disagreements over political methods, the Congress was soon opposed by the Muslim League, an organization formed to protect Muslims against Hindu domination.

The Indian nationalist movement began to change from a passive, patient movement to an aggressive, demanding one during and after the First World War. Disappointed by Britain's rejection of their wartime requests for additional rights, and outraged by the passage of the Rowlatt Acts and by the tragic Amritsar Massacre, nationalists were only partially appeased by the Montagu-Chelmsford Reforms. The Reforms gave them a larger share in their government, but the clamor for self-government never died.

The appearance of Mahatma Gandhi upon the scene transformed the nationalist movement into a struggle against British rule. Popular with Hindus because of his religious and moral qualities, Gandhi was also a masterful political strategist. He is remembered in India both for his success in awakening the people to their need for self-government and for his humanitarian efforts.

The nationalist movement was revived in the late 1920's by the Simon Commission Report. A new generation of Indian leaders, including Jawaharlal Nehru, began to press for independence. Through the Round-Table Conferences, Great Britain unsuccessfully tried to satisfy the conflicting demands and interests of the Congress, the Muslim League, the princes, and other groups. Parliament finally passed the Government of India Act in 1935. However, the legislation was only partially successful in quieting the unrest.

The Second World War brought about the final split between Parliament and the Indian National Congress. Nehru, Gandhi, and their followers refused to support the British war effort unless their demands for immediate independence were met. The Muslim League, while cooperating with Britain in the prosecution of the war, was now committed to establishing a separate state. At war's end the British government withdrew from its Indian empire. Amid unprecedented violence and disorder two new nations, India and Pakistan, came into being.

CHAPTER REVIEW

Can You Identify?

Indian National Congress	Government of India Act	hartal
National Congress Party	Cripps Mission	Muslim League
communal representation	Tilak	Jinnah
Civil Disobedience Movement	Gandhi	Rowlatt Acts
Simon Commission	Nehru	swaraj
dominion status		

What Do You Think?

1. What was the reaction of Indians to English ideals of liberty and respect for the individual? Why did these ideals add to Indian unrest?

2. Not many Muslims joined the Indian National Congress. Why was this so?

3. What was Gandhi's position with respect to cooperation with Britain in World War I? in World War II? Explain why in each case.

4. Why was Britain unable to formulate a plan for the government of India that was acceptable to virtually all Indian leaders?

5. In 1939 the Viceroy proclaimed India to be in a state of war. Soon afterwards the Congress Party ministries in various provinces resigned. Was this action wise? Explain.

6. Should Britain have stayed longer in the subcontinent instead of withdrawing in 1947? Why, or why not?

Extending and Applying Your Knowledge

1. Among the books which provide the reader with insight into Gandhi's philosophy of non-violent resistance is Vincent Sheean's *Mahatma Gandhi* (Knopf, 1955). After reading the book, report to the class about Gandhi's use of this approach. Was it effective? Where have similar methods been used?

2. A vivid account of Gandhi's assassination is given in "A Time of Sorrow," in *India: Selected Readings*.

7

AFTER
INDEPENDENCE

. . . .

The violence and bloodshed which marked the birth of India and Pakistan were only the beginning of troubles on the subcontinent. No longer dependent on Britain, the two nations were faced with a multitude of difficult problems which they had to solve on their own. They had to find their place in world affairs, no easy task on a globe divided by conflicting ideologies. On the domestic scene, they had to form governments, expand industry, overcome poverty, and improve health. National leaders soon found that the struggle to establish strong and secure states was even more demanding than the fight to break away from British rule.

The leaders of India and Pakistan have not found ready answers for the many problems. For millions of Indians and Pakistanis, pride over the winning of national independence is unimportant when compared with their struggle for life. Year after year hunger, disease, and grinding poverty have prevented them from enjoying their status as independent peoples. Indian leaders, realizing that domestic problems must be solved, have largely withdrawn from contention for world leadership, trimmed programs for industrial expansion, and tried to launch sweeping social reforms. Pakistan has followed a different course, but its people live no better than the Indians.

Meanwhile, a new state has emerged on the Indian subcontinent. Years of bitter disagreement between Pakistan's national government and political leaders in East Pakistan erupted in a bloody civil war in 1971. The issue was settled, for a time at least, by India's military intervention on the side of East Pakistan. As a result, this region won its independence, but like the other countries of South Asia, the new nation of Bangladesh faces a bleak future. Without heavy international aid it is difficult to see how this infant nation, or India and Pakistan either, can solve their enormous problems. Nevertheless, it is the peoples of the subcontinent who must choose the paths their nations will follow.

1. Independent India Constructed a New System of Government

The leaders of newly independent India faced the task of bringing order out of turmoil. Even after the initial violence was over, the problem of stabilizing the political situation remained. Nehru, leader of the new India, made it unmistakably clear that the country would be a democracy committed to the advancement of the people's welfare. The lengthy constitution which went into effect in 1950 set forth in detail a plan calling for a democratic political system, a social structure based on full equality, and a program for eliminating poverty and establishing a sound economy.

The Indian constitution drew heavily on many sources. The ideas of many systems and philosophies can be found in the Indian constitution. Nehru's socialist leanings are especially noticeable. So, too, are ideas borrowed from the United States Constitution. For example, the written bill of rights in the Indian constitution strongly resembles that of the United States. As might be expected, the most extensively used source was English law and tradition. India had become more Anglicized than many nationalists cared to admit, and the basic plan of government was patterned after England's.

India's constitution is unusual in that it devotes much space to social problems. It includes a ban on caste distinctions, and it guarantees free and compulsory education for all children to age 14, a living wage for all, equal pay for equal work, and public assistance for the needy. India's leaders wrote these provisions into their constitution knowing full well that they could not enforce them immediately. India had to overcome many problems before it could make significant gains in the field of social welfare. Such provisions reflected ideals and goals, however impractical at the moment, which the leaders held for the Indian people.

The constitution establishes India as a democratic federal republic. This means that (1) the central government is made up of representatives of the people, elected by popular vote; and (2) the individual provinces, having surrendered certain powers to the central government, retain much authority. Thus India is, according to the constitution, a "Union" of equal, self-governing states. In actual fact the powers of the central government are extensive while those of the member states are limited.

India has a parliamentary system of government. India, like Britain, has a parliament consisting of an upper and a lower house. The upper house, the *Rajya Sabha* (*ruhj'*yuh *sub'*huh) or Council of the States, has very little power. Council members serve for six years, with a third of them being elected every two years. A dozen members are distinguished writers, artists, scholars, and scientists appointed by the President of India, the country's constitutional head of state. The rest of the 250 members are elected by the state legislatures. The real law-making body is the lower house, the *Lok Sabha* (House of the People). Its 500 representatives serve for five years and are elected by the people. The actual head of the Indian government is the Prime Minister, the leader of the majority party in the lower house of Parliament. He chooses an advisory council consisting of members of his party who are also members of Parliament. The Prime Minister and his council perform the executive functions of government.

India's President is elected jointly by its parliament and the state legislatures. His term of office is five years. Although the constitution states that "the executive power of the Union shall be vested in the President," in practice the chief executive is largely a ceremonial figure. He appoints the Prime Minister, has the power to dissolve Parliament and to call for a new election, and constitutionally has broad powers over the state governments. However, generally the President exercises his powers only upon the request of the Prime Minister.

Unlike the United States, which has both federal and state courts, India has only federal courts. The judges of these courts enjoy a large measure of independence. They cannot easily be influenced by either the executive or legislative branches of government.

The state governments are modeled on the national system. The structure of the state government is similar to that of the nation. The nominal head of each of the 20 states is a governor appointed by

(*Continued on page 179*)

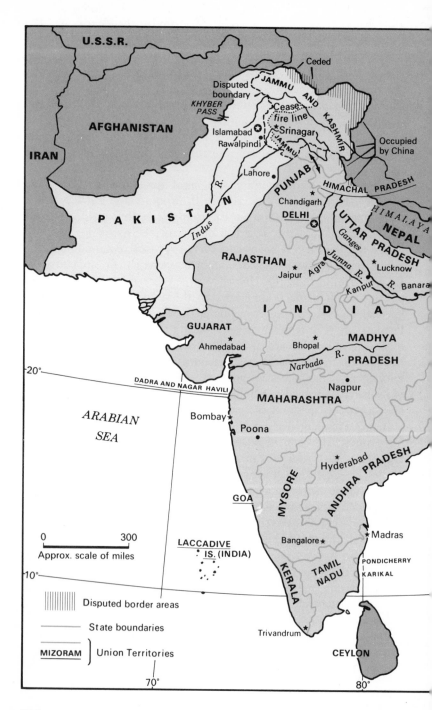

INDIA IN PROFILE

Capital: New Delhi

Government: Democratic Republic; 20 States, 10 Territories

Official Language: Hindi; 13 regional languages

Currency: Rupee
(13½ U.S. cents)

Area: 1,262,000 sq. mi. (approx.)

Population: 547,000,000 (1971 est.)

Largest cities (1971 est.):

Bombay	5,931,981
Delhi	3,629,842
Calcutta	3,438,887
Madras	2,470,288
Hyderabad	1,798,910

Chief products:

Agriculture—cotton, jute, peanuts, pepper, rice, sugar cane, tea, tobacco, wheat

Manufacturing—brass and silverware, cotton and silk, fertilizer, iron and steel, jute bags and rope, leather goods, paper, rugs, sugar, woodwork

Mining—bauxite, coal, iron ore, manganese ore, mica, salt

177

Constitutional Government in India

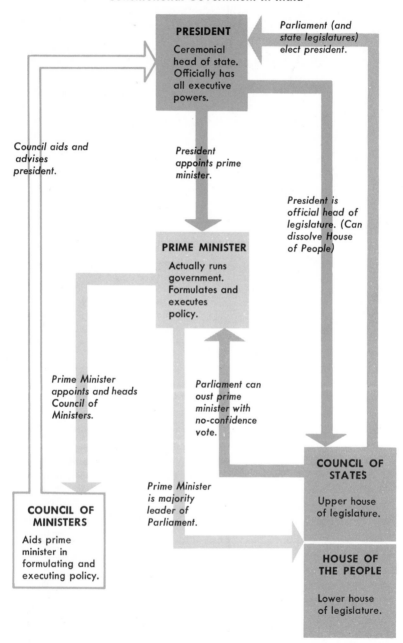

PRESIDENT

Ceremonial head of state. Officially has all executive powers.

Parliament (and state legislatures) elect president.

Council aids and advises president.

President appoints prime minister.

President is official head of legislature. (Can dissolve House of People)

PRIME MINISTER

Actually runs government. Formulates and executes policy.

Prime Minister appoints and heads Council of Ministers.

Parliament can oust prime minister with no-confidence vote.

Prime Minister is majority leader of Parliament.

COUNCIL OF MINISTERS

Aids prime minister in formulating and executing policy.

COUNCIL OF STATES

Upper house of legislature.

HOUSE OF THE PEOPLE

Lower house of legislature.

the President. This governor chooses as chief minister the leader of the majority party in the state legislative assembly. The members of the state council of ministers, headed by the chief minister, are appointed by the governor on the advice of the chief minister. Most states have bicaméral (two-house) legislatures, but some have a single house. State legislators are chosen by direct election.

In addition to the 20 states, India has 10 union territories. These territories, administered by the central government, have less self-government than the states. Their people do not elect legislatures but they do elect members of advisory councils.

The district is a major political subdivision in India. Most of India's states are divided into districts, a system inherited from the days of British rule. Under the British the district commissioner was the key official in the administrative system. Now appointed by the President, the district commissioner remains the most important government official in rural India. The commissioners have general responsibility for developing projects to further economic development and social welfare in their respective districts. They also collect revenue and have authority to maintain law and order.

Within each district are hundreds or even thousands of villages. Each village has a headman who is responsible for collecting revenue and keeping order in his community. The headman is a member of the panchayat (page 83), the governing council of the village. To the millions of peasants, many of whom are only vaguely aware of state and federal systems, the more than 212,000 panchayats are the most important units of government.

India's government was long dominated by the National Congress Party. India has many political parties, but the National Congress Party held a near-monopoly on government offices for many years after independence. Since its leaders for decades had been in the forefront of the struggle for national freedom, their names were familiar to millions of Indians, many of whom knew nothing about national politics. Moreover, only the National Congress Party had a truly nationwide organization with branches in every major city and town.

The rivals of the Congress Party represented many shades of political opinion. Some political groups, such as the Socialists and the Communists, had been active before independence; others were founded after the Union was established. Among competitors of the Congress Party were political parties seeking to preserve Hinduism intact, parties devoted to the interests of factory workers, organizations concerned with the special problems of farmers, and parties which advocated rapid social change. But for many years no party was able to make a significant showing against the firmly entrenched Congress Party.

National elections in India have brought out the largest vote in the free world. Although almost a quarter of a billion people were eligible to vote in postwar India, only about half that number exercised this right in the early elections. One of the major obstacles to voting was widespread illiteracy. This problem was solved by continuing a practice devised during British times: parties and their candidates used familiar symbols to identify themselves. Thus, in campaign materials and on the ballot the Congress Party was represented by a pair of yoked bullocks; the Communists by ears of corn and a sickle; the Socialists by a hut; and the Jan Sangh (jun sung), orthodox Hindus, by an earthen lamp.

Over the years the Indian voter has become increasingly more concerned about government. Since he weighs his political choices with ever greater care, one can no longer predict with any certainty the outcome of an election. Candidates for office must campaign vigorously in each election. The returns have demonstrated that voters in India have a grasp of major issues. Every political party, for example, has experienced ups and downs in popularity, depending on its stand on domestic issues especially.

Nehru towered above all other Indian leaders in the postwar era. From the end of the Second World War until 1964, Jawaharlal Nehru remained at the helm of India's government. The leader of the National Congress Party, he led it to victory in three successive national elections. Nehru was India's first Prime Minister, and as long as he lived no other Indian could even hope to gain that office.

Nehru was the only Indian leader to gain a respect and popularity approaching that enjoyed by Mahatma Gandhi. Nehru's word was virtually law in India, for all Nehru needed to do to get his way in Parliament was to threaten to resign. Whatever progress India made during the early years of independence must be credited to Nehru. Nehru made mistakes; he himself admitted this. Still, he retained the confidence of the Indian people until his death in 1964.

Nehru's passing marked a turning point in the politics of modern India. Nehru was the symbol of the generation which had struggled for independence. But by the final years of his life a new generation had arisen, one that had taken no part in the nationalist movement. These young men and women admired Nehru, but they were less enchanted with other of the older nationalist leaders. However, the older nationalists retained control of the party's power structure and showed no interest in sharing positions of leadership with newcomers. Moreover, the Congress was split into factions, and only the magnetism of Nehru kept the huge party reasonably united. Excluded from the power structure of the Congress Party and disillusioned by its lack of real unity, newcomers to politics turned increasingly to other parties. Even before Nehru's death, the popularity of the Congress Party had begun to decline.

With the death of Nehru the decline of the Congress Party became more rapid. Lal Bahadur Shastri (lul buh-*huh'*door *shuhs'*tree), a veteran warrior in the fight for independence, became Prime Minister. Shastri lacked his predecessor's prestige and charm. During his brief tenure as leader of the country, the split in party ranks widened, even though the Congress Party remained in firm control of the Indian government.

New life was breathed into the Congress Party by Indira Gandhi. On Shastri's death in 1966, Indira Gandhi became Prime Minister. She was the daughter and only child of Nehru (her late husband was not related to Mahatma Gandhi). Despite her efforts to restore unity, the Congress Party continued its quarrels over issues of leadership and policy. In the national elections of 1967 the party's decline was made painfully evident. Mrs. Gandhi's party lost almost one quarter of its seats in the lower house of Parliament, and fully half the states voted Congress Party governments out of office. At no time since the winning of independence had the power and prestige of the Congress Party sunk so low.

These political setbacks convinced Mrs. Gandhi that the Congress Party had to be revitalized. Even at the cost of further splitting the party, she launched a basic shake-up in leadership. The Prime Minister also decided that the party had to pursue more liberal policies than ever before.

For several years political warfare raged within the party, but Mrs. Gandhi succeeded in winning the upper hand. In the national elections held in 1971, her supporters, running as the New Congress Party, captured more than two-thirds of the seats in the lower house of Parliament. This landslide victory firmly established Prime Minister Gandhi's power and popularity.

• CHECK-UP
1. What are the chief provisions of India's constitution?
2. How does India's parliamentary system of government work?
3. What types of political parties developed in India?
4. Why was Nehru considered independent India's greatest leader? How did the Congress Party fare after his death?

2. India Has Made Slow Economic Headway

Nehru and his lieutenants recognized the urgency of strengthening the Indian economy. Among the major nations of the world none had a more wretched standard of living. At the time of independence India's per capita annual income was estimated to be about $50. But this was the average; millions of Indians lived on less. Raising the living standard of the Indian people, therefore, was the most important task of the new government.

An expanding economy is one of India's major goals. The leaders of the new India were determined to raise standards of living, but they did not agree on how this should be done. Many top-ranking members of the Congress Party were industrialists and businessmen. They believed that India could best make economic progress by encouraging free enterprise, the system that had made them wealthy. They pointed to Britain and the United States as examples of countries which had built healthy economies along the lines of free enterprise. But Nehru and most of his supporters blamed Britain and its economic system for many of India's problems. Also, Nehru was convinced that a capitalistic system such as Britain's could not work in an emerging country, since not enough private capital would be available to develop new industries. He believed that socialism (economic development through government planning and government ownership of important industries) was the answer.

Per Capita Income in Current U.S. Dollars		
	INDIA	UNITED STATES
1950	$56	$1501
1960	68	2219
1970	80 (est.)	3910

Indian leaders finally agreed to establish a "mixed economy," one which combined free enterprise and socialism. Both private capital and public funds would be used to develop industry, mining, and farming. The overall framework, however, was socialist, for it was agreed that the government should prepare a master plan for developing the nation's resources. That master plan has been implemented in a series of five year plans. The First Five Year Plan went into effect in 1951; the Fourth, in 1969.

Agricultural expansion was stressed in early plans. Nehru believed that the nation should give highest priority to boosting the output of food. The crop yield per acre in India was one of the lowest in the world. Farmers were too poor to buy fertilizers, improved seed, and insecticides. Farming methods were antiquated; peasants continued to use methods developed by their ancestors centuries ago. Moreover, land holdings were small. The average farm was five acres, but millions of peasants had only an acre or two.

The First Five Year Plan was largely an attempt to carry out British plans for putting more land into cultivation. All the agricultural goals were met or exceeded. Almost 17 million additional acres of land were brought under cultivation through the expansion of irrigation systems. Food grain production was increased by more than 11 million tons per year. Later plans were also successful. A quarter century after independence, food production in India had doubled.

Food remains a problem. Despite the increase in agricultural production, there has been great uneasiness in India over the food situation. High hopes were raised when the "green revolution" got under way. This was a movement to increase grain yields by encouraging farmers to use new, improved seeds. The "green revolution" brought impressive results in such countries as the Philippines, Pakistan, and Mexico. And it also has led to larger wheat crops in India. But for many years India's rice production was scarcely affected. Unless much more rice can be raised, India's overall food situation will continue to be gloomy. Moreover, many of the people simply cannot afford to buy adequate food, even when markets have abundant supplies.

The population explosion wiped out agricultural gains. A complicating factor in India's attack on the food problem has been its rapidly growing population. The sharp rise in number of people is not due to a rise in birth rate. Rather it can be traced to the use of modern medicines, other new methods of fighting disease, and the

Population Growth in India

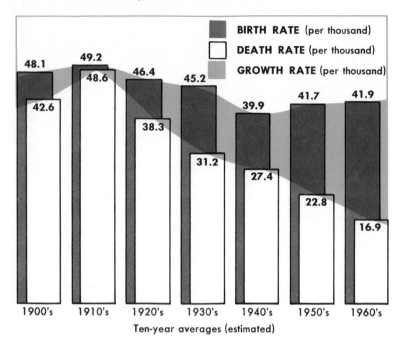

This chart illustrates why a country's population can increase even when its birth rate does not. India's birth rate has declined since 1910, but its death rate has decreased even more. As a result, the growth rate, or rate of population increase, has reached alarming proportions.

development of an efficient system of famine relief. All these measures, started by the British, caused the death rate to fall sharply. With fewer babies dying soon after birth and with people living longer, India's food needs remain critical.

The seriousness of India's population problem can be judged from census figures. After partition the population of India was 345 million. That figure reached 392 million in 1957 and passed the half-billion mark in the mid-1960's. Even in a year free of damaging droughts and floods, population growth more than offsets agricultural gains.

India has tried to expand its industry. By world standards India had a modest industrial system when it became independent. Britain, being a highly industrialized nation, had developed India as a market rather than as a supplier of finished goods. Once in charge of its own destiny, however, India began to encourage industrialization. Today it is not only the country's rich heritage that Indian leaders

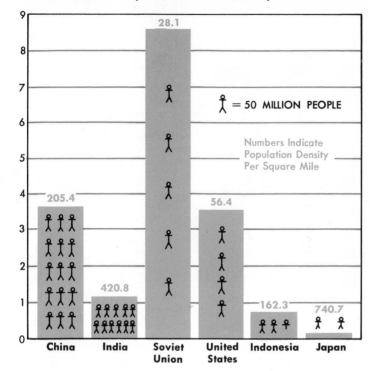

Land Area Vs. Population — Six Most Populous Nations

$\text{❊} = 50$ MILLION PEOPLE

Numbers Indicate
Population Density
Per Square Mile

Of the six most heavily populated nations, India is first in number of people per square mile. Further population growth could be disastrous.

emphasize before the world; it is also India's manufacturing, the source, they hope, of future prosperity. For the present, however, output per capita remains pathetically low.

The road to industrial development has not been an easy one for India. A continuing problem is lack of capital. Without money new industries cannot be developed nor established ones be expanded. And India has a problem common to all developing nations — a reluctance on the part of capitalists to invest in uncertain ventures. The fact that government leaders advocated socialism did nothing to loosen purse strings. Many foreign capitalists assumed that fewer governmental controls would mean more profit for themselves. Under a socialist system such as India's, they expected government interference.

Unexpected problems upset India's industrial plans. In 1961 the government launched the Third Five Year Plan, India's most ambitious economic offensive up to that time. Unfortunately India soon

THE FOOD PROBLEM. Grain became scarce and prices high during the terrible drought that hit India in the mid-1960's. The women pictured above were able to buy reasonably priced rice at a government store. Whether the "green revolution" will adequately expand India's food supply is an urgent question for the future. Right, crop experts at an Indian agricultural university study seeds of high-yield varieties of corn.

found itself in its most serious crisis since becoming independent. In 1962 a boundary dispute with China reached a climax when that country occupied disputed territories in the Himalayan frontier region (page 199). Fearing the worst, Indian leaders hastened to strengthen military defenses. They could do this only by scrapping plans for economic development.

In the following years, more crises developed. In 1965 India experienced the worst drought in a century. Faced with the threat of famine, the government drew heavily on its own funds and also had to ask for tremendous amounts of foreign aid. The United States, one of the responding nations, sent thousands of bushels of wheat. When the tragic drought continued into the following year, India made a new appeal for help. Again the United States responded, sending India a million tons of wheat every month for over a year. By the time the Third Five Year Plan ended in 1966, India seemed to be little better off than when the plan was launched.

Foreign trade contributed little to the growth of India's economy. As a developing nation, India has had to buy more from other nations than it sells. For the first 20 years of its existence as a nation the value of its exports was half that of its imports. The reason for this unfavorable balance of trade was that India had little except low-priced agricultural commodities to exchange for expensive industrial goods. Jute and tea were the main products that India offered for sale abroad. Moreover, India did not have a large world market. Its chief trading partners were the United States, Great Britain, and the Soviet Union. Together with West Germany, these countries were also the main investors and creditors for the government of India.

As India's economy expands, its income from world trade also grows. More and more goods labeled "Made in India" are reaching world markets. However, India continues to buy from the outside world more than it sells. Regardless of how fast India's productivity increases, the needs of its people seem to grow even faster.

• CHECK-UP

1. How did India go about building a stronger economy? Why was agriculture stressed? With what success?
2. How has India sought to expand its industry? What factors slowed industrial growth?
3. Why does India have an unfavorable balance of trade?

3. India's Social Needs Are of Gigantic Proportions

For the long-suffering people of India, the nation's leaders realize that more than food, clothing, and shelter are needed. Nehru and his successors hoped to raise the level of education, to improve public health, and to eliminate the social injustices which made many Indians "second-class" citizens. In short, government leaders have wanted to create a way of life characterized by freedom and human dignity. Despite many handicaps, India has made some progress in social reform.

Who was to be educated? India can boast of a tradition of education dating back many centuries. Until the 1800's, schooling was essentially religious, and the few upper-class Hindus and Muslims who learned to read and write did so in connection with religious studies. These privileged individuals were of course only a tiny percentage of the population. Even the Western-style education introduced by the British was on a modest scale. At the time India became independent, only about 15 per cent of the population could read and write.

India's leaders believed that the country could develop a modern democratic society only if every Indian were literate. But they also realized that the task of educating all of India's millions was beyond the country's resources. Government officials decided that modest goals would have to do for the meantime.

India manages to educate only a small number of its young people. India has made gains in education but still has a long way to go. Though primary schools have doubled in number since independence, illiteracy has been reduced only a little. And of the roughly 50 million students who attend the primary schools annually, only a small percentage will get more than a meager education. While the Indian government has made a strong effort to get most children into school, not many of them stay very long. An American observer described the problem:

> Although the lack of interest on the part of rural parents in education for their children is perhaps diminishing, it is still not at all uncommon for parents to withdraw their children from school after one or two years. Out of every hundred pupils who enter the first class, only 35 reach the fifth class. It is at the primary level that stagnation and wastage in the educational process are especially marked.[1]

[1] Beatrice Pitney Lamb, *India; A World in Transition* (New York, Frederick Praeger, 1966), p. 291.

The high drop-out rate has delayed fulfillment of India's educational goals. Less than one fourth of the country's school children continue their schooling beyond the primary level, and only a small percentage go on to high school.

The "brain drain" has handicapped India. Many graduates of Indian universities have traveled to the United States and Europe for further training in their special fields. After completing their studies, many of them have decided not to return to their homeland. Since India is so much less developed than most Western countries, it can offer only limited opportunities in many specialized occupations. Indian scientists especially find this to be true. At home they do not have the laboratories and expensive equipment that are available for research in wealthier countries. Moreover, Indians with graduate degrees are attracted by higher salaries and better living conditions overseas. How to deal with the "brain drain" is a critical problem for India. Simply forbidding students and scholars to study abroad would be pointless. But talented people continue to leave a country that badly needs their services.

Competition for admission to universities is fierce. A person with a university education is still unusual in modern India. Although institutions of higher education were founded during the British era, only a few Indians were able to attend them. Since 1947 many new colleges and universities have been started. However, they have not kept pace with demand. Competition for admission to first-rate universities, therefore, is intense. Even the less distinguished colleges have more applicants than they can admit.

Having attended a college or university has long been a source of pride to Indian students. Higher education is so valued that many Indians proudly identify themselves as "Failed Scholars." They could not pass the final examinations and receive degrees, but they are proud of the fact that even for a time they were part of the academic world.

The language controversy has troubled India. No sooner had India's leaders organized a new government than the issue of a national language was raised. Because so many languages and dialects were spoken in the subcontinent, it seemed that no agreement on the issue was possible. Most leaders spoke and wrote English, but few thought it should be the national language. After all, English was the symbol of British imperial rule, something many of them had fought for years.

The most logical choice for a national language was Hindi, the mother tongue of almost half the people. Accordingly, a provision was added to the Constitution of 1950 which said that Hindi would become the official language on January 26, 1965. However, many people opposed giving Hindi that special status. Most speakers of Hindi live in North India, and residents of other regions feared that the use of that one language would weaken their cultures. In an effort to satisfy everyone, the framers of the constitution gave 13 other languages an official status as regional languages.

The constitutional provision for language differences has failed to be a solution. Feeling against Hindi is so strong that the government has not tried to force its acceptance as the national language. On the other hand, the backers of Hindi are upset because English continues to be used to "bridge" the language barrier. Never, they say, will Hindi or any other language become a national language as long as English is used. But the equally determined opponents of Hindi declare that the day will never come when all India accepts Hindi as the national language. They insist that English, although spoken by only three per cent of the people, is understood by so many of India's leaders that it can be used for all official purposes. These opponents of Hindi see no reason for changing the present system of regional languages.

As a concession to the anti-Hindi point of view, the government decided in 1967 to keep English as an official "associate national language." It was hoped that when knowledge and use of Hindi became more widespread, the controversy would fade.

India's government has tried to improve health. Over the years India has repeatedly suffered epidemics of such fatal diseases as malaria, smallpox, cholera, typhoid fever, and tuberculosis. Many Indians also have died from supposedly "non-fatal" illnesses, such as intestinal and respiratory ailments. To still other Indians, diseases related to malnutrition have been fatal. The introduction of modern medicine during the British era greatly reduced the death rate, but it could scarcely be said that the Indian people enjoyed good health. The British had slowed down, but not halted, the epidemics which periodically broke out in various parts of India.

Since independence, the improvement of health has been a major goal of the Indian government. Among the campaigns launched for this purpose have been efforts to get villages to avoid polluting water supplies and to eliminate vermin. The government has paid for the education of doctors and nurses, built hospitals and clinics, and sponsored medical research. India's health programs have also been aided by other countries, especially the United States, and by the World Health Organization of the United Nations. These efforts have resulted in some progress, but India's health problems still are far from solved.

Health programs call for widespread reeducation. Indian leaders realize that disease cannot be eliminated simply by providing doctors, medical equipment, and drugs. Just as important is the modifying of people's attitudes. Villagers have to be persuaded to abandon traditional treatments which do no good. In many cases time-honored practices contribute to the spread of disease in India, but villagers often refuse to admit that this is so.

One factor working against the acceptance of new medical ideas is India's widespread poverty. People cannot afford to make proposed changes. An American scholar who studied village life in India reported the following conversation:

Q. Why can't you wash your clothes, if, as you say, dirty clothes cause disease?

A. We are lucky if we have one complete set of clothes. We can't find time to wash them, but have to wear them twenty-four hours a day.

Q. Why can't you keep your house clean, though, if an unclean house also causes sickness?

A. I have two rooms. In the back room the buffalo is kept at night all winter. She drops dung and passes urine there. It is impossible to keep the place really clean. There is one living room for us. I do my weaving there. The food is cooked there, and we all sleep there at night. During the day the other family members stay in that room. It is hard to keep it clean.[2]

India recognizes the need for birth control. Since the rapid rise in population has been of major concern in India, the government has proposed birth control as a solution to the problem. Various birth control programs have been started, but their impact has not been great. Many Indians who would like to limit their families make no use of these programs because of fear, ignorance, or mistaken information. Moreover, India has not been able to recruit enough qualified

---

[2] Oscar Lewis, *Village Life in Northern India: Studies in a Delhi Village* (Urbana, University of Illinois Press, 1958), p. 264.

SOCIAL CHANGE IN INDIA. At the root of India's many problems are illiteracy and a soaring population. To combat these problems, the Indian government has opened hundreds of new schools (left) and birth control clinics (center). The task is great, however, and the obstacles are many. Considering what remains to be done, progress hitherto has been slow.

In one area, India has made considerable progress. The status of women has improved greatly. The woman instructor in the birth control clinic and the nurse in one of India's thousands of health clinics (right) are illustrative of the increasing importance of women in Indian life. Not many years ago very few women indeed were employed outside the home.

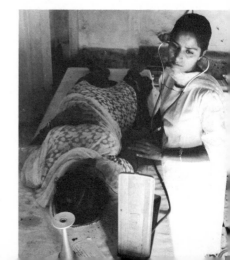

192

instructors to make the programs effective. Nevertheless, the government has adopted as one of its primary goals for the nation an effective birth control program. It realizes that India can never hope to solve its other problems as long as the population increases more rapidly than the ability of the economy to provide for additional people.

The government has acted to raise the status of Untouchables. Perhaps India's oldest problem is the plight of the Untouchables. (In the constitution and other official documents, Untouchables are referred to as the "Scheduled Castes.") To help Untouchables overcome their many handicaps, the framers of India's constitution officially outlawed Untouchability. All buildings, institutions, and services supported by government funds were opened to the Scheduled Castes. Professions and trade were opened to them, and advisory councils and departments for promoting their welfare were set up in all the states. Blocs of seats in Parliament and in the state legislatures were also reserved for Untouchables.

In the years since the constitution was written, Parliament has given additional help to the Untouchables. Penalties for discrimination were provided, and laws were passed assuring to Untouchables specific government jobs. Also, universities were required to admit a certain number of applicants from this group. And since the living conditions of the outcastes were even worse than those of Indians in general, the government gave them financial aid.

Certainly the condition of India's millions of Untouchables is now better than it was. Some have found places in political life and have filled jobs formerly closed to them. But the great mass of the Untouchables have experienced no major change in their lot. Legislation on their behalf is one thing; the acceptance of change by Hindus is another. Deep-rooted attitudes and customs are not easy to sweep away.

The position of women in Hindu life has changed. A very obvious social advance in India is the improved status of women. For many centuries they held an inferior position. For example, they could not inherit property; at the death of a husband, his estate went to a son or brother rather than to his wife. In some regions a widow could be deprived of her children. Marriage laws, too, were strongly weighted in favor of the husband.

In the postwar period the leaders of the new India passed laws to give women equality in marriage, property rights, and other matters. Moreover, positions in public life and in private industry were opened to women. Today many Indian women pursue careers in government, education, medicine, and the arts. The fact that Indira Gandhi could become Prime Minister is proof that new opportunities are available to Indian women.

• CHECK-UP

1. Why did independent India greatly expand schools and colleges? What has handicapped these efforts?
2. Why did the question of a national language provoke controversy?
3. How has India tried to improve the health of its people? What have been the results?
4. What efforts have been made to raise the status of Untouchables? of women?

4. India Seeks Its Place in the World Order

When independent India was born, the "old order" was being ripped apart in many parts of the world. Germany and Japan, defeated in war, no longer were great powers. A Communist government was established in mainland China, and a number of European nations were coming under the domination of Soviet communism. The mighty empires of Britain and France were collapsing as former colonies demanded and achieved independence. India, of course, was one of these former colonies. The "new order" which was emerging in international affairs consisted of three camps—Communist nations,

TIMETABLE	India Since Independence
1947	Partition of India
1947–64	Nehru is Prime Minister
1948	Gandhi assassinated
1950	Constitution adopted
1951	First Five Year Plan begins
1964–66	Shastri is Prime Minister
1966	Indira Gandhi becomes Prime Minister
1971	Victory in war with Pakistan

the United States and its allies and friends, and non-aligned nations. India had to decide which of these camps to join and how active a part to play on the world scene.

India adopted a policy of non-alignment. As one of the new nations of the post-World War II era, India was not satisfied with its image as a "former colony." At the time of partition India became a self-governing dominion within the Commonwealth of Nations (the organization which replaced the British Empire). But in 1950, when its new constitution went into effect, India renounced dominion status. It remained a member of the Commonwealth but as a "sovereign democratic republic."

India's struggle for independence had made it a foe of imperialism. It is not surprising, therefore, that Nehru put India forward as the champion of Asian and African peoples who wanted freedom from colonial rule. Ways in which India's foreign policy reflected its bitter experiences as a British colony were brought out by one of Nehru's biographers:

> The pillars [of Indian foreign policy] may be summed up as follows: *anti-colonialism* or, in more positive terms, active support for all peoples in Asia and Africa who strive to eliminate the remnants of foreign rule; *anti-racialism*, i.e., a demand for *full equality among all races*, particularly recognition of equal rights for colored peoples of the world over; *non-alignment* with power blocs . . . *the recognition of Asia* as a new, vital force in the world arena and the right of Asian states to decide the issues of direct concern to them; *mediation* with a view to relaxing international tension and to creating an atmosphere conducive to Indian economic development . . . and *non-violence* as the preferred means of settling international disputes. . . .[3]

One "pillar" that attracted a great deal of attention was Nehru's policy of non-alignment with power blocs. With respect to the cold war between Communist and Western camps, India refused to line up with either the United States or the Soviet Union. Nehru's government held to a policy of judging each international issue separately.

The problem of Kashmir continued to plague India. The bitter controversy over Kashmir (page 168) was a major factor in keeping

[3] Michael Brecher, *Nehru: A Political Biography* (New York, Oxford University Press, 1959), pp. 563–64.

tension alive between India and Pakistan. Kashmir was important to each country as a "buffer zone" against the other and against China. The province also was important because its rivers supplied water for the Indus irrigation system, which was used by both India and Pakistan. Each country was afraid its neighbor might monopolize this water if it controlled the source.

For a time, it seemed that the United Nations might bring about a settlement of the Kashmir dispute. In early 1949 the UN arranged a truce to end the fighting which had broken out between India and Pakistan. The UN also worked out an arrangement for sharing the water of the Indus River system. The water arrangement proved successful, but the truce did not last.

Renewed trouble over Kashmir was precipitated by India's actions. The Indian government had agreed to allow the people of Kashmir to decide by popular vote which country to join, but it soon retracted its pledge. Muslims greatly outnumbered Hindus in the province, and Indian officials knew all too well how such a plebiscite would turn out. In 1956 India proclaimed that the part of Kashmir it was occupying was a permanent part of Indian territory. Tension over the Kashmir issue built up steadily until large-scale fighting erupted between the two countries in 1965.

India used force to recover European-held land on its coastline. The Kashmir dispute enabled Nehru's critics to charge that India could ignore its professed ideals whenever they conflicted with Indian interests. This view was strengthened when India took steps to annex several small European possessions along its coasts. These "foreign enclaves," as they were called, were the last remnants of Portuguese and French power in India. None of them, with the possible exception of Portuguese-held Goa, had much strategic or economic importance. But these "pimples on the face of India"—Nehru's expression — reminded Indians of the former colonial status of their country. Because of national pride as much as anything else, most Indian leaders thought the enclaves should be eliminated.

France put up little opposition when India demanded the cession of its possessions in the subcontinent. In 1954 France surrendered its five small holdings on India's east coast. Portugal, however, having held its three small territories for more than four centuries, refused to give them up. Finally, in 1961, India moved troops into the Portuguese enclaves and took them by force. This action shocked many of

India's friends. They had heard Indian spokesmen condemn force as a means of settling international disputes, and now India itself had used strong-arm methods.

India's First Lady

Indira Gandhi, daughter of the late Jawaharlal Nehru, and India's first woman prime minister, was born in 1917. She grew up during the years when her father was blazing a path to the leadership of the Indian nationalist movement. After attending college in India, Indira went to England in 1937 to study at Oxford University. Shortly after her return to India, she married — against her father's wishes — a lawyer and journalist named Feroze Gandhi (no relation to the Mahatma). The marriage was not a happy one and, after a few years, the Gandhis separated.

During the Second World War, while Nehru was in prison along with many other nationalists, he wrote many letters about India's past to his daughter (page 164). When Nehru became Prime Minister of independent India, Indira became his official hostess (Mrs. Nehru had died in 1936). Soon Mrs. Gandhi became active in the Congress Party, and in 1959–1960 served as its president. In 1964 she was appointed India's Minister for Information and Broadcasting.

When Bahadur Shastri, who had followed her father as Prime Minister, died in 1966, Indira Gandhi was moved up to the position of Prime Minister. Faced with bitter opposition from the conservative wing of the Congress Party, she built up her own following and in the 1971 national elections scored a smashing victory. This not only confirmed Prime Minister Gandhi's great popularity in India but also insured her status as a major world figure.

The 1962 border dispute between India and China concerned some of the most rugged land in the subcontinent. Pictured here is a mountain path, over which supplies were carried to Indian soldiers.

India's policy toward China changed from friendship to tension. When Communists came to power in China in 1949, Nehru was confident that India could maintain peaceful relations with the new rulers. For several years the actions of the Indian government reflected this attitude. India was one of the first countries to break off relations with the defeated Chinese Nationalist government and recognize the new regime. India consistently led the annual attempt to have Communist China seated in the United Nations. In 1954 Nehru and the Chinese foreign minister agreed on "Five Principles of Peaceful Coexistence," a pledge of peaceful and neighborly relations between India and China.

The time came when India began to have second thoughts about the policy of its neighbor to the north. After China occupied Tibet in 1950, the presence of Chinese forces along the borders of India, Bhutan, and Nepal disturbed Nehru. In 1959 India's relations with China took a sudden turn for the worse when a widespread rebellion in Tibet was cruelly suppressed by the Chinese. The Dalai Lama, the spiritual leader of Tibet, and some 13,000 of his followers sought sanctuary in India. Over the next few years skirmishes between Indian and Chinese troops occurred from time to time along the frontier. In 1962 serious fighting suddenly broke out, and Chinese

198

troops advanced deeply into Indian border areas. Before a full-scale war could erupt, however, the Chinese withdrew from many of the areas they had occupied. Nevertheless, China had made its point, namely, that it did not recognize India's claim to sovereignty over the disputed frontier territories.

Since their frontier clashes in 1962, relations between India and Communist China have remained strained. The dispute over the Himalayan frontier areas has not yet been resolved. And as relations between China and the Soviet Union became increasingly tense during the 1960's, India and Russia drew closer to each other. Communist China was now recognized to be a common enemy of both.

India maintained cordial relations with the USSR. Although India refused to join either of the two great power blocs, it has been consistently friendly with Russia. Indian Socialists were inspired by the success of the Soviet Union in modernizing its industry within a socialist framework. Russia responded to Indian friendship by granting economic, technical, and military aid from time to time. Though less substantial than similar American programs, the Russian aid was deeply appreciated in India.

In the late 1960's the widening split between Russia and China tended to draw India and Russia closer together, especially as Chinese leaders directed propaganda attacks against both countries. In 1971 Russia and India cemented their closer relations with a 20-year treaty of friendship. And when war flared up between India and Pakistan over the secession of the new state of Bangladesh, Soviet Russia made clear its support of Prime Minister Gandhi's stand.

Relations with the United States gradually shifted. Relations between India and the United States were friendly but formal for many years. Americans felt deep sympathy for India, and Nehru had many admirers in the United States. As American concern over Asian affairs mounted, the volume of aid to India increased. American funds for economic development and technical assistance, and credits for the purchase of food, played a vital role in India's five year plans. But American offers of military aid were for a long time turned down. By refusing military aid, India hoped to keep free of American influence in foreign affairs.

Gradually India had to change its policy toward the United States. The Chinese military ventures along the frontier exposed glaring weaknesses in India's defenses. Nehru and later Shastri had to turn to the United States for military aid. But when Indian and Pakistani troops clashed in 1965, the United States suspended arms shipments to both countries.[4]

During the next few years American relations with India were played out in a low key. It was no easy matter for the United States government to adjust to the conflicting positions of India and its rival, Pakistan. American-Indian relations finally came to a head in 1971 when India dispatched military forces across the frontier into East Pakistan. Since the United States officially frowned on this action, relations between the American and Indian governments became very cool.

India's role in world affairs became less active. During its first decade of independence India enjoyed great popularity among the new nations of Asia and Africa and was highly respected by other nations as well. Nehru was the idol of the developing countries and the hero of anti-imperialists. When he spoke on international issues, the whole world listened. But by the late 1960's India's prestige had waned. Failure to solve internal problems, the sacrifice of professed ideals to advance national interest, and setbacks in international affairs had damaged India's image. Today, burdened with grim problems at home and faced with explosive situations along its frontiers, India concentrates its energies on domestic and regional affairs rather than on international matters.

● CHECK-UP

1. What were the "pillars" of India's foreign policy under Nehru? Why were these desirable for India?
2. How did India take over the last foreign holdings in the subcontinent? Why?
3. Why did India's relations with China worsen? Why did India and Russia draw closer together?
4. Trace relations between the United States and India since the latter became independent.

5. Pakistan Has Had a Stormy Existence

For years before the partition of the British Indian Empire, Muslim leaders in India had dreamed about a separate nation of their own. That dream became a reality with the creation of the independent

[4] As a member of the Southeast Asia Treaty Organization (SEATO), Pakistan had received military aid from the United States.

state of Pakistan (page 166). Unfortunately, Pakistan was even less ready for independence than India. Not only were its scars of partition particularly deep, but it had nothing on which to base national policy and little with which to build its economy.

Independent Pakistan had many problems. Few states of the postwar world were founded under less favorable conditions than Pakistan. The first hard fact was that the country was divided. A thousand miles separated East Pakistan from West Pakistan. Since an unfriendly India lay between the two parts, most messages and goods passing from one section to the other had to follow air and sea routes that avoided India. Moreover, each section had its own distinctive culture, a factor which greatly hindered national unity. The chief language in West Pakistan was Urdu; in East Pakistan, Bengali. West Pakistan looked to the Middle East for inspiration, while East Pakistan had more in common with the countries of Southeast Asia. About the only bonds between the two sections of Pakistan were the Muslim religion and mutual distrust of India.

The same problems of partition that hit India also affected Pakistan, but they were even more serious in the latter country. Over six million Muslims fled from India into West Pakistan alone. This

TIMETABLE	Pakistan Since Independence
1947	Partition of India
1948	Death of Mohammed Ali Jinnah
1950	First constitution adopted
1955	First Five Year Plan begins
1956	Second constitution adopted
1958–69	Government headed by Mohammed Ayub Khan
1962	Third constitution adopted
1965	War with India over Kashmir
1966	Tashkent Declaration
1971	Secession of Bangladesh. Pakistan defeated in war with India

meant that one out of every five persons in that area was a refugee who had to be resettled. Pakistan was left with almost no military supplies, since the lion's share of the British military system was absorbed by India. Moreover, Pakistan lost most of its merchants, moneylenders, and civil servants, as well as many doctors, lawyers, and teachers. Most of these people in pre-partition Pakistan were Hindus and they fled to India after partition.

In addition to these problems, Pakistan had to create a new central government. India was able to build on the British governmental system, but Pakistan had only provincial governments. It had no central legislature, no central executive, no foreign policy, no agency to handle economic development. For the first decade of its existence, Pakistan found it difficult simply to survive.

Pakistan's first years were politically stormy. India had the firmly established Congress Party to guide its destiny, but Pakistan had no strong political party to take it through the early critical years. If Mohammed Ali Jinnah had lived, he might have brought a measure of stability to the land. In 1947 he had virtually taken over the new government and kept it from falling apart. But the founding father of Pakistan died in September, 1948.

The passing of Jinnah led to bitter political struggles. Rivalries between leaders and parties threatened to tear the state apart. Cooperation between East and West Pakistan proved difficult; each was afraid of domination by the other. For a number of years Pakistan changed leaders with confusing frequency. Not even the adoption of a new constitution in 1956 helped to settle political unrest.

Ayub Khan brought a period of stability to Pakistan. In 1958 a "strong man" emerged to take control of the government. Army leaders had suspended the constitution and declared martial law. Soon General Mohammed Ayub Khan (*ah' yub kahn'*) became supreme. Taking the title of president, Ayub governed the country with a firm hand. Corrupt officials were turned out of office, economic abuses were checked, and social reforms were started. In 1962 a new constitution granted the president almost unlimited powers. Three years later presidential elections were held, and the popular Ayub easily won. Ayub Khan was credited with saving Pakistan from disaster. The country was so divided that an effective government could probably never have been formed under a democratic process. Ayub's government gave Pakistan strong central leadership.

Under Ayub Khan (above right), who gained power in 1958, Pakistan had a period of stability, but mounting unrest forced him to resign in 1969. Following Pakistan's humiliating defeat and dismemberment in 1971, Ali Bhutto (above left, with his daughter) took charge of the Pakistani government.

Political differences finally broke up the country. Despite the benefits of efficient government, simmering opposition to Ayub Khan's strong-man rule came to a head in 1969. Faced with continued riots and protest demonstrations, Ayub proclaimed martial law and resigned from the presidency. His place as head of state was taken by General Agha Mohammed Yahya Khan (*yah'* yah *kahn'*), the commander-in-chief of the Pakistani army.

Yahya Khan made a serious effort to satisfy the demands of the government's critics. He relaxed many of the military controls over Pakistani life, cracked down on corruption by state officials, and permitted greater freedom of political expression. He also promised to hold elections for Parliament (which had been dissolved several months before).

When the elections were held late in 1970, an East Pakistani political party called the Awami League scored a landslide victory. The Awami League had for several years agitated for greater self-rule for East Pakistan. The Pakistan People's Party, a socialist group led by Zulfikar Ali Bhutto (*boo'* toh), won many of the parliamentary seats in West Pakistan. The first responsibility of the newly elected parliament was to draw up a new constitution for the nation.

But Yahya Khan twice postponed the first session of the new parliament. When leaders of the Awami League protested and rioting broke out, the government sent armed forces into East Pakistan to enforce its authority. The confrontation between Yahya Khan's regime and the East Pakistani protesters erupted in a continuous wave of violence throughout 1971. Finally, in December, India entered the tragic conflict. In a short but bitterly fought war, the Indian army overwhelmed the Pakistani forces in East Pakistan.

As a result of India's victory, East Pakistan successfully broke away from its parent state and a new country, Bangladesh, was established. This setback cost Pakistan about one-sixth of its territory and more than half of its population. Yahya Khan was held responsible for the defeat. He was replaced as leader of what remained of Pakistan (that is, the West) by Ali Bhutto.

The government of Pakistan encouraged industrial growth. Like India, the new state of Pakistan in its early years established as a main goal the development of industry. In pursuit of this goal, however, Pakistani leaders took a course different from that of their Indian counterparts. The Pakistani placed their faith in private enterprise. The government of Pakistan long followed the policy of helping businessmen who were willing to develop needed industries. Although a number of state-run enterprises were set up, whenever one of these projects began to function efficiently, it was usually sold to a private company. The government also made credit available to industrialists and encouraged investments by foreign capitalists.

Until Ali Bhutto came to power late in 1971, capitalism was strongly encouraged in Pakistan. This did not mean that, under the regimes of Ayub Khan and Yahya Khan, central planning (the heart of socialism) had been ignored. In fact, like India, Pakistan sought to develop its industry, agriculture, and mining through a series of five year plans. For many years increases in farm production barely met the needs of the steadily rising population. As a result of the "green revolution" (page 183), sharp increases in wheat production were scored in West Pakistan starting in the late 1960's. In East Pakistan, however, food production did not keep pace. As opposed to the overall picture in agriculture, Pakistan's industrial record was far more impressive.

The growth of Pakistani industry has been one of Asia's success stories. Thanks to efficient planning, Pakistan continued year after year to make great strides in industrial development. A steady uphill fight was needed, for at the time of partition Pakistan had almost no modern industries. The mills which had processed Pakistan's jute and cotton had been lost to India in the partition. Moreover, the areas inherited by Pakistan were poor in resources of such raw materials as coal and iron ore. Therefore, when the Pakistani government decided to promote industrialization, it had little to work with.

Many plants and mills were built to replace those taken over by India at the time of partition. Eventually Pakistani mills turned out sufficient cotton cloth and sacking for national needs and also for export. Modest starts were made in establishing plants and factories to produce iron and steel, railroad equipment, light machinery, cement, glass, paper, and a variety of consumer goods. Moreover, all this was done at relatively little expense to the government. Much of the capital invested in the five year plans came from private business. The government created necessary facilities such as power plants, transportation, and communication systems, but wherever possible it left industrial development to private companies.

Bhutto called for nationalization of industries. On the completion of the Third Five Year Plan (1965–1970), a Fourth Five Year Plan was launched. But, after the loss of East Pakistan, Ali Bhutto's government was forced to reconsider the targets of this plan. Immediately after he came to power, Bhutto ordered the nationalization of major Pakistani industries. Nevertheless, Bhutto declared it was his intention "to have a happy blend of the public and private sectors."

Pakistan's foreign policy has revolved about the "India problem." Because of the way the state of Pakistan was created, its leaders were especially sensitive about national security. The borders of their new country were very long, and the two parts of the state were separated by a thousand miles. Pakistani leaders were outraged when Indian forces invaded and occupied a large part of the state of Kashmir. They believed that until they found ways to cope with these problems, Pakistan dared not relax its guard against India. Pakistani foreign policy, therefore, consistently reflected fear of its stronger and larger neighbor. As a result, Pakistani leaders sought to make friends with nations that might help it in its contest with India. An

ECONOMIC DEVELOPMENT IN PAKISTAN. The Republic of Pakistan has called itself "an economic showcase." There is truth in the claim, for the country has made great progress in developing irrigation systems, industry, and job-training programs. In the picture above (left) workers are building a dam across the Indus River. The dam has since been completed, and now irrigates some 2,500,000 acres of land. Next to this picture is one showing a trainee learning welding. He is in one of the schools opened to help meet Pakistan's need for more technicians. In the lower photograph a worker observes the action of weaving machines in one of the many new silk mills opened in Pakistan in recent years.

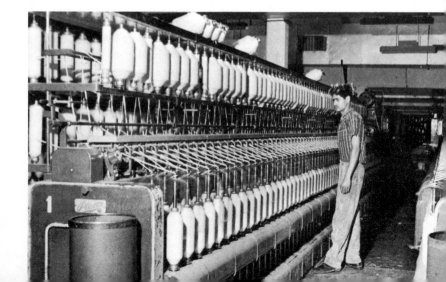

old Arab proverb is "The enemy of my enemy is my friend." To some extent, this saying has applied to Pakistan's foreign policy since 1947.

When Pakistan and India became independent in that year, India established itself as a non-aligned nation. Not so Pakistan. Having received assurance of American military aid, Pakistan aligned itself with the United States in the cold war between that country and the Soviet Union. Though it did not play an active role, Pakistan joined both the Southeast Asia Treaty Organization (SEATO) and the Central Treaty Organization (CENTO). These international alliances had been formed at the encouragement of the United States for mutual defense against Communist expansion.

Pakistan joined these organizations not only because it feared Russia but because it wanted to be well-armed in its quarrels with India. From 1954 to 1965 the United States gave Pakistan one and a half billion dollars in military aid. (This figure does not include a tremendous amount of economic and technical assistance.) The United States furnished this aid in order to shore up Pakistan's defenses against Russia. By having Pakistan as an ally, the United States was able to maintain radar stations and air bases in that country to check on the movements and locations of Soviet military forces and installations. But both Pakistan and India recognized that American aid also strengthened Pakistan's military posture against India. This aid was deeply resented by India, which for many years would accept only economic and technical assistance from the United States (page 199).

India's war with China made Pakistan and China friendlier. The worsening of relations between India and Communist China inspired Ayub Khan to seek closer relations with the latter. (Despite Pakistan's membership in SEATO and CENTO, Pakistan and Communist China had never had serious differences.) In 1962 the two countries began discussions aimed at settling a disagreement over their boundaries. The beginning of these talks coincided with the most serious phase of the border war between India and China (page 199). Early the next year, an agreement was reached. Thereafter China not only supported Pakistan in the dispute over Kashmir but also supplied Ayub Khan with military equipment from time to time. When war between Pakistan and India broke out in 1965, China gave token assistance to the Pakistani by provoking incidents along the China-India frontier.

The Soviet Union helped arrange a truce over Kashmir. The fighting between India and Pakistan over Kashmir alarmed the Soviet Union. Since Russia had extended much aid to both India and Pakistan, it had considerable influence in both countries. Therefore, when the United Nations brought about a cease-fire between the two nations in 1965, the Soviet Union was one of the chief supporters of the measure. Moreover, Soviet Premier Kosygin arranged for Prime Minister Shastri and President Ayub Khan to meet for peace talks in the Soviet city of Tashkent. As a result, the Tashkent Declaration was signed by India and Pakistan in early 1966. This agreement did not settle the dispute over Kashmir, but it did bind each of the countries to withdraw their forces from areas occupied during the war.

Pakistani foreign policy was reshaped after the Tashkent Declaration. After the 1965 war with India, Pakistan began to revise the direction of its foreign policy. Disappointed because the American government had refused to provide military aid, relations with the United States started to cool. Increasingly the Pakistani government sought military and economic assistance from Communist states. Trade with the Soviet Union was gradually stepped up; meanwhile, Soviet assistance to Pakistan increased. Even more notable was the improvement in Pakistan's relations with Communist China. In all of these maneuvers, Pakistan did not forget that its mortal enemy was India.

A third war between Pakistan and India erupted in 1971. Many people expected that India and Pakistan would go to war again some day over Kashmir. When a new war did erupt in 1971, however, the issue that touched it off was the situation in East Pakistan. India's military intervention in aid of the Bangladesh secession led to violent fighting which alarmed nations throughout the world.

It soon became apparent where the sympathies of each of the big powers rested. Soviet Russia made clear that it supported India, and Communist China showed its sympathy with Pakistan. Confusion was raised by the stand of the United States. The American government said that it was neutral, but there was reason to believe that its policy was "tilted" in favor of Pakistan.

When Ali Bhutto came to power in Pakistan soon after the war with India, he began to work out a new foreign policy for his defeated country. While seeking for ways to improve Pakistan's relations with India, he undertook a review of the nation's policy towards the United States, the Soviet Union, and Communist China as well.

1. What problems plagued Pakistan after it achieved independence? How did the country fare under Ayub Khan's leadership?
2. What crisis hit Pakistan in the early 1970's? What was the outcome?
3. What has been the chief goal of Pakistan's foreign policy? Relate this goal to Pakistan's relations with the United States and China.

6. Bangladesh Is the Newest Nation in South Asia

Bengal was a key state in the British Indian Empire (map, page 123). At the time of partition in 1947, this large and heavily populated province in the northeastern part of the Indian subcontinent was divided between India and Pakistan. The eastern two-thirds of Bengal became Pakistani territory and thereafter was known as East Pakistan. For many years the people of East Pakistan believed they were discriminated against by the central government situated in West Pakistan. In the late 1960's the resentments of the East Pakistani began to boil over, and by the end of 1971 they had successfully revolted from Pakistan and set up the new nation called Bangladesh.

Bengal is a well-watered region of the Indian subcontinent. For many centuries the state of Bengal dominated the northeastern sector of the Indian subcontinent. It was bounded on the north by the eastern Himalaya foothills and on the east by the almost impassable jungles of Burma. On the west the lower Indo-Gangetic Plain extended into Bengal. To the south were the broad waters of the Bay of Bengal, the oceanic bridge between the Indian continental land mass and the lands of Southeast Asia. It is in lower Bengal that the eastward-flowing Ganges River joins the southward-flowing Brahmaputra River. These two mighty rivers, coming together about two hundred miles from the sea, have formed one of the largest delta areas in the world. Watered by countless streams and having a heavy rainfall throughout most of the year, a large part of Bengal is covered with thick jungle growth and swamps. Roads have always been scarce here, and most travel and transportation has depended on boats. The famines that sometimes ravage Bengal are caused by floods and tidal waves, not by drought.

Most of the people of Bangladesh are Bengali. An overwhelming majority of the inhabitants of Bengal speak the Bengali language. In physical appearance, many of the Bengali are short, slight of build, and dark-skinned. They more generally resemble the peoples of the

Gangetic River Plain and South India rather than the tall, muscular, and fairer-skinned people of the Indus River region. Besides the Bengali, various small ethnic groups have long dwelt in the area.

Bengal has been chiefly an agricultural region. The fertile lands of the Ganges-Brahmaputra delta have been worked by farmers since early times. Long ago they learned how to cope with flooding waters and to make a living from the rich soil. Over the centuries Bengal became one of the most heavily populated areas in the world.

It is a land of few cities. Near the southwestern coast, Calcutta (in India) has flourished as one of the busiest ports of the Indian sub-continent. In very recent years, Chittagong (in Bangladesh) has blossomed into a lively port city along the southeastern coast. The city of Dacca lies in the interior of eastern Bengal. Once the center of ancient kingdoms, it was designated the capital of East Pakistan and then of its successor, Bangladesh. Most Bengali people, however, live in the thousands of farming villages that dot the landscape, particularly in the delta area.

Thanks to the fertile soil, the year-long warm climate, and the abundance of water, agriculture in Bengal has been able to support a huge population. Several crops of rice, the staple product, are raised annually. About three-quarters of the cultivated land is given over to this crop. Other important crops are jute and tea. Jute is used for the manufacture of sacking, long Bengal's major export. Most Bengali tea is raised in the hilly country to the north. The extensive forests have been a valuable source of commercial timber. Unfortunately Bengal has few mineral deposits and few sources of power other than water. For these reasons, there has been little effort to promote industry in East Bengal, nor do future prospects for industrialization appear promising.

Bengal was ripped in two when the British left India. The principal guideline for the partition of Britain's Indian Empire in 1947 was religion. Most strongly affected were the peoples of Bengal province. About half its inhabitants were Hindu; the rest were largely Muslim. The Hindus, living mainly in the western part of the province (which became the state of West Bengal), remained within the new republic of India. The Muslim people in the eastern two-thirds of Bengal became citizens of the new nation of Pakistan. But, except for their religious faith, the Bengali Muslims in East Pakistan had nothing in common with their fellow-countrymen in

West Pakistan, situated a thousand miles away. In language and way of life, they were totally different.

East Pakistani people came to feel like second-class citizens. From the outset, many East Pakistani people believed that their needs and problems were given little attention by the national government. For a while they reluctantly accepted explanations by government leaders that the nation's resources had to be devoted mainly to strengthening national defense. But gradually they became convinced that Pakistan's rulers were mainly concerned with the interests of West Pakistan. They noted that the heads of state were, one after another, West Pakistani leaders and that most of the other high government offices were also monopolized by West Pakistani. It was impossible

One Nation Becomes Two

	PAKISTAN (old West Pakistan)	BANGLADESH (old East Pakistan)
Area	310,403 sq. miles	55,126 sq. miles
Capital cities	Islamabad	Dacca
Population (est.)	55 million	75 million
Population density (est.)	183 persons per sq. mile	1364 persons per sq. mile
Ethnic background	Punjabi, Pathan, Sindhi, Baluchi	Chiefly Bengali
Religion	99% Muslim	89% Muslim
Climate and terrain	Ranges from hot desert to cold mountain ranges	Warm and humid lowlands
Economy	Principal products: wheat and cotton. Industry is growing.	Principal products: rice, jute, and tea. Virtually no industry.
Annual per capita income (est.)	$130	$77
Neighbors	Afghanistan, Iran, China, India	Burma, India

BIRTH OF A NATION. **Happy Bangladesh patriots welcomed Indian troops in
Dacca (below) following the victory over
Pakistan in late 1971. But grim problems
faced the new nation, including the disrupted lives of millions of refugees
(left). Mujibur Rahman, Bangladesh's
national hero and first prime minister,**
received arms surrendered by a left-wing student leader in a ceremony symbolizing
hopes for an end to guerrilla actions (above, right).

to ignore the fact that control of the nation's military forces was kept tightly in the hands of West Pakistani officers. And the nation's revenues and loans and grants from abroad seemed always to be used for the development of West Pakistan. Thus, while West Pakistan's economy advanced dramatically, East Pakistan struggled to survive as best it could.

The East Pakistani began to protest openly. The anger of the East Pakistani against the central government mounted steadily. Not even Ayub Khan, who ruled with a strong hand for eleven years, could quell the outbursts of protest by the Bengali people. Riots and demonstrations continued to flare up. Increasingly Bengali political leaders demanded a greater voice in government and especially a large measure of regional autonomy (control over local affairs) for East Pakistan. Sheikh Mujibur Rahman (moo-jee-*boor'* rah-*mahn'*) emerged as spokesman for the protesters. A militant and lively speaker, he rapidly won enormous popularity in East Pakistan.

In late 1968 and early 1969 a wave of riots forced Ayub Khan to make concessions to his critics but these came too late. Bowing to pressure, Ayub resigned from office and General Yahya Khan took over the Pakistan government (page 203).

Yahya Khan failed to solve the crisis. As told earlier, Yahya Khan promised to hold elections for Parliament. But agitation for drastic political change did not quiet down. In particular, the Awami League, led by Mujib,[5] continued to clamor for regional autonomy for East Pakistan. Finally, in late 1970, the long-awaited elections were held. The Awami League won a clear majority in Parliament by taking almost every parliamentary seat in East Pakistan. (In West Pakistan the anti-government party led by Ali Bhutto won many seats.)

A deadlock immediately emerged between Yahya Khan and the victorious political parties. Yahya refused to allow the new parliament to meet, and a protest campaign was launched in East Pakistan. When national troops moved into the rebellious province, bloody fighting broke out. In March, 1971, Mujibur Rahman and his supporters proclaimed the independence of East Pakistan. The new state was to be called Bangladesh ("Bengali Nation"). Mujib was arrested and imprisoned in West Pakistan. Now there was to be no turning back for the Bengali rebels.

[5] Mujibur Rahman is widely known by this shortened form of his first name.

Violence swept over East Pakistan. Government forces moved rapidly to crush the rebellion in East Pakistan. The defenders of Bangladesh, realizing it was folly to confront the national army in open combat, waged guerrilla warfare. Soon the Pakistani government charged that India was secretly supplying the guerrilla forces. It also claimed that the Indian government was permitting guerrillas eluding government troops to escape to sanctuary across the frontier. The infuriated and frustrated West Pakistani soldiers reacted by launching a reign of terror. They slaughtered tens of thousands of Bengalis, guerrilla fighters and civilians alike. Villages were sacked and burned, and Bengali women and girls were raped. A living nightmare seemed to have enveloped large parts of East Pakistan.

Meanwhile, an unbroken stream of Bengali refugees fled across the frontier seeking safety in India. Perhaps as many as ten million men, women, and children poured into hastily established refugee camps across the border in West Bengal. The Indian government and also nations around the world sought to provide emergency relief for the refugees.

India intervened and Pakistan was defeated. In December, Indian military forces began to move across the frontier into East Pakistan to help the Bengali fighters. The outraged Pakistani government protested. From its point of view, it was dealing with an internal rebellion, the outcome of which would affect the very survival of the Pakistani state. But India could not pass up the chance to help in the creation of a friendly independent nation on its eastern border.

Fighting between Indian and Pakistani forces also erupted along India's border with West Pakistan. Before the end of 1971, the isolated and outnumbered Pakistani forces in East Pakistan surrendered, and a cease-fire was declared in the west as well. As a result of its defeat, Pakistan had to acknowledge the loss of its eastern province. Bangladesh had gained its independence. Returning home to a hero's welcome, Sheikh Mujibur Rahman became leader of the new nation. Many nations around the world soon recognized the government of Bangladesh, and in the spring of 1972 the new government was also recognized by the United States.

Bangladesh faces a troubled future. The people of Bangladesh celebrated their new political freedom, but they had won at a tremendous cost. And as an independent nation they faced gigantic problems. It was not simply that the old governmental system had to be overhauled. A workable economic system capable of supporting a huge population had somehow to be created. And resettling the refugees who returned from India would require much time, patience, and sacrifice. Though many nations pledged help, whether Bangladesh would be able to meet the challenges of independence was a question raised by concerned people everywhere. One conclusion seemed unavoidable: Bangladesh faced an uncertain, and probably turbulent, future.

• CHECK-UP

1. Why were two distant regions joined in the new nation of Pakistan in 1947?
2. Why were the people of East Pakistan dissatisfied with their political status? Why did this feeling finally erupt into rebellion?
3. What problems make a troubled future seem likely for Bangladesh?

Summing Up

In 1947 Britain withdrew from its Indian empire. The subcontinent was divided into two independent states: India and Pakistan. Independent India, led by Nehru, committed itself to democracy. A constitution was drafted and a new political structure erected. India's federal system provided the central government with broad political powers. The newborn state sought to promote the welfare of its people by passing laws to eliminate social abuses and by launching five year plans for economic improvement. But India continued to struggle with tremendous problems. On the international scene India has sought to play only a limited role. Until its domestic problems are solved, India cannot hope to become a world leader.

Like India, newly independent Pakistan faced difficult problems. More than a decade passed before a government emerged which was capable of handling the many nearly impossible tasks. State planning backed up by large-scale private investment resulted in a great expansion of industry. In foreign affairs Pakistan was chiefly concerned with India, its unfriendly neighbor on the subcontinent. In the cold war Pakistan sided with the United States but later also became friendly with Communist China.

From the outset, relations between the eastern and western sectors of Pakistan were strained. The peoples of the two areas had little in common except their religion. Feelings of hostility between them finally exploded in a tragic civil war. This led to a new round of conflict between India and Pakistan and to the birth of the new state of Bangladesh in what had been East Pakistan.

CHAPTER REVIEW

Can You Identify?

Kashmir   Council of the States   Indira Gandhi
autonomy   House of the People   West Bengal
Ayub Khan   parliamentary system   Mujibur Rahman
Yahya Khan   anti-colonialism   five year plan
Ali Bhutto   green revolution

What Do You Think?

1. Why would Nehru have thought the foreign policy he developed to be the best possible one for India at the time?

2. What are the advantages and limitations of a parliamentary system of government?

3. Why have India and other developing countries experimented with a socialist economy?

4. Why is the population explosion a problem in developing countries?

5. Why has Pakistan found it useful to be friendly with both the United States and China?

Extending and Applying Your Knowledge

1. How well is India coping with its domestic problems? For an early account, see Taya Zinken's *India Changes!* (Oxford Press).

2. How have India, Pakistan, and the United States sought to solve issues of common concern? See for example, *India, Pakistan, and the West,* fourth edition (Oxford Press), by Percival Spear.

3. To get a better idea of India's goals read the Preamble from the Indian Constitution. This, together with selected articles, is found in "A Nation Is Born" in *India: Selected Readings.*

BIBLIOGRAPHY

Basham, A. L., *The Wonder That Was India*, rev. ed. Hawthorn, 1963. Surveys Indian civilization from ancient times to the advent of Islam.

Bhutto, Zulfikar Ali, *The Myth of Independence*. Oxford University Press, 1969. Sets forth in hard-hitting fashion some of the basic political beliefs of a major Pakistani leader.

Bolitho, Hector, *Jinnah: Creator of Pakistan*. Lawrence Verry, 1964. A good account of the life and career of the founding father of modern Pakistan.

Brown, Donald MacKenzie, *Indian Political Thought from Ranade to Bhave: The Nationalist Movement*. University of California Press, 1961. Representative writings of modern India's nationalist leaders.

Brown, William Norman, *The United States and India and Pakistan*, rev. ed. Harvard University Press, 1963. An authoritative survey of Indian civilization, emphasizing modern culture, life, and affairs.

De Bary, William T. (ed.) and others, *Sources of Indian Tradition*. Columbia University Press, 1964. A superb collection of selections from the Indian philosophical, religious, and literary heritage.

Fischer, Louis, *The Life of Mahatma Gandhi*. Harper, 1950. A warm and moving biography.

Fisher, Margaret W. and others, *Himalayan Battleground*. Frederick Praeger, 1963. A sound appraisal of the Sino-Indian clash in the northwest Himalaya border region.

Ghosh, Sudhir, *Gandhi's Emissary*. Houghton Mifflin, 1967. The role of Gandhi in the independence movement, seen through the eyes of a trusted aide.

Gibb, Hamilton A. R., *Mohammedanism; An Historical Survey*. Oxford University Press, 1953. A fine review of the history and teachings of Islam, containing good material on India and Pakistan.

Goetz, Hermann, *The Art of India*. Crown, 1959. One of the better surveys of India's long artistic heritage.

Herold, A. Ferdinand, *The Life of Buddha*, trans. by Paul C. Blum. Charles E. Tuttle, 1954. A sensitive sketch of the life and teachings of the Buddha.

Hesse, Herman, *Siddhartha*, trans. by Hilda Rosner. New Directions, 1951. A delicate portrayal of the Buddha in fictive style by a recipient of the Nobel Prize in Literature.

Isaacs, Harold R., *India's Ex-Untouchables*. John Day, 1965. A hardheaded but sympathetic appraisal.

Kalidasa, *Shakuntala and Other Writings*, trans. by Arthur Ryder. Dutton, 1959. Polished translations from the writings of one of the greatest dramatists in Indian history.

Kublin, Hyman, *India: Selected Readings*. Houghton Mifflin, 1973. A collection of readings, with introductory texts, on Indian history and civilization.

Lamb, Alastair, *The Kashmir Problem: A Historical Survey*. Frederick Praeger, 1967. A brief, objective review.

Lamb, Beatrice Pitney, *India: A World in Transition*, rev. ed. Frederick Praeger, 1966. An informative appraisal of modern Indian affairs, achievements, and problems.

Lin Yutang (ed.), *The Wisdom of China and India*. Random, 1942. Selections from the finest of Chinese and Indian writings.

Lord, John, *The Maharajahs*. Random, 1971. Fascinating accounts of the lives of some of India's most colorful princes, both past and present.

Markandaya, Kamala, *Nectar in a Sieve*. John Day, 1955. A moving novel of life in a modern Indian village.

Mehta, Ved, *Face to Face*. Little, Brown, 1957. A young blind man from India tells about his quest for an education in that country and in America.

Moon, Penderel, *Divide and Quit*. University of California Press, 1961. An incisive account of the background and implementation of the partition of India.

Nair, Kusum, *Blossoms in the Dust*. Frederick Praeger, 1962. A hardheaded evaluation of the efforts of India to modernize her society and economy.

Nanda, Bal R., *Shapers of History, Mahatma Gandhi*. Barron's Press, 1965. A solid and detailed biography.

Narayan, R. K., *The Financial Expert*. Michigan State University Press, 1953. A delightfully roguish novel by one of modern India's most gifted writers.

Nehru, Jawaharlal, *Toward Freedom*. Beacon Press, 1958. The reminiscences of India's great nationalist leader; particularly useful for the study of his earlier life and career.

Palmer, Norman D., *The Indian Political System*. Houghton Mifflin, 1962. A lucid introduction to the structure and operations of the government of independent India.

Piggott, Stuart, *Prehistoric India*. Barnes and Noble, 1962. The best introduction to the India of prehistoric times.

Pitt, Malcolm, *Introducing Hinduism*. Friendship Press, 1956. A brief and intelligible introduction especially useful for beginners.

Rawlinson, H. G., *India; A Short Cultural History*, rev. ed. Frederick Praeger, 1952. A well-written survey; particularly good on ancient and medieval times.

Rice, Edward, *Mother India's Children; Meeting Today's Generation in India*. Pantheon, 1971. Absorbing vignettes of modern Indian youth in all walks of life.

Sayeed, Khalid B., *The Political System of Pakistan*. Houghton Mifflin, 1967. Thorough coverage of Pakistan's economic and political institutions.

Segal, Ronald, *The Anguish of India*. New American Library, 1966. A critical account of Indian civilization, past and present.

Spear, Percival, *India, A Modern History*. University of Michigan Press, 1961. One of the best general studies of modern Indian history.
The Nabobs, rev. ed. Oxford University Press, 1963. Rich sketches of the life and manners of the English in eighteenth-century India.

Stephens, Ian, *Pakistan*, rev. ed. Frederick Praeger, 1967. A brief but rounded survey.

Tagore, Rabindranath, *A Tagore Reader*, ed. by Amiya Chakravarty. Beacon Press, 1966. Selections from the voluminous writings of India's Nobel Prize winner in Literature.

Tandon, Prakash, *Beyond Punjab*. University of California Press, 1971. Sketches showing recent social and cultural change in the Punjab.

Ward, Barbara, *India and the West,* rev. ed. Norton, 1964. A thoughtful interpretation of the interacting influences between India and the West.

Weekes, Richard V., *Pakistan: Birth and Growth of a Muslim Nation.* D. Van Nostrand, 1964. A carefully written history, useful especially for the formative years of the new state.

Wilber, Donald N., *Pakistan, Yesterday and Today.* Holt, Rinehart, and Winston, 1964. A popular but sound account of the history, land, and people of Pakistan.

Wiser, William and Charlotte, *Behind Mud Walls, 1930–1960.* University of California Press, 1963. A classic account of Indian village life written by an American missionary couple.

Woodruff, Philip, *The Men Who Ruled India,* 2 vols. Verry, 1963. An unusually illuminating study of the founders, builders, and rulers of the British Empire in India.

Ziring, Lawrence, *The Ayub Khan Era: Politics in Pakistan, 1958–1969.* Syracuse University Press, 1971. A detailed review and analysis of political developments in Pakistan during Ayub's administration.

ACKNOWLEDGMENTS

Thanks are extended to the following persons and organizations for making pictures available for reproduction:

13 — top, Government of India Information Service; center left, UNESCO/Vaidya 1961; center right, Harrison Forman; bottom, BP Singer Features
16 — BP Singer Features
20 — top, Government of India Information Service; bottom, WHO photo by P. N. Sharma
25 — top left, Deane Dickason from Ewing Galloway, N.Y.; top right, Government of India Information Service; center left, WHO photo by Eric Schwab; center right, United Nations; bottom, WHO photo by P. N. Sharma
27 — Wide World Photos
37 — top, bottom, Harrison Forman; center left, middle, Archaeological Survey of India, Government of India; center right, Government of India Information Service
54 — left, UNESCO/Christopher Hills; right, Government of India Information Service
57 — top, Government of India Information Service; center, Yale University Art Gallery; bottom, Archaeological Survey of India, Government of India
65 — top left, Courtesy, Fogg Art Museum, Harvard University; center right, WHO photo; bottom, Consulate General of the Republic of Indonesia, N.Y.
68 — UNESCO
73 — top left, The Metropolitan Museum of Art, Eggleston Fund, 1927; top right, Courtesy, Museum of Fine Arts, Boston, Marianne Brimmer Fund; bottom, The Cleveland Museum of Art, Dudley P. Allen Collection
79 — Government of India Information Service

98 — top, Radio Times Hulton Picture Library; bottom left, Courtesy, India Office Library; bottom right, Government of India Information Service
99 — Government of India Information Service
104 — United Nations
110 — Government of India Information Service
115 — Radio Times Hulton Picture Library
118 — Radio Times Hulton Picture Library
129 — Culver Pictures, Inc.
132 — Radio Times Hulton Picture Library
136 — Courtesy, India Office Library
147 — left, Wide World Photos; right, Culver Pictures, Inc.
151 — Courtesy, India Office Library
152 — Keystone Press Agency
155 — Culver Pictures, Inc.
158 — United Press International
166, 167 — Government of India Information Service except 167 background photo, Keystone Press Agency
169 — United Press International
186 — top, FAO photo; bottom, Philip Boucas for World Bank
192 — top, UNESCO; center, Government of India Information Service; bottom, WHO photo by T. S. Satyan
197 — Black Star
198 — Government of India Information Service
203 — left, Keystone; right, Embassy of Pakistan
206 — top left and right, United Nations; bottom, Embassy of Pakistan
212 — top left, Black Star (Santash K. Basak); top right and bottom, Wide World Photos

Maps by Lilli Tanzer. Drawings by John Gretzer.

INDEX

This Index includes references not only to the text of the book but also to charts, maps, and pictures. These may be identified as follows: *c* refers to a chart; *m* refers to a map; *p* refers to a picture.